Identity and Institutions

SUNY series in Global Politics
James N. Rosenau, editor

and

SUNY series in National Identities
Thomas M. Wilson, editor

Identity and Institutions

Conflict Reduction
in Divided Societies

Neal G. Jesse
and
Kristen P. Williams

STATE UNIVERSITY OF NEW YORK PRESS

Published by
State University of New York Press, Albany

For information, address State University of New York Press,
90 State Street, Suite 700, Albany, NY 12207

Production by Diane Ganeles
мк Marketing by Susan Petrie

Library of Congress Cataloging in Publication Data

Jesse, Neal G., 1967–
  Identity and institutions : conflict reduction in divided societies / Neal G.
Jesse and Kristen P. Williams.
      p. cm. — (SUNY series in global politics) (SUNY series in national
identities)
  Includes bibliographical references and index.
  ISBN 0-7914-6451-2 (hardcover : alk. paper)
  1. International relations and culture. 2. Conflict management.
3. International organization. 4. International agencies. 5. Minorities—
Civil rights. 6. Ethnic groups—Civil rights. 7. Social justice. I. Williams,
Kristen P., 1964– II. Title. III. Series.

JZ1251.J47 2005
303.6'9—dc22

                                                          2004016208

10 9 8 7 6 5 4 3 2 1

To Paula, Jess, and Stewart
and
James, Anne, and Matthew

Contents

Illustrations

Figures

Map

Tables

Preface

The first decade following the end of the Cold War did not bring an end to conflicts between nationalist/ethnic groups around the world. Such conflicts revolve around issues of identity; territorial control; access to policy making; and political, economic, and social resources. These conflicts pose a challenge to scholars and policy makers searching for practical solutions. Thus, the question arises: how can conflicts within and between states among various ethnic/nationalist groups be ameliorated or reduced? In this book we seek to understand the link between identity and institutions as a means to reduce ethnic/nationalist conflicts. We challenge the consociational and federal models on the grounds that internal solutions are unlikely to foster overlapping identities. Differing from consociational theories, we make the novel argument that cross-border (external) parliamentary institutions can ameliorate ethnic conflict by promoting and/or constructing overlapping identities. These institutions provide multiple forums of representation and pool sovereignty across ethnic divisions. Increased access and representation leads to a reduction in political tension and ethnic/nationalist conflict by reducing threat perceptions and ethnic security dilemmas, and increasing trust. Moreover, through external institutions, outside parties can make credible commitments to the conflicting parties, which cannot be done with consociational or federal institutions. This commitment is needed to reduce the ethnic security dilemma faced by groups that have unequal access to policy making. Thus, this book contributes to the theoretical debate over the utility of internal institutions as a means to resolve ethnic/nationalist conflicts.

The book illustrates the argument in more detail through an examination of cases that explore the link between identity and institutions. Three cases are investigated: the efforts of the Spanish government to address the continuing conflict from two groups, the Basques and Catalans, through federalism; the development and evolution of the European Union (EU), along with the deliberate effort by the institution to promote a European identity that transcends the national identities of its member states; and the attempt to resolve the conflict between Protestants and Catholics in Northern Ireland through the 1998 Good Friday Agreement. We hope that students of international relations and comparative politics will come away with a better understanding of the connection between an overlapping identity and representative institutions as a means to reduce conflict between nationalist and ethnic groups who seek to overcome issues of inequality in access to political, social, and economic resources.

We would like to thank four people for their valuable comments on the manuscript. We thank Nathan Richardson of Bowling Green State University and Shawn Reichert of Central Florida University for their comments on the chapters on Spain and the EU, respectively. We also thank the two anonymous reviewers of the State University of New York Press for their helpful suggestions.

Portions of chapters 1 and 4 appeared as an article, "Resolving Nationalist Conflicts: Promoting Overlapping Identities and Pooling Sovereignty-The 1998 Northern Irish Peace Agreement," *Political Psychology* (September 2001). We are grateful to Blackwell Publishing for permission to reproduce parts of this article. We also thank the following undergraduate and graduate students for their research assistance: Peter Clayson, Katie Dilworth, John Dreyer, Adam Hunt, Eric Kintner, Jennifer Lambert, Nicole Oberthur, Daniela Tepe, Karl Vogel, Angela Whitely, Stephanie Whitely, and Amie Wynn. We also thank Deborah Larson and George Tsebelis for their mentorship so many years ago which contributed to our intellectual and professional maturation.

We would like to thank a number of people at State University of New York Press for their contribution toward this endeavor. In no particular order we thank Acquisitions Editor Michael Rinella, Senior Production Editor Diane Ganeles, Copyeditor Marilyn Silverman, and Marketing Manager Susan Petrie.

Finally, Neal G. Jesse would like to thank his parents, Jess and Paula, and his brother Stewart for their support. Kristen P. Williams thanks her husband, James, and her children, Anne and Matthew. To these family members, we dedicate this book.

1

Theory of Identity and Institutions

Quarrels would not last long if only one side were wrong.
— Francois de la Rochefoucauld, *Maxims*

The end of the Cold War brought about the end to the East-West conflict between the United States and the former Soviet Union. And yet, the first decade of the post-Cold War period did not bring about an end to conflicts between nationalist/ethnic groups around the world, as witnessed by the conflicts in Bosnia-Herzegovina, Kosovo, Rwanda, East Timor, Sri Lanka, and other countries. Such conflicts revolve around issues of identity, territorial control, and access to policy making. These conflicts are the result, in large part, of unequal access to economic, political, and social resources.

These conflicts pose a challenge to scholars and policy makers searching for practical solutions. Thus, the question arises: how can conflicts within and between states among various nationalist/ethnic groups be ameliorated, or reduced, so that inequality in wealth and power can be overcome and peace be achieved? This book examines the role of international institutions in promoting overlapping (superordinate) identities as a means to resolve nationalist/ethnic conflicts through the pooling of sovereignty. Pooled sovereignty provides a mechanism for groups and states to obtain greater access to policy making, thereby enabling them to gain equality in resources.

Importantly, we develop an argument that links resolving issues of identity and perceptions of inequality to the establishment of cross-national, democratic institutions. We posit that cross-border parliamentary institutions can affect deeply held attitudes by promoting overlapping identities and pooling sovereignty. Moreover, we distinguish our argument from that of consociationalism, which relies solely on internal, national parliamentary/federal institutions.[1] Pooling sovereignty across a number of international (and national) representative bodies leads to increased access to governmental policy making for all the parties involved, with each principal actor having a stake in government. Increased access, therefore, leads to a reduction in political tension and ethnic/ nationalist conflict that results from real and/or perceived unequal access to resources. Increased access reduces threat perceptions and ethnic security dilemmas, and increases trust. Thus, cross-national parliamentary institutions may provide a solution to these conflicts.

The first section of this chapter discusses the argument in detail, particularly the role that cross-border institutions play in promoting multiple (and overlapping) group identities. The next section addresses the link between identity and institutions, through an examination of the literature on social identity theory, enemy images, and the security dilemma, as well as the literature on institutions (both domestic and international) as applied to ethnic/nationalist conflicts.

The third section presents our research method and design. In this section we proffer a new theory of conflict resolution in terms of the role that cross-border institutions play as a means of resolving ethnic group conflict resulting from inequality. We also elucidate our hypotheses and discuss why we chose the cases that are presented in subsequent chapters of the book. The chapter concludes with an overview of the remainder of the book's structure.

The Argument

We argue that national and cross-border parliamentary institutions allow multiple forums for representation for any group with possible overlapping identities. Such institutions promote political trust, and allow for credible commitments and pool sovereignty, leading to an amelioration of conflict over unequal access to resources by promoting overlapping identities among the warring communities. We make the novel argument that cross-border institutions have an effect on the expression of multiple group identities. It is this expression of multiple (and overlapping) identities that reduces tension by creating an atmosphere where different ethnic groups lose their strict definitions of the self and other (i.e., enemy images). Thus, we look to the interaction between the two independent variables, international institutions and overlapping identities, to account for the reduction in ethnic/nationalist conflict. The argument diagrammed is as follows: *international institutions (with representation and pooled sovereignty)* → *promotion of overlapping identities (common interests)* → *decrease in ethnic/nationalist conflict*.

To some degree our argument is consistent with the consociationalism and federalism literature; to some degree it is not. Specifically, we embrace the consociational prescriptions of proportional representation, grand coalition, and minority veto as well as federal prescriptions for autonomy for ethnic groups.[2] We assert that these *internal* mechanisms can create both a forum for representation of all groups and pool governing responsibility. However, we assert that the cross-border derivation of ethnic identities limits the ability of internal institutions to reduce conflict, especially federalism and autonomy. Thus, internal arrangements alone *will not* succeed in the future when the sources of ethnic division are at least in part derived from external sources.

Cross-border institutions promote overlapping identities in three important ways. First, they provide an alternative forum for representation in addition to the national or regional ones. Second, representation in a cross-border institution permits the expression of an overlapping identity for each group. The ethnic group can still express its local (or community) identity, but it also can express its national (or transnational) identity. For example, a political party delegation to the European Parliament (EP) denotes its national affiliation (i.e., local in this usage, British Labour) and also a European affiliation (e.g., Party of European Socialists). The potential for groups at the local level to use the other layers of representation to get what they want pushes these groups to reach across the community and to develop cross-cutting identities in the process.[3]

Third, cross-border institutions pool sovereignty. This pooling of responsibility and governance creates an opportunity for leaders to seek accommodation and consensus. Rather than having sovereignty divided into federal regions, these institutions unite regions into a larger governing structure. Moreover, they bring external actors into direct contact with internal actors in an environment of mutual recognition.

As much as our theory relies on the argument that institutions can promote a change in group/individual identity expression, it agrees with (and can be criticized along with) the consociational/ federalism literature about the direction of causation. Turning to this point, we believe that it is not possible at this time for us to untangle the complex relationship of cause and effect in identity formation and conflict resolution. It is certainly probable that reciprocal effects exist. A change in identity, however caused, may lead to a change in institutions in some instances. And of course, more than just institutional change can elicit a change in the expression of identity. We do not seek to solve this dilemma in this book. Rather, we merely posit that cross-border institutions con- tribute to the overall relationship and that this contribution has been neglected. It is our hope that by focusing on this neglected piece of the puzzle a greater understanding of the overall pattern becomes clearer.

Identity and Institutions: The Link

Intractable conflicts within and between states often revolve around issues of inequality in access to political, social, and eco- nomic resources. Issues of "property rights, jobs, scholarships, edu- cational admissions, language rights, government contracts, and developments all confer benefits on individuals and groups."[4] Scarcity of resources means that some groups win while others lose, leading to inequality. This inequality often manifests itself in group identity and threats to identity in the form of enemy images and ethnic security dilemmas. This section brings together the social psychology literature on social identity and the link to enemy images and security dilemmas, followed by a discussion of the political science literature on institutions.

Social Identity, Enemy Images, and Security Dilemmas

Individuals and groups have a social psychological "need to belong," and express this need through their social identities (or such cate- gories as ethnic group, nationality, or political identification).[5] According to Henri Tajfel's Social Identity Theory (SIT), individuals and groups have social identities that enhance their self-esteem and cohesiveness through the comparison of their group with others, the out-group.[6] These social identities are descriptive (what the attributes of the group's members are), prescriptive (how the members should behave and think), and evaluative (how the group compares to other groups).[7] As Ted Hopf notes, identities have three functions: tell you who you are, tell others who you are, and tell you who others are. The function of telling you who you are—your identity—indicates interests or preferences.[8]

In building on social identity theory, Marilynn B. Brewer's theory of "optimal distinctiveness" further explains the process of social identification. Individuals have two important, yet opposing, needs: (1) the need for assimilation and inclusion (need to belong leads individuals to become members of groups), and (2) the need for differentiation from others (acting in opposition to the need for assimilation in a group). These opposing individual needs are assuaged through membership in a social identity group (need for inclusion and belonging) that distinguishes itself from other groups (need for differentiation from out-groups).[9] In the case of nationalist (or ethnic) groups, individuals' need for inclusion leads to socialization into perceiving themselves as belonging to a particular nationalist (or ethnic) group, in contrast (differentiation) to another group or nationality.[10] For example, Catholics in Northern Ireland perceive themselves as Irish, in opposition to Protestants, who perceive themselves as British.[11]

Social identity theory further posits that the need for a positive in-group evaluation and perception can lead to comparisons with the out-group as negative. This in-group favoritism can lead to conflictual relations with other groups, particularly if there is a perception of a threat to group identity.[12] From the perception of a threat to one's group identity, enemy images about the other group emerge based on exaggerated differences, historical antagonisms, past experience, and collective memories.[13] Moreover, according to Shannon Lindsey Blanton, the "adherence to rigid images reduces the likelihood that even genuine attempts to resolve issues will be successful."[14]

As long as the in-group views the out-group in negative terms (enemy image) and perceives a threat to its own identity, a lack of trust between the groups is likely. Mistrust reinforces the negative perceptions each group has of the other, especially hostile intentions, and thus each group may be inclined to threaten the other, leading to counterthreats and to a spiral of escalation of the conflict.[15] This cycle of mistrust and perception of hostile intentions

results in the *security dilemma*, a concept found in the international relations literature within political science.[16] In essence,
"what one does to enhance one's own security causes reactions that,
in the end, can make one less secure."[17] The security dilemma can
also apply to ethnic and nationalist groups.[18] When one group
threatens another, the competition fuels the mutual mistrust that
further aggravates the already tense relationship. Rather than
backing down in the face of threats, the other group may react with
counterthreats, thereby leading to a spiral of conflict.[19] For example, in the few short years leading to the breakup of Yugoslavia,
actions by both Serbs and Croats reinforced the mistrust both sides
had of the other and of threats to each other's identity. As noted by
Barry R. Posen, "in the spring of 1990, Serbs in Croatia were rede-
fined as a minority, rather than a constituent nation, and were
asked to take a loyalty oath. Serbian police were to be replaced
with Croats, as were some local Serbian officials. No offer of cultural autonomy was made at the time. These Croatian policies
undoubtedly intensified Serbian fears about the future and further
tempted them to exploit their military superiority."[20]

Moreover, the security dilemma and concomitant mistrust can
lead to group conflict if one group is dominant over another, as is
the case in Northern Ireland, where the Protestants are the majority within the police forces, professional services, government
services, non-manual labor, and overall employment. The dispro-
portional dominance of Protestants in these areas has led to long-
term inequality and tensions with Catholics. The out-group, or
minority (in this case, Irish Catholics), may perceive itself as
having no recourse to address its complaints, furthering the conflict between the groups.[21]

Trying to overcome the security dilemma is crucial to resolving
conflicts, including nationalist and ethnic ones. The need to reduce
the security dilemma involves establishing trust, credible commitments, and a changed image of the enemy. If groups maintain mistrust resulting from the security dilemma, they are unlikely to be
able to reach agreement in order to resolve their differences. Alter-
natively, mutual trust makes it possible for groups and states to
negotiate agreements and to increase cooperation.[22] To demonstrate trust, groups (and individuals) can make costly concessions.
According to Deborah W. Larson, costly concessions are those that
have an effect "on a state's [or group's] bargaining reputation,
image, or tactical advantage" and are believed to be irrevocable,
such as formal recognition.[23] For example, in the 1998 Good Friday

Agreement the Republic of Ireland revised Articles 2 and 3 of its Constitution, which explicitly called for the unification of both parts of Ireland. The Agreement specifically stipulates: "It is the firm will of the Irish nation in harmony and friendship, to unite all the people who share the territory of the island of Ireland, . . . recognizing that a united Ireland shall be brought about only by peaceful means with the consent of a majority of the people, democratically expressed, in both jurisdictions in the Island."[24] Thus, the Republic of Ireland made a costly concession to the Unionists in Northern Ireland by ending its constitutional claim to the North. The Irish government's concession was costly because it involved a complete reversal of a constitutional provision in existence since 1937 and could have triggered domestic political opposition toward the Irish government.

An example of a costly concession can also be found in the Catalan nationalist movement and its relationship to the post-Franco Spanish state. After the general elections of 1977, but before the approval of the 1978 constitution, Catalan nationalists had many aspirations. Of central concern to the main Catalan political parties was whether the monarchy had a legitimate role in a democracy and in the purging of former Francoists from the state apparatus (the "democratic break" or "rupture strategy"—*la estrategia de ruptura*). The Spanish state persuaded the Catalan parties to abandon these demands and to take a more moderate stance. The government conceded to nationalist demands for greater regional autonomy and for official legitimacy for non-Castilian languages in the Constitution. Thus, the credible concession by the government led to a credible and costly concession by the Catalan nationalists. As a striking counterexample, the Basque nationalist parties refused to make concessions and opposed the Constitution. This difference in approach has led to a large difference in conflict reduction in Catalan versus Basque areas.[25]

By fulfilling its obligations, a group demonstrates its credible commitment to an agreement.[26] For example, in 1998 the British and Irish governments were required to hold referenda in their respective countries on the Good Friday Agreement. Each country fulfilled its commitment by holding a referendum on May 22, 1998: the result was overwhelming support for the Agreement. However, Larson argues that mutual trust is a necessary but not sufficient condition for states to incorporate their agendas. Other factors may hinder agreement and cooperation, including domestic public opinion, ideology, opposition from allies, and strategic interests.[27] In the case of Northern Ireland, opposition from some political groups in the North affected the negotiation process of the Agreement. For instance, the Democratic Unionist Party (DUP), under the leadership of the Reverend Ian Paisley, opposed the inclusion of Sinn Fein in the all-party talks. The DUP also encouraged its supporters to vote against the Agreement in the referendum that ratified the Agreement.

What, then, connects social identity, changing enemy images, and reducing the ethnic security dilemma that emerges from inequality so as to resolve such conflicts? A key to solving the puzzle is the agreement among many scholars that identities are *socially constructed*:[28] through social interactions, the values and beliefs that define one's identity are shaped and molded (i.e., constructed).[29] As Alexander Wendt notes, "*social* identities are sets of meanings that an actor attributes to itself while taking the perspective of others, that is, as a social object." Moreover, these "actors normally have multiple social identities that vary in salience.[30]

In the case of national identities, leaders can mobilize people by appealing to the primordial attachment individuals have toward their nation, thereby socially constructing national identity. Symbols of the nation, such as parades, holidays, flags, national anthems, and ties to the family and community (e.g., "the sons of Ireland" and "defending the homeland"), are means by which leaders can promote national identity and nationalism. In turn, appeals to national identity and nationalism can explain why individuals are willing to engage in conflict with others. Additionally, when leaders are successful in appealing to nationalism and national identity, other identities are attenuated.[31]

The question arises: if identities are socially constructed, can that not also mean that they are malleable? If so, can altering the salience of particular identities then help to resolve previous conflicts between groups by making some identities more important than others, given that people have multiple identities?[32] We argue that this is the case. It is important to bear in mind that ethnic or nationalist identities are not necessarily incompatible with other identities. Groups and individuals may have other social identities that overlap or crosscut.[33] For example, a person may identify with Edinburgh, Scotland, the United Kingdom, and Europe. Overlapping identities in Northern Ireland include religious identification, political party identification, and national identification. A person could be a Protestant, a member of the Ulster Unionist Party, and

British. In addition, recent survey research demonstrates that a considerable number of Catholics and Protestants in Northern Ireland claim a Northern Irish identity—a more inclusive identity.[34] These overlapping, or multiple, identities may be the key to reducing intergroup bias.

Overlapping or multiple identities (or memberships) are examined in the social psychology literature on cross-categorization that augments social identity theory. The literature demonstrates that overlapping memberships in different groups can lead to decreased intergroup bias and decreased conflict between in-groups and out-groups.[35] In synthesizing the literature, Lynn M. Urban and Norman Miller found that when in-group members had opportunities for interaction with out-group members, increased personalization and less stressful and negative moods led to less intergroup bias.[36] In the case of Northern Ireland, the leaders of the various political parties involved in the Good Friday Agreement negotiations maintained overlapping identities/memberships: identities as members of their political parties, identities as people of Northern Ireland, and identities as negotiators. During the negotiations the leaders came to know each other through the personalization of the intergroup interactions. Indeed, even when the talks stalled over the issue of decommissioning of weaponry, the parties continued to meet as members of the larger group involved in the negotiations, intent on continuing their dialogue as the first step in resolving the conflict. The chair of the talks, former senator George Mitchell, noted: "Merely continuing the talks had become an important objective. There was a broad consensus that if they ended without an agreement there would be an immediate resumption of sectarian violence, possibly on a scale more deadly than ever before."[37] As part of a larger (overlapping) group, the positive (but sometimes acrimonious) interaction between in-groups and out-groups during the negotiations reinforced their commitment to finding an agreement despite their differences over particular issues.

Consequently, a mechanism that can promote overlapping identities may afford the means to resolve, or at least reduce, conflict between opposing groups that result from inequality.[38] The creation of institutions that overlap identities (structure cross-categorization) and provide credible commitments can overcome the enemy images and security dilemmas that hinder the development of trust between conflicting groups. As will be discussed in the next section, by creating institutions that promote overlapping identities, individuals and groups have more than one avenue for self-identification and means for reducing polarization of interests between groups and, therefore, for reducing conflict.

Creating Institutions to Overcome Inequality and to Reduce Nationalist Conflicts

The neoliberal institutionalist paradigm in political science argues that international institutions can provide the necessary conditions for states that want to reach cooperative agreements and arrangements. Unlike neorealism, neoliberal institutionalism asserts that states need not always be in conflict. Through communication, interdependence, and interaction, expectations and policies converge to the point of creating common institutions. Through politics, these institutions, in turn, can lead to new relationships and identities built on trust and cooperation.[39] Institutions provide information, establish rules, safeguard expectations, and reduce uncertainty. Furthermore, institutions make commitments more credible and facilitate reciprocity, in addition to creating issue linkages. Institutions matter because they can change state preferences and, therefore, behavior.[40]

In terms of ethnic and nationalist groups, institutions may promote cooperation if they are structured in such ways that they change the behavior of previously conflicting groups to one of cooperation. Both majority and minority groups must have access to policy making and be able to express their grievances and interests. Importantly, internal reforms can promote inclusion of groups within the state: all groups in the society have an opportunity to be represented and have a voice. When groups are deprived, perceiving political and economic inequalities, they are likely to feel frustrated, often leading to conflict with the existing regime and with other groups.[41] Consociationalism and federal autonomy are two such institutional arrangements *within states* that seek to deal with nationalist and ethnic cleavages. In either institutional arrangement the central government must take measures to protect the rights of minorities as well as to promote civic nationalism. Civic nationalism, which is based on the conception of citizenship, is inclusive; ethnic nationalism, which is based on ethnic identity, is exclusive. As such, civic nationalism is more likely to promote harmony and less divisiveness and separation than ethnic nationalism.[42]

Federalism offers a solution to ethnic conflict when ethnic groups are territorially (regionally) concentrated because "federalism deflects hostility from the central government by creating new political institutions and political competition at the local level."[43] Moreover, federalism can be successful if it raises the costs of secession. For example, in certain towns in Kenya, such as Nairobi and Mombasa, the Luo occupy important positions "outside their regions." Therefore, for the Luo, secession is costly because of the loss of significant opportunities in other regions in Kenya were they to secede.[44]

Many scholars make persuasive arguments that federalism provides the best possible government for a nation of considerable ethnic and regional disparity. Especially in territorial federations,[45] federalism is an institutional arrangement that provides ethnic and/or regional communities with due territorial recognition.[46] Federalism may also aid in the management of conflict by providing many political centers, each of which may be the locus of resolving disputes.[47] Federalism may also constrain central power, thus allowing for more regional autonomy.[48] Alexander Murphy posits that federal systems provide incentives for groups to create separate policy within their territorial unit. While such policy variance may be difficult for the state as a whole, it may eliminate, or at least ameliorate, conflict between regional units.[49] More generally, Sharda Rath goes so far as to say that federalism promotes peace, security, strength, democracy, liberty, and identity.[50]

Federalism is not without its detractors. K. C. Wheare agrees that federalism is one method by which to solve ethnic conflict. However, he argues that federalism may produce a constitutional crisis in some instances. Such a crisis can occur because of the built-in disequilibrium in federalism: the struggle between the imposition of common values by the central government and the jealous protection of local powers by regional units.[51] Jonathan Lemco elucidates a dozen prerequisites for federalism to be an effective method of stemming state dissolution in multi-ethnic states.[52]

Federalism also suffers from the problem that minority groups within the state remain a minority in positions at the federal level.[53] For example, in the former Yugoslavia, each federal republic became ethnically based.[54] The minority groups within Serbian territory felt threatened by the increasingly ethnically focused actions of the Serbian government, and President Slobodan Milosevic in particular. Each group sought to further its interests, thereby contributing to the ethnic security dilemma within each republic. Moreover, the fear always exists that regional leaders will seek further autonomy and separation from the central government, leading to demands for independence.[55]

When ethnic groups are intermingled, consociational institutions offer a solution because minority groups are represented in the central government and thus have an opportunity to engage in the act of governing.[56] Importantly, the consociational literature emphasizes the need to match the proper set of institutions to divided societies. The right institutions (e.g., a proportional representation electoral system, a power-sharing executive, federalism, and a grand coalition) are said to promote elite accommodation. Elite cooperation would then ameliorate the community conflict.[57] I. William Zartman argues that consociational institutions can create new and overlapping identities, such as multi-ethnic or transethnic coalitions that move beyond singularly ethnic parties and ethnic majorities.[58] Indeed, Arend Lijphart argues that consociational institutions are responsible for the ethnic cooperation that has brought peace and harmony to divided Belgium.[59]

However, not everyone agrees that consociational and federal institutions are so benevolent or successful. Setting aside until later the disagreements on whether the bulk of empirical cases support or reject these theories, critics make several arguments. First, one line of thought suggests that the direction of causation points the wrong way. Institutional change does not lead to social change. Rather, the moderation of cleavages allows the successful implementation of democratic institutions.[60] Conflict reduction requires mechanisms to disperse the loci of power, emphasize intra-ethnic divisions, provide incentives for interethnic conflict, and so forth. Second, elite accommodation may lead to political compromise, but it does not lead to a long-term solution to the divided society, which is the source of the conflict. Cameron Ross argues that federalism allows authoritarianism to flourish in many of Russia's eighty-nine regions and republics.[61] Third, ethnic groups often do not want to cooperate with each other, cooperation that is necessary for effective government under a proportional representation system as found in consociational structures. Fourth, such a structure invariably solidifies (and perhaps exacerbates) ethnic divisions by making ethnicity more salient. Institutions that separate groups into hierarchical/geographic political units (e.g., federalism) sharpen social divisions.[62] Political parties tend to reflect this salience by promoting themselves as ethnically based.[63] For example, as Yugoslavia's breakup occurred, political parties defined themselves in ethnic terms, and voting in elections held in 1990 reflected the nationalist/ethnic divisions within the republics.

Additionally, if the allocation of proportionality is considered unalterable, problems may arise when the actual proportional distribution of groups changes.[64] For example, Lebanon's government was structured as a consociational democracy from the time of independence in 1943 until 1975, when civil war erupted. The consociational formula was constructed such that the relative importance of the top government positions reflected the proportion of the population of each sect: a Maronite Christian president, a Sunni Muslim prime minister, a Shiite Muslim chair of the legislature, and a Greek Orthodox deputy chair and deputy prime minister. While this arrangement worked for three decades, it faced the challenge of the changing proportionality of the population. The Christian sects had been a majority in the earlier census and thus allocated the position of president. Over time, however, the proportion of the Muslim population overtook the Christian population, thereby leading to demands by the Muslim sects that the composition of the government reflect the changed status. Soon, periodic clashes between groups erupted into full-scale civil war.[65]

Ian S. Lustick takes a different approach by attacking the research heuristic behind the consociationalist literature. Lustick argues that the "success of the consociational research program cannot be explained on the basis of its explanatory power."[66] He points out that even early into the "consociational research program" critiques existed. In particular, Lustick cites Eric A. Nordlinger and his criticism of Lijphart with "the imprecision of his terms, the awkwardness of his typology, and his mischaracterization of key cases."[67] Lustick includes a quote from the work of M. P. C. van Schendelen, a Dutch scholar, who disagrees with Lijphart's classification of the Netherlands (the bedrock case) as a consociational democracy. Van Schendelen "concludes that Lijphart probably cared little about the empirical validity of his theory"[68]; he "seems to attach more value to the theory's potential for engineering societies than to any other criterion of science."[69] Lustick shows in a convincing manner that Lijphart advances consociationalism as a valid normative prescription for divided societies "(almost) regardless of its scientific status, because it serves the ends he values."[70]

Lustick is quite critical in his treatment of Lijphart's research agenda in the 1980s and 1990s. He marshals evidence and argument from David D. Laitin to illustrate that Lijphart's extension of his work to South Africa is problematic. Lustick employs John McGarry and S. J. R. Noel and their criticism of the same case. But Lijphart himself supplies Lustick with his most damning argument. Lustick points out that in a move typical of the "late-Lakatosian" mode (i.e., the mode in which a research agenda moves forward despite a lack of scientific rigor or contribution), Lijphart finds the ability to "transform an anomaly into a profoundly confirming case of its [research agenda] hard-core theoretical propositions."[71] Lijphart argues that India is indeed a consociational democracy.[72] This, despite Lijphart's own earlier analysis that labeled India as neither a consociational nor a long-term democracy.

Returning to empirical evidence of consociational success or failure, a number of scholars even criticize some of the foundation examples of successful consociational democracy. Maureen Covell argues that bargaining theory better explains the tenuous grasp on unity that exists in Belgium. She posits that the actual process of accommodation, and not the institutional devices, leads to stable negotiations between political elites. She echoes the worries of Brian Barry that "the extension of these [consociational] 'devices' to countries marked by sharp political conflicts will be futile at best and possible dangerous."[73] Peride Kaleagasi posits that "it is incredible to think that federalism has worked well so far and that more federalism is going to be the solution to Belgium's problems." She says further that federalism "has helped to mitigate ethnic conflict, but has not been enough by itself to eliminate it."[74] Michael O'Neill inquires as to whether increased globalization will lead Belgian ethnic groups to consider surviving alone and cutting adrift "from the drag of a larger polity that submerges and discounts their particular interest."[75]

Clive H. Church puts forth the argument that Switzerland is not a good example of consociationalism either. He gives three reasons. First, Church states that Switzerland has a "consensus" democracy and not a consociational one. His reasoning seems to rely on at least two components: direct democracy through the referendum and the extensive process of policy consultation. While we do not fully agree with this, we do agree with Church's second reason: the divisions within Swiss society do not approximate Lijphart's "pillar" model of ethnic division. Church argues that the society is stable because ethnic groups are "all divided up inside or among cantons so that cross cutting cleavages are the norm."[76] He argues that there are no simple pillars and thus wise elites are not needed. Church's third reason is the complex web of context and behavior that promotes the unique Swiss political culture. He states that Swiss political culture encourages power-sharing and consensus.[77] Robert Senelle agrees, stating that strong cultural diversity unites Switzerland and that sub-cultural segmentation does not dominate.[78] Kaleagasi points out that the Swiss political parties do not resemble ethnic parties. There is a complete absence of ethnic parties at the national level. Moreover, political parties do not correspond to language regions.[79]

In a similar vein, Rotimi T. Suberu argues that federalism has not been a panacea for nationalist problems in Nigeria. Suberu acknowledges that "Nigeria is perhaps the paradigmatic African case of the innovative use of federal principles and institutions to accommodate diverse communal constituencies within the power structure of the state."[80] He finds five ways in which federalism has been useful for Nigeria. First, it devolves ethnic conflict from the national capital to regional capitals. Second, it fragments the identities of the three largest ethnic groups. Third, federalism protects the smaller minorities from the larger three. Fourth, it promotes a state-based identity, particularly through administrative units. Last, federalism devolves resources and opportunities to diverse territorial interests. Despite these advantages, federalism is still an incomplete answer to ethnic conflict. Suberu argues that federalism in Nigeria is flawed because it emphasizes distribution of resources over development, breeds corruption, and encourages further political fragmentation.[81]

Adding to the criticisms of Nordlinger, Donald L. Horowitz, and others, we argue that the internal focus of these approaches neglects any external components that shape the group identities. Consociational and federal solutions have failed because they refuse to recognize the external derivation of identities and groups. Because these institutions rely on the very divisions that cause conflict, they cannot and do not promote overlapping identities. In the end, such consociational and federal institutions will only be successful in the future if states pair them with cross-border institutions.

It follows that institutional arrangements that address ethnic and nationalist conflicts need not, and should not, be located solely within the domain of a single state. States are members of international institutions, which provide another arena or layer for policy making, representation, and, thus, identity. For example, members of the European Union (EU) have representation in the European

Parliament (EP). In addition, the EU has created a EU flag, anthem, and passport. Therefore, citizens of the EU may perceive themselves as having an ethnic, regional, national, *and* European identity as a result of these various avenues for representation (including transnational political parties) provided by the respective national and European institutions.[82] Indeed, recent *Eurobarometer* (EB) surveys indicate that significant numbers of people in the EU feel *both* a national and European identity.[83] Likewise, group identity that derives from cross-border identities (e.g., the British and Irish identities in Northern Ireland) can be represented in cross-border institutions. For example, in the EP, Northern Ireland is a single constituency with three Members of the European Parliament (MEPs). These MEPs are also members of the various political parties in Northern Ireland and yet "speak with one voice" in the various committees on which they serve.[84] In essence, the fact that they speak with one voice indicates a possible common group identity as "Northern Irish" MEPs. The implications can be far-reaching even in terms of nationalist strategies. Ferran Requejo points out that the enshrinement of European regionalism in the Maastricht Treaty has fundamentally altered the strategies of Catalan nationalists:

> So, from the perspective of present-day Catalan nationalism, it is no longer a question of achieving the highest number of instrumental "state" competences as possible, as this is clearly obsolete in view of the current process of economic and technological internationalization. It is more important to achieve the highest possible level of democratic self-government (symbolic, institutional and functional/financial presence) in those areas that reinforce and develop Catalonia's national personality as far beyond its borders as possible.[85]

Of course, any institution, whether national or cross-border, needs to promote fair representation of the competing groups. Ideally, agreements and institutions that deal with ethnic and nationalist groups should focus on "the rights and responsibilities, political privileges, and access to resources of each group."[86] However, in trying to design such institutions to resolve ethnic and nationalist conflicts, the problem of *credible commitment* arises. With uncertainty and lack of full information about each other's intentions, groups may fear the worst and be reluctant to accept mutually beneficial agreements. Conflict results because groups are unable to commit credibly to agreements that would be advantageous to all groups. One or more groups may believe that the others cannot guarantee that they will fulfill the terms of the agreement in the future; rather, maybe they will abandon the terms, particularly if the ethnic/nationalist demographic balance changes.[87] The fear of the uncertain future makes groups less likely and less willing to commit to such agreements, and conflict continues.

According to James D. Fearon, one way to overcome the credible commitment problem is through *external guarantees*, namely a "powerful third party willing and able to commit to intervene if the majority does not respect political commitments to the minority."[88] Fearon asserts that international organizations, for the most part, are unable to make such credible commitments; however, external states in close proximity to the conflicting state may be able to do so, particularly if kin from the conflicting state reside within the external state. Fearon cautions, nevertheless, that in the case of "nested minorities" the spread of ethnic conflict is high. Nested minorities are those situations in which members of group X are a minority within a political/administrative system dominated by another group, Y. Yet group Y is a minority within an even larger system in which group X is the majority. He notes the example of Ireland: Irish Catholics are the minority within Northern Ireland dominated by Protestants (and also within the UK), but Protestants would be a minority within a unified Ireland. Situations of nested minorities increase the likelihood of the spread of ethnic conflict.[89]

We disagree that nested minorities necessarily lead to an increase in ethnic conflict. Could not institutional arrangements that include third parties connected to the conflict possibly reduce tensions and resolve, or at the least ameliorate, the conflict? The idea of helpful, external third parties is congruent with our argument for the inclusion of cross-border institutions. For example, in the case of the Northern Ireland conflict, the Republic of Ireland (with its Irish Catholic population) and Britain (with its Protestant population) are more likely to make credible commitments to the 1998 Good Friday Agreement than the ethnic communities in Northern Ireland. Moreover, the institutions of the Agreement, which provide varying layers of representation, can reduce the uncertainty of the future, as well as provide information about interests, intentions, and concerns of the various groups.

Research Method and Design

To restate our puzzle: how can conflicts within and between states among various nationalist/ethnic groups be ameliorated, or reduced, so that inequality in wealth and power can be overcome? In order to develop our argument and present our analysis, we combine the social psychology literature on identity and cross-categorization and the political science literature on institutions. We show how social identity theory posits that "in-groups" distinguish themselves from "out-groups," thus producing mutually exclusive group identities. We integrate the political science literature on security dilemmas to show how exclusive identity groups living in distrust of each other fuel mutual antagonism. We hypothesize that cross-border parliamentary institutions are key to the solution to community conflict. Cross-border institutions can promote (and perhaps construct) overlapping social identities if they possess the following attributes: (1) allow multiple forums for group representation, (2) promote cross-community trust and, (3) encourage groups to see a common identity in pooled sovereignty.

Consequently, in this book we set out to develop a new theory of conflict resolution. We have made some fairly strong claims about the role of cross-border institutions as a means to solve, or reduce, ethnic group conflict that often results from perceived inequality. From the theory we derive some testable hypotheses. First, the establishment of cross-border institutions should promote the growth of overlapping identities among the groups in conflict. If our theory is correct, as communities gain representation in new forums, they should begin to express multiple, and overlapping, identities. This should be evident in cross-community cooperation and alliances in these new forums. If groups refuse to work together and maintain strict, unitary identities, such evidence would disprove our hypothesis. Second, the intensity with which an individual holds her primary identity should decline with the continuation of functioning cross-border institutions. Third, group identification of the self and other should become more complex and less antagonistic over time. Such a reduction in antagonism would reduce the ethnic security dilemma. Evidence that the intensity of primary identity increases with involvement in cross-border institutions or that each group's definition of self and other becomes more monolithic would disprove our theory. Last, the final indicator of the success or failure of the theory is the eventual amelioration of the conflict.

To test the hypotheses, we use the method of comparative case study of three cases of identity and institutions, recognizing the limitations of a small-N study (and thus the importance of "intentional selection of observations").[90] For each case, we discuss the identity issues of the various parties to the conflict, and the inequality of access to resources, as well as the existing institutions, both external and internal. The evidence we examine includes attitude surveys and the secondary literature on the background history of the conflicts. As there is significant research on the three cases examined, the information can be corroborated, and thus no one interpretation is relied upon. As for the attitude surveys, we are confident in the interpretation of surveys done by other scholars. We have also utilized primary survey data (e.g., the biannual *Eurobarometer* surveys conducted by the EU, and Coopers and Lybrand surveys conducted for the BBC Northern Ireland) as evidence for our cases.

The three cases used to illustrate the argument are as follows. First, the efforts by the Spanish government to address the continuing conflict from two groups, the Basques and Catalans. Second, the development and evolution of the EU, along with the conscious effort by the institution to promote a European identity that transcends national identities. Third, the attempt to resolve the conflict between Protestants and Catholics in Northern Ireland through the 1998 Good Friday Agreement.

These cases were chosen because of variance along the independent and dependent variables.[91] In terms of the independent variables, in some cases international (cross-border) institutions were established in order to address the various grievances among the ethnic groups. In one case (Spain), the government promoted an internal (federal) institution. In each case there is evidence of an overlapping identity (Spanish, European, and Northern Irish, respectively). There is also variance in terms of the dependent variable (reduction of ethnic/nationalist conflict). In the case of Spain, despite a federal system, conflict between the Basque region and the center remains. The jury is still out on Northern Ireland, as the Good Friday Agreement has yet to be implemented fully. In the case of the EU, while not a case of ethnic/nationalist conflict per se, the promotion of an overlapping identity has reduced the level of conflict and tension among its member states.

As is evident from the geographic location of the cases, we readily acknowledge that there is an inherent European focus. The limitations in utilizing cases from other parts of the world arises due to the fact that there have been relatively few attempts at the creation of both international, cross-border legislative institutions and the promotion of an overlapping identity—and where attempts have been made, they have failed. For example, two attempts at the creation of a supranational state, one in the Middle East, and one in the Caribbean, failed after only a few years. In the case of the United Arab Republic (UAR, 1958–1961), Egypt and Syria formed a political union, partially based on "a general and vague spirit of Pan-Arabism"—an overlapping identity. Moreover, the institutional structure was weak, and importantly, unequal as Egypt was the dominant partner. After three years, the UAR collapsed when Syria seceded.[92] In 1958, under the direction of Britain, several islands in the Caribbean attempted to form The Federation of the West Indies. While focused on anticolonialism as a unifying slogan, citizens' identity with their island was stronger than "with the federation or the 'West Indian Nation.'"[93] Additionally, divisions between the larger (islands Trinidad and Jamaica) and smaller islands (including Antigua, St. Kitts, and Barbados) challenged the effectiveness of the federation, particularly given that Britain favored the smaller islands. Following Jamaica's secession in 1962, the Federation fell apart.[94]

Conclusion

This chapter addressed the main argument that we propose: cross-border institutions can affect deeply held attitudes by promoting overlapping identities and pooling sovereignty. Pooling sovereignty across a number of international (and national) representative bodies leads to increased access to governmental policy making for all parties involved, with each having a stake in government. Increased access may lead to a reduction in political tension and ethnic/nationalist conflict that results from unequal access to resources, through reducing threat perceptions and ethnic security dilemmas, and increasing trust. Thus, international institutions may provide a solution to these conflicts.

This book, therefore, contributes to the theoretical debate over the utility of internal institutions as a means to resolve ethnic/nationalist conflicts. We challenge the consociational and federal models on the grounds that internal solutions are unlikely to foster overlapping identities. Neither consociational institutions nor federalist structures entail a credible commitment from outside parties. This commitment is needed to reduce the ethnic security dilemma faced by groups that have unequal access to policy making. Moreover, we link the literature from two disciplines: the social psychology literature on social identity and enemy images with the political science literature on institutions and conflict resolution. This interdisciplinary approach permits a richer exploration of the issues involved, namely ethnic security dilemmas and inequality.

The conclusions of this book are important for both academic research and for normative prescriptions. First, our analysis opens up a new path in the exploration of conflict reduction. We bring identity back into the calculus. Lijphart and others in the consociational school treat identity as non-malleable: identity is fixed. Therefore it cannot be an explanatory variable for change in the level of conflict. The consociational school thus must look elsewhere. This reduction in the importance of identity has been the dominant paradigm for over two decades. We reintroduce identity as an explanatory factor. By showing that identities not only change, but can also be constructed, we demonstrate that this change can lead to a change in the level of conflict. Second, by examining the connection between identities and institutions, we are linking the literature on international relations and comparative politics to that in social psychology. Thus our work is interdisciplinary. Third, our analysis opens up new normative conclusions. Primarily based on the consociational school but also on other works, institutional engineering has been dominant in trying to bring stability to divided societies. For decades constitutional engineers have sought to tinker with institutions, hoping to get just the perfect match for each society. The failures of constitutional engineering (documented earlier) have been dramatic and heartbreaking. Our study points to a different approach. Institutions should be chosen to help construct overlapping identities. Once citizens possess overlapping identities there will be a reduction in conflict with almost any institutional arrangement. Our prescription is to create institutions that allow for change in identity and promote cross-national cooperation. Our approach denies a role for institutions such as the minority veto that operate on the sole understanding that societal division is permanent.

The remainder of the book is as follows. Chapters 2 through 4 examine three cases to illustrate the argument: Spain, the EU, and Northern Ireland, respectively. In chapter 2, we examine the state of inequality of the Basques and Catalans as expressed through nationalist concerns in Spain, the failure of federalism (an internal solution), and the potential promise of the EU (an international/ external solution) to accommodate nationalist claims in this country. Importantly, this case demonstrates that federal solutions can exacerbate sub-national demands by segmenting the society into exclusive political communities as well as failing to promote an overlapping state identity.

We then explore the case of the EU in chapter 3. While there are no intractable ethnic/nationalist conflicts between the fifteen members of the EU (and soon to be expanded by an additional ten members), the case does provide interesting insights into the establishment of an international institution that has purposefully promoted a European identity. This Europe-wide identity overlaps with national identities, with the concomitant representation of the citizens of Europe in the EP through transnational groups and in national and sub-national governments and legislatures. In this way, groups are able to rectify perceived inequalities through representation in such institutions.

In chapter 4, the last case study examines the protracted conflict between Protestants and Catholics in Northern Ireland. We examine the historical background of the conflict, including the attempts by the British government to establish internal solutions that ultimately failed. We also provide evidence of a Northern Irish identity that transcends strict definitions of Protestant and Catholic. The existence of such a Northern Irish identity provides an opportunity for both groups to focus on viewing common interests. The chapter then looks at the 1998 Good Friday Agreement that contains both internal and international (cross-border) institutions as a means of increasing representation for both groups, but particularly Catholics, the minority. The Agreement also stipulates the role of the two main governments, the Republic of Ireland and the United Kingdom, as well as a role for the EU. The concluding chapter revisits the theoretical argument and recaps the analysis of the three cases. We then provide suggestions for areas of future research.

2

Inequality and Nationalist Conflicts

The Dual Process of State-Building
and Nation-Building in Spain

De ponent ni gent ni vent!
(From the West neither people nor wind).
—Benplantat the Giant, the mythical leader of the Catalan
spirit, warning against dealing with other nations

Joseph Carner Ribalta, *The Catalan Nation and Its People*

Spain is an instructive example of state-building in a multinational polity. The centralization of a Spanish state has progressed along with nation-building, especially among the historical minority nationalities. This dual process of state-building and nation-building maintains an uneasy, juxtaposed relationship. The centralization of Castilian authority in the nineteenth century and the efforts at centralization that the Franco dictatorship attempted in the twentieth century have done little to stop the forward motion of nation-building among, in particular, the Catalan and Basque communities. The failure of Spanish centralism is important because it is the main impetus for the contemporary federal Spanish state that emerged in the post-Franco period. To some degree, federalism is the new answer to the multinational makeup of the Spanish state.

Spain is an instructive example for a second reason: it provides a look into identity building in a postauthoritarian state. Gen.

Francisco Franco, dictatorial ruler of Spain from the end of the Spanish Civil War to his death (1939–1975), enlisted the power of the state in an attempt to homogenize the minority cultures in Spain. He tried to create a highly centralized, uniform image of Spain centered on the Castilian culture and language. To this end, the Spanish state oppressed its ethnic/cultural minority groups, in particular the Basques and the Catalans. The historical mistrust of the central government, a view held by the minority groups, worsened under the Franco dictatorship. The post-Franco transition to democracy combines two seemingly divergent processes: the creation of autonomous regions and federalism, with the subsequent building of national identities and the integration of Spain into the European Union (EU) and the building of a European identity.

Taking these two issues together, we argue in this chapter that the federal system does not solve the inherent tension between state-building and nation-building. The nature of the autonomous communities and the federal system promotes nation-building at the expense of state-building. The decentralization of politics and issues of identity has led to a renewal of calls for subnational government and independence. While we do not predict that the Spanish state will fracture under the federal arrangement, we do argue that the climate of increased sub-national demands inhibits state-building and fuels sub-nationalist movements and even terrorist/paramilitary activity. The formation of exclusive identities is the link between federalism and nationalist tensions. The division of the Spanish state into autonomous communities promotes the building of an exclusive identity in each community. This is more pronounced in the "historical" communities of Catalonia and the Basque Country, but it is also evident in the newly created communities.

The central thesis of this book is that cross-border parliamentary institutions are necessary in order to promote overlapping identities. These institutions in turn ameliorate conflict by promoting compromise and concession between national/ethnic groups. Spain is an example of how increasing the number of governing jurisdictions and providing a degree of regional governance and autonomy does not insure a reduction in sub-national demands. Rather, federalism exacerbates sub-national demands by segmenting the society into exclusive political communities. These exclusive communities use their autonomous position in an attempt to secure further devolution or even independence. The failure of federalism is that it institutionalizes ethnic/national differences; it does not promote recognition of an overarching state identity. Therefore, we argue that the federal Spanish state is unlikely to contain or channel sub-national demands into the greater project of state-building. Consequently, we conclude that federalism is a poor model for state-building in a state with ethno-nationalist divisions. The current constitutional arrangement does not encourage the nationalities to work together. It encourages instead the slow disintegration of the Spanish state.

The first section of this chapter provides some background information on the multinational character of the Spanish state. It highlights the long historical presence of a number of national communities and the lack of any early centralization of the state. It also provides a brief description of the centralization under the Kingdom of Castille-Leon. The second section looks at the Franco regime (1939–1975) and at the second attempt by the Spanish state to centralize authority. Franco also engaged in a forced normalization of the population through assimilation into the Castilian culture (i.e., the Spanish culture). We depict how these efforts by the regime laid the foundations of the current sub-national demands for increased autonomy.

The third section examines the transition to democracy and the development of federal Spain. It highlights the tension between creating a democratic, Spanish state and the accommodation of ethno-national demands. We demonstrate that while nationalist groups supported the ratification of the democratic Constitution, they did not agree unanimously to support the federal division of Spain. The Basques sought greater autonomy and recognition of their status as an historical community; thus they did not support the Constitution. In the last decade, there have been demands by the Basques and by other nationalities to alter the federal arrangement to provide the autonomous communities with even greater autonomy. We also examine the tension between national demands and state-centralization and the unfortunate degradation of the political dialogue to violent and military action. The fourth section focuses on identity building in federal Spain. It elaborates the counterproductive building of exclusive and sub-national identities in the autonomous communities. We argue that the inability of the federal arrangement to promote overlapping identities will hinder state-building. The fifth section provides an analysis of the connection between state-building and identity building. It outlines the reciprocal of our thesis: that the reduction of overlapping identities and the promotion of sub-national identity by institutions (i.e., federalism) leads to an exacerbation of tension and conflict rather than an amelioration.

The Multinational Spanish State

Our goal in this section is to provide a brief overview of the multinational character of modern Spain for the reader who may not possess extensive knowledge of the subject. As such, we do not intend to provide a complete picture of Spanish society or culture.[1] Our emphasis is on outlining the national and regional divisions within the Spanish state. We strive to show that modern Spain is now and always has been a divided state. Moreover, this section highlights the context in which we examine topics in later sections: the battle between center and periphery, between a Castilian (or "Spanish") identity and other national identities and even between state-building and nation-building.

Political, national, and linguistic borders divide modern Spain. Understanding the regional differences is paramount to understanding contemporary Spanish politics. As one scholar claims, "since the nineteenth century, regional demands have constituted one of the central issues in Spanish politics."[2] But the word "regional," especially as it relates to the term *periphery,* can mean two different and separate things. First, it can refer to political division (i.e., separate legislative and administrative jurisdiction) with the connotation that the current Spanish states and their demands are a central issue. Second, the word "regional" can refer to national division (i.e., separate communities) and nationalist demands under the central Spanish state. There is of course some overlap between these two definitions, as the minority nationalities tend to reside in well-defined and exclusive political communities. But there is a degree of divergence as well. Certain national groups, such as the Basques, reside in more than one political community. In the analysis that follows we endeavor to untangle these different meanings and show the diversity of multinational Spain.

That Spain is multicultural is evident. The diversity of culture is most obvious in the diversity of languages spoken within the borders of the Spanish state. While Spanish is universal in Spain not every citizen uses it as her first language. Table 2.1 lists the relative and absolute number of Spaniards who use a language other than Spanish as their first language.[3] Roughly 18% of the population uses a non-Spanish language as their language of choice and

Table 2.1. Linguistic Groups in Spain

Autonomous Communities	Language	Population (est.)	Percent of Pop.	% Having own Lang. as 1st Lang.
Whole of Spain		38,473,000	100	
Catalonia	Catalan	6,000,000	16.4	50
Balearic Islands	Balearic (Catalan)	680,000	1.76	64
Valencia	Valencian (Catalan)	3,700,000	9.7	40
Galicia	Galician	2,800,000	7.39	55
Basque Country	Basque	2,100,000	5.55	20
Navarre Vascuence	Basque	515,000	1.34	9

Source: Miquel Siguan, *Multilingual Spain* (Amsterdam: Swets and Zeitlinger, 1993).

24% can speak a non-Castilian language.[4] Four different languages reside in Spain: Spanish (or Castilian), Catalan, Basque, and Galician, in descending order of usage.

The distribution of non-Spanish speakers is concentrated in certain regions. Map 2.1 portrays the political and geographic boundaries of modern Spain. It is clear from map 2.1 that the linguistic minorities reside primarily on the periphery. For instance, almost all speakers of Galician reside in the Autonomous Community of Galicia. Likewise, almost all Basque speakers reside in the Basque Country and Navarre. Catalan is spoken in a number of different areas: Catalonia, the Balearic Islands, and Valencia (where the name of the regional dialect of Catalan is called Valencian).[5] The 1978 Constitution provides for the official recognition of these languages as coequal with Spanish. Roughly 42% of the Spanish population resides in Autonomous Communities (*Comunidades Autónomas*) that recognize a coequal language.[6]

National identity is a harder concept to measure, although once again, it is clear that a number of nationalities reside within Spain. As we discussed in chapter 1 an individual can possess more than one national identity (i.e., overlapping identities). As such it is difficult to identify with precision what percentage of the population of Spain holds a particular national identity. National identity tends to coincide with cultural and linguistic divisions, although not in every case. The residents of Andalucía do not speak a non-Spanish language, yet 89% of Andalucians purport to possess an Andalucian nationality.[7] Studies estimate that over 50% of those in

Map 2.1. Map of Spain and Subnational Linguistic Groups

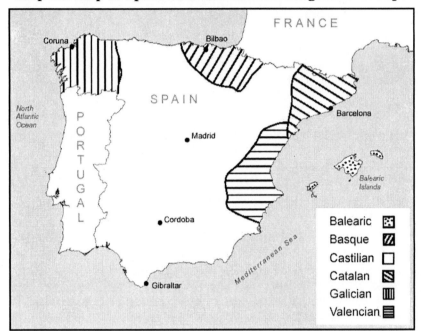

Source: Jose Terrero, *Geografia de Espana* (Barcelona: Editorial Ramon Sopena, 1978).

the Basque Country self-identify as "more Basque than Spanish" or "only Basque" while over 43% in Catalonia self-identify as "more Catalan than Spanish" or "only Catalan."[8] If such numbers are accurate, then anywhere from one-tenth to one-sixth of Spaniards identify more with a non-Spanish nationality than a with Spanish nationality.

Political division is easier to understand. The 1978 Constitution creates a federal Spanish state. It divides Spain into a central government and seventeen Autonomous Communities. The new federal arrangement is complex and contains contradictory and ambiguous conditions (we discuss this further in the next section). In short, the Constitution entails the "recognition of [the] regions' right to some form of autonomy, but with no statement on the definition of such autonomy, nor what powers it would entail."[9] Each Autonomous Community defines its own arrangement with the federal government through its own "Statute of Autonomy." All have in common "a president, an executive and a unicameral parliament . . . administrative organizations and a High Court of Justice."[10]

Each Autonomous Community has its own different set of competencies. The "specific areas of competency assigned . . . are established by a complex mechanism, dependent . . . on the particular route to autonomy . . . and . . . on the basis of negotiation between the Community and the central state, subject to approval by the Constitutional Tribunal."[11] Also, while the primary source of revenue for each community is from grants from the central budget, some communities have the ability to collect a limited set of taxes, thus raising additional revenue. In particular, the Basque Country and Navarre collect "contracted" taxes to support their historical form of administration. Because of these differences, scholars often portray federalism in Spain as asymmetrical.

The division of the Autonomous Communities also is a bit irregular. It recognizes the "historic" regions of Catalonia, the Basque Country, and Galicia while at the same time creating "new" regions without any "distinctive, historic tradition of autonomous identity," such as La Rioja and Murcia.[12] The institutionalization of regional identities in the separate Autonomous Communities has tended to promote these identities. Unexpectedly, it has also promoted "new" regional identities in the non-historic communities. We will return to this topic later in this chapter.

The multinational composition of Spain is a recent phenomenon. The process of state-building in Spain is separate from that of nation-building. The inherent contradiction between the centralizing dynamic of state-building and the focus on the locality in nation-building emerged with the centralization of the state in Castile in the fifteenth century. Thus, the center-periphery cleavage developed as the centralized state developed.[13] The next section outlines the development of the Spanish state, the process of centralization, and resistance by the nations on the periphery.

Building of the Spanish State: Castilian and Francoist Attempts at Centralization

Both the Catalans and the Basques resisted attempts at domination and centralism by Castile. But eventually both were conquered by the superior military might of the Spanish state. Centralization of the Spanish state began in the fifteenth century and continued through the building of the absolutist state in the seventeenth century. Catalan resistance to the rising Castilian regime ended in 1714 with the surrender of Barcelona to Philip V and his Franco-Spanish army. The Basques traditionally ruled themselves according to *fueros*, Basque historical administrative systems that dated back to the seventh century. Through two long civil wars, the Castilian regime abolished the *fueros* in 1876. Thus, Castile brought the two largest national minorities into union under the rule of the Spanish king.[14] In the following section we detail the process by which the Castilian state sought to centralize Spain. We highlight the incompleteness of assimilation and the continuation of regional identity.

The Crowns of Castile and Aragon (incorporating the Catalan-speaking community) united in 1479, creating the Kingdom of Spain. The actual Spanish state emerged in 1492 when the army of the Catholic monarchs, Ferdinand and Isabella, conquered Granada, displacing the last Muslim kingdom on the Iberian Peninsula. The incorporation of Navare (with its Basque-speaking community) in 1512 completed the acquisition of territory that is now part of modern Spain. This loose confederation of regions also was united with the Holy Roman Empire, led by the Habsburgs. Under the Habsburg monarchy, Spain would colonize Latin America, extend her European possessions, and be the staunchest defender of the Catholic Church.[15]

Thus, Spain was a strong, maritime, colonizing state, yet at the same time it lacked any effective centralization of power.[16] The separate kingdoms possessed different legislative bodies and autonomous institutions. For example, the Crown of Aragon maintained its own parliament (the *Cortes*), while the Basque provinces maintained their *fueros*.[17] Furthermore, each of the Basque provinces had separate *fueros* as each had separate autonomy.[18] While the elite in Castile used a single language, the common people spoke a number of different languages. In conjunction with the inability of this loose confederation to centralize effectively the Spanish state, the power of the Habsburg Empire slowly declined from the seventeenth to the nineteenth centuries.[19]

How successful were the Castilians in centralizing the Spanish state and introducing a single national identity? Did a "proto-nationalist" identity within the Spanish state exist by the eighteenth century? Scholars disagree. José Alvarez Junco suggests that a pre- or protonational identity (which he terms ethno-

patriotic) did in fact exist. He says that while Spain comprises separate kingdoms the subjects of the Spanish state shared the same
religion (i.e., Catholicism), shared common enemies (e.g., the
French and English), and shared a common literary culture. All of
which leads to a collective Spanish identity. While Alvarez Junco
admits that the "general population felt much more linked to their
local communities than to any 'imaginary community' spanning
territory beyond the immediate area" he argues that overarching
institutions, such as the Catholic Church, provided a means to
transmit a Spanish identity.[20]

Alvarez Junco asserts that this Spanish identity comprised
four features. The first feature was "a fusion of religious and political identity."[21] The Catholic identity of Spain became the most
salient identity for Spaniards versus outside nations. The second
feature was "a deep-rooted xenophobia."[22] In particular, Spaniards
feared the English and the French. Spain had fought the former
constantly for centuries both in Europe and in the Americas. From
the latter, Spain adopted its administrative-political system. Its
adoption uprooted many historical and cultural traditions and
engendered in the population an anti-French sentiment. The third
feature was Eurocentrism. The Spanish conquests in America were
secondary to Spanish concerns on the European continent. The last
feature was a "defensive, victimized and self-pitying tone."[23] Spain
saw itself as battered by numerous foes whose superior might pre-
vented Spain from achieving any triumphant victories.

Other authors insist that alternate identities, particularly
among the historical nations, were stronger and maintained their
salience well into the nineteenth century. A number of works
explaining Catalan and Basque nationalism chronicle the existence
and maintenance of these identities despite Castilian attempts at
centralization.[24] Consequently, the centralization of the Spanish
state under the Castilian throne did not lead to the rapid homoge-
nization of all Spaniards. National minorities retained their cultural and linguistic identity.

Economic differences between Castile and the periphery also
contributed to the lack of cultural standardization. At the time of
the Castilian conquest of Catalonia and the Basque Country, both
regions were among the more modern and industrial areas of
Spain. Their subjugation opened both regions to migration from
the less advanced regions, primarily from the central and rural
areas. Thus, both found themselves governed by a militarily

superior, but economically (and perhaps politically) backward state. The new immigrants, new language, new laws, and new culture now threatened the cultural separatism of the two communities. This led to social and economic transformations that upset the traditional culture and society in both regions.[25] The national minorities were forced to accept an unequal position in which their cultures were devalued and judged as being unequal. Preference in politics and economics was given to those of Castilian nationality.

Pressures for centralization gained momentum during the nineteenth century. The Napoleonic wars and the Napoleonic army brought the modern conceptualization of "nationalism" into Spain. The new presence of nationalism had two effects. First, it led to calls for a Spanish national identity and for a stronger Spanish state. In response to the French attempt to change the ruling dynasty in Spain to one more friendly to France, the Spanish state rallied in its own defense. In what would later be termed the *War of Independence,* the citizens of Spain rallied to protect their cities from sieges by Napoleonic troops. In this war the supporters of Ferdinand presented "the struggle as a national uprising of the Spanish people against a French attempt to dominate them."[26] In this way the mythology of a unified, Spanish state was born.

Second, nationalism spawned prenationalist movements. These "prenationalisms" would later transmute into full-blown national movements. Spain did not get to bask in the limelight of its new nationalism very long before critics questioned its legitimacy. The period from 1808 to 1875 saw the rapid replacement of governments and criticism of the Spanish state from autocrats, liberals, and the military. The Carlist Wars (1834–1837, 1870–1876) sapped the strength, and quite possibly retarded the economic and political development, of Spain. After the Napoleonic invasion "a small 'liberal' elite sought to impose a rationalized, uniform and highly centralized form of state authority, modeled on the French post-Revolutionary model."[27] The Carlists (i.e., supporters of Don Carlos, a claimant to the Spanish throne) rebelled against this new centralization. Support for the Carlists was greatest in the rural regions of Spain and in the Basque region. In the latter, the peasants fought in support of the *fuero*s (and Catholicism) and against the centralizing political authority and urbanization of the cities. The eventual defeat of the Carlists led to the abolishment of the *fuero*s (1876) and an end to local authority in the Basque region.[28]

As Ken Medhurst points out, the founder of modern Basque nationalism, Sabino Arana, came from a Carlist family.[29] Arana's new formulation of Basque nationalism incorporated two principles fundamental to Carlism: affinity for the provincial rights (i.e., *fueros*) and a defense of Catholicism. However, he added two modern nationalist concepts: race as a basis to espouse an exclusive Basque identity and a call for Basque national independence (as opposed to just local control). It is important to note here that Arana studied in Barcelona and to some degree imitated the emerging Catalan nationalism. The major difference is that while Catalan nationalism expressed itself through a linguistic and literary renewal (*Renaixença*) the Basque nationalism of Arana stressed ethnicity.[30] We will return to this distinction later in this chapter and show how it has shaped the long-term differences between Basque and Catalan nationalism.

During the nineteenth century, the Spanish state never became the liberal nation nor democratic polity that Britain and France became.[31] The Catholic Church, the nobility, the monarchy and the military maintained power in Spain during this period. Alvarez Junco points out that this conservative leadership of Spain failed to support a nationalizing process and did little to build a national identity. Moreover, the loss of the Spanish navy and its possessions in the Americas, as well as other factors such as fiscal mismanagement, placed the Spanish state into a chronic position of indebtedness. The inability of the Spanish state to rule effectively led to constant opposition to the state by reform-minded movements.[32]

The Bourbon Restoration Monarchy (1875–1923), succeeding the chaotic First Republic (1872–1873), ushered in a period of relative stability. A consensus between the industrial bourgeoise, the military, and the aristocracy led to a pseudodemocracy in which the conservative elements of Spanish society maintained control over the political realm.[33] The two wars of the late nineteenth century (Spanish-Cuban, 1895–1898 and Spanish-American, 1898)[34] exposed the inability of the Restoration Monarchy to create a strong, central Spanish state. It also exposed the association of Spanish nationalism with the imagery of the aristocracy. Sebastian Balfour points out that the monarchy developed Spanish nationalism in its efforts to fight the Americans and that this nationalism was accepted by the Spanish society as it mobilized for war.[35] The defeat of the respondent and powerful Spanish "lion" by the "plebian, gluttonous, dirty, cowardly and mercenary" American "pig" was almost impossible for the Restoration government to fathom.[36] The Spanish defeat struck at the heart of the Spanish identity as a traditional, conservative society by displaying how powerful the modern, commercial state (i.e., the U.S.) was in comparison.

The modernization of Spain and the industrialization, urbanization, and migration that it brought meshed with the Spanish defeats to create a crisis of Spanish identity. Challengers to the Restoration accommodation emerged from seemingly everywhere. Socialists and working-class movements sprung up on the left. Anarchists and Republicans sprouted on the right. And, perhaps more central to this work, regional nationalisms gained in strength. Catalan nationalism espoused devolution to the regions and to a multinational Spanish state.[37] Basque nationalism, primarily reacting to modernization, spread among the peasantry and rural clergy.[38] The ideology of the military moved rapidly to the right during this period, posing another threat to the Spanish state.

The Restoration collapsed in 1923 under enormous pressure from these unaligned but all-threatening forces. The Conservative and Liberal parties, the two parties that alternated in power under the Restoration through support of the traditional *caciques*, had a falling-out in 1909 after a failed attempt at reform by the Conservative leader Antonio Maura. The *Mauristas*, supporters of Maura, became the first true right-wing group in Spain. The Socialists (PSOE) struggled to gain acceptance from the proletariat and anarchist groups grew in strength. The end result was the destabilization of Spanish politics.[39]

Spanish neutrality during the First World War did little to quell the unrest and may have even exacerbated the tension for two reasons. First, it polarized opinion in Spain into pro-German and pro-Western camps. Spanish neutrality was initially popular among almost all groups. However, continued German sinking of Spanish merchant shipping, the entry of the United States into the war, and a growing sympathy for the Western democracies led to calls for Spanish entry on the side of the Western Allies. However, the king of Spain, Alfonso XIII, continued to veto any shift from neutrality as he regarded such a move as dangerous to the Spanish state. Alfonso XIII feared that he might be the next Nicholas II if the war started going badly. He also was apprehensive about siding with the wrong side in the conflict, that is, the Western democracies, for fear that this might undermine his rule.[40]

Second, the war had a profound impact on the Spanish economy. Industrialization expanded greatly as Spain used its neutral stance to supply both sides in the conflict. However, the economic boom was asymmetrical. Industrialization and urbanization led to the strengthening of the Catalan region and organized labor while rural areas experienced food shortages and unemployment. The government had neither the will nor the resources to address this differential effect of the wartime economy.[41] In 1917 the army entered directly into politics. Gen. Miguel Primo de Rivera intervened in 1923, establishing a dictatorship under his rule that would last until 1930 and the founding of the Second Republic.[42]

The divisions of the Spanish society that had been building over the last few decades beset the Second Republic (1931–1936).[43] These divisions included a class division (i.e., workers vs. owners); a church-state division (i.e., clerical vs. secular); a center-periphery division (i.e., central state vs. regions); and a conservative-liberal division (i.e., Monarchists vs. Republicans). Helen Graham points out that this polarization of Spanish society and politics accompanied the fragmentation of each component.[44] She indicates that organized labor and the progressive Republicans, two groups instrumental to the health of the Republic, were both internally fragmented. Graham continues that this fragmentation helps explain why from 1931 to 1933 the government could not deliver social or economic reform. In short, she argues that while the military coup of July 17–18, 1936, did not achieve control of the Spanish state, it did expose the polarization and fragmentation of Spanish politics, therefore, "precipitating a state crisis of unprecedented proportions."[45]

The period of Civil War (1936–1939) is fascinating in Spanish history, if not European and world history in general.[46] One point that we stress as important to identity building is that the Basque community divided its loyalties among the Nationalists and Republicans during the war. Basque nationalism revived after the fall of Primo de Rivera. The repressive nature of Primo's dictatorship led to a resurgence of radical nationalism in the Basque regions.[47] The Basque population voted for autonomy in a referendum in 1936 and subsequently established a local government. But Basque political sympathies were fragmented. While the Basque regions of Vizcaya and Guipúzcoa supported the Republicans, principally because the Republicans promised them autonomy, much of Álava and Navare sided with the Nationalists (i.e., Francoists).[48] Many elements of the *Partido Nacional Vasco* (PNV) felt more comfortable with the heirs of the Carlists than with the Anarchists, radical Socialists, and Communists fighting for the Republic.[49] However, with the occupation of the Basque regions by the Franco forces, most Basques turned toward opposition. In a display of national identity and after the signing of the Pact of Santoña, the Basque army declared the war with the Nationalists over and refused to fight for them outside of the Basque territories.[50] This action highlights the belief that the Basque participation in the Civil War was coincidental. The Basque struggle against the Francoist forces was just one chapter in the Basque struggle against the centralized Spanish state.[51]

The significance of this continued struggle of the periphery versus the central state is that it continued to simmer under the Franco dictatorship (1939–1975) in spite of Franco's attempt at centralization of authority and *hispanolizacion* of culture and society.[52] We emphasize the following two points. First, nationalist sentiments became latent under Franco's rule but did not dissolve. Second, Catalan and Basque nationalism diverged greatly under Franco's rule, not just in their formulation but also in their expression.

The Franco dictatorship was repressive and resistance was a dangerous business. Franco initially imposed a series of measures that sought to eliminate all surviving opposition. His use of the army, especially in the Basque regions, subjected portions of the Spanish population to state-directed terror. Franco directed the *Falange* (the Francoist fascist party), the state (primarily through laws such as the 1939 Law of Political Responsibilities), and the Church to form a new national identity.[53] Franco's direction of the Church was important in his control of social organization in Spain.[54]

In the process, these same institutions sought to eradicate "all vestiges of ethnopolitical identity."[55] Literary and cultural works would no longer be conducted in Basque or Catalan. Initially, the almost full ban on the use of national languages devastated the national minorities, sending hundreds of thousands into exile. But with the Allied victory in World War II and the slow move of Franco away from fascist ideology, nationalism in the Basque regions and Catalonia grew slowly in a clandestine environment.[56]

But Basque and Catalan nationalism did not emerge in the same form. Basque nationalism became radical and violent. Frustration among PNV members led to the establishment of the *Euskadi Ta Askatasuna* (ETA, Basque Homeland and Liberty) in 1959 and a shift toward armed, terrorist resistance. Conversi explains that the increasing inability of PNV to respond to the

Franco measures led to nationalist unrest, particularly among the Basque youths. He summarizes that "the 'emerging' generation were young enough to be impatient with the inertia of the their fathers, but old enough to remember the atrocities committed by Madrid after the fall of the Republic."[57] The first ETA act was a bombing in 1961, with the first victim of ETA violence in 1968 and the first premeditated political murder by ETA later in 1968.[58] On the other hand, Catalan nationalism became more moderate. The focus of the resurgent Catalan identity was on cultural and linguistic revival. This may be due to the more elite-driven and practical nature of Catalan nationalism.[59] We will return to the difference between Basque and Catalan nationalism in a later section of this chapter.

By the end of the Franco regime its attempts to homogenize the ethnic minorities had failed clearly. There is ample evidence to show that far from eradicating non-Spanish, national identities, these identities "dug in" and maintained themselves.[60] The level of mistrust between the central government and the regional national groups worsened under Franco, but the centralized government kept it hidden. With the end of state repression, these nationalisms became free to express themselves. Just as the end of the Primo dictatorship brought nationalist calls for autonomy, so would the end of the Franco dictatorship. We explore the nature of nationalism under democratic governance in the next section.

The Transition to Democracy in Spain: The Constitution, Federalism, and Regional Autonomy

Under the 1969 Law of Succession, Prince Juan Carlos assumed the position of head of state upon the death of Francisco Franco. Thus began a process by which the dictatorship dismantled itself. The entire process of democratization would occur within the boundaries of the Francoist constitutional framework.[61] Franco's death presented Spain with a genuine opportunity to reinstitute democracy and to join the mainstream of European political current.[62]

Evident at the time were the dangers in the democratizing process. Spain's previous attempts at democratic governance had ended in right-wing dictatorships. Moreover, some of the conservative institutions that had supported these dictatorships were still powerful, for example, the army and the Church. Moreover, Franco had groomed Juan Carlos since he was a child. Thus, many questioned the commitment of Juan Carlos to democracy and true reform. Juan Carlos's eventual selection of Adolfo Suárez proved both his true loyalty to democracy and led to a process of reform in which there was no constitutional crisis or breakdown in state authority. Suárez even managed to get the Francoist institutions to legislate themselves out of power.[63]

Of special interest to this study is the foundation and workings of the seven-member *ponencia*. The Committee on Constitutional Matters and Public Liberties commissioned the *ponencia* to create a draft of the new Constitution. The members include three from the *Unión de Centro Democrático* (UCD, Center-right, former Francoists), one from the *Partido Socialista Obrero Español* (PSOE, Socialists), one from the Alianza Popular (AP, Right Populist), one from the *Partido Comunista de Español-Partit Socialista Unificat de Catalunya* (PCE-PSUC, Communist), and one from the *Convergència i Unió* (CiU, Catalan moderate). This committee completed two drafts, one of which the Constitutional Committee, the Congress, and the Senate, and the people through Public Referendum endorsed in 1978.[64] Basque discontent with the constitution (detailed further in the next section) arises from many issues. However, the exclusion of the PNV, or any other Basque representative, from the *ponencia* signaled to the Basques that the Spanish parties would not hear their concerns. One author argues that the PNV may have been less oppositional, and certainly less critical, of the eventual Constitution if they had been included in its framing.[65] As an example of how disturbing the exclusion was to the PNV, in May of 1978 when the PNV heard that secret deals were being brokered in the *ponencia* they withdrew their membership from the Constitutional Committee. Thus, the main issue of whether to have a unitary or decentralized state was made with some input from the Catalans but none from the Basques. In this instance, the Basques felt that they lacked representation in decisionmaking that impacted them. The PNV would negotiate directly with Suárez to obtain promises of some degree of self-determination, leading to the July 1978 Statute of Guernica. This distinction is important when we consider later the differences in Catalan and Basque acceptance of the current federal framework.[66]

The 1978 Spanish Constitution replaced the extreme centralization and conservatism of the Franco regime with a democratic state and the recognition of national minorities.[67] The new federal Spain would be based on a model of symmetrical decentralization, referred to colloquially as *café para todos* (coffee for everyone). The

Constitution created seventeen Autonomous Communities, of which some represent culturally distinct minorities (Catalonia, the Basque Country, and Galicia) while the others do not. The Constitution grants these regional communities a wide range of competencies (including health, education, and agriculture) while reserving certain powers (e.g., justice and defense) to the national government. The 1978 Constitution provided a staggered recognition of the autonomy of the new Autonomous Communities. The Constitution granted immediate "full autonomy" to the three historical nationalities (*nationalidades históricos*, i.e., Catalonia, the Basque Country, and Galicia) while the other fourteen communities underwent a five-year period of "restricted autonomy" (we talk more about this process in the next section). This restricted devolution created resentment among the fourteen non-historical communities. These fourteen felt that the "historical" nationalities were receiving privileges denied the new, territorial nationalities.[68] All communities share a common structure: a unicameral regional legislature and a community presidency.

Federalism was introduced into the new Constitution as a solution to the nationalist demands of two regional and cultural minority groups in Spain, the Basques and the Catalans. The prospects of democracy allowed submerged nationalist feelings to rise. Popular demonstrations erupted in most Spanish cities, with the largest occurring in Barcelona and Vitoria. More than a million people rallied in Barcelona, pressing demands for "freedom, amnesty and [a] statute of autonomy."[69] The situation was more tense in the Basque Country. Police brutality and repression was excessive toward the Basques during late Francoism. At the time of Franco's death, the Basque Country had the largest prison population in Spain.[70] The Basque perception of unequal standing and unequal treatment within a Castilian state contributed to the outbreak of violence just before and during the transition to democracy. As a result. ETA and its political wing, *Herri Batasuna* (Basque Homeland and Freedom Party, HB), gained in popularity and Basque nationalism became more radical.

This federal arrangement has not been fully successful in accommodating the demands of the Basques nor Catalans. Both communities want to be recognized as nations within a multinational Spain. In particular, the Basques argued that the Constitution was ambiguous about Basque rights. Moreover, it treated the Basque nationality as equal with the pseudonationalities, as opposed to its rightful position as one of the historic nationalities.[71]

Paradoxically, it was this equal treatment of all regional autonomies that Basques perceived as unfair.[72]

A number of scholars point out that the constitution is ambiguous about some very important aspects of the Spanish democracy.[73] The three ambiguities regarding the role of the head of state, the duties of the armed forces, and the status of the Catholic Church do not play an important role in this study. The fourth, the structure of the Spanish state is of tantamount importance. Many authors conclude that the definition of the "state" in the Spanish Constitution is unclear at best, and used in an inconsistent manner at worst.[74] Paul Heywood points out that the term *state* has at least two separate and perhaps irreconcilable meanings in the Constitution. It sometimes refers to "the group of general and central institutions . . . specifically counterposing these to institutions which belong to the Autonomous Communities" and other times refers to "the entire juridico-political apparatus of the Spanish nation, including those organizations which are specific to the nationalities and regions."[75] Through comparison with the equally ambiguous Italian Constitution, another author identifies three different usages of the term *state*: *Estado-comunidad* (state as community, similar to the second usage), *Estado-aparato* (state as apparatus, similar to the first usage), and *Estado-ordenamiento* (state as ordinance, meaning the totality of all elements and encompassing both usages).[76]

This ambiguity over the definition of the state takes on greater importance when we juxtapose it to the new federal, decentralized system of Autonomous Communities (*el estado de las autonomías*). The Constitution provides for three separate relationships between the central state and the Autonomous Communities: powers exclusive to the central state, powers shared between the state and Autonomous Communities, and powers exclusive to the Autonomous Communities. The last set of powers devolved to the regions through either the "fast route" (Article 151) or the "slow route" (Article 143). As we mentioned previously, the Basque Country, Catalonia, and Galicia (i.e., the historic nationalities) compose the three on the fast track.[77] Negotiations between Suárez and the Basques and Catalan nationalists set the precedent for the remaining regions (i.e., the regions without a historic minority) to press for greater autonomy.

Despite this two-track approach, the Constitution also left alternate routes to autonomy open for exploitation. In particular, the Constitution allows the *Cortes* to pass laws that devolve extra powers to the Autonomous Communities. Furthermore, the regional governments could determine the level of shared powers through each region's statute of autonomy.[78] A particularly telling quote comes from an UCD member from Andalusia emphasizing the psychological effect of the process and how it pushed the Autonomous Communities into a race toward autonomy sometimes called "autonomy fever":[79]

> The UCD made a great error by not understanding the Andalusian mentality, in the sense that Andalusians . . . are not autonomists. We are not. But we are not less than the Basques, not historically, not in any way, because we have a more ancient civilization than the Basques and the Catalans. . . . The Basques and the Catalans by [Article] 151, and Andalusians by [Article] 143. Why? . . . Everybody in the same way, or not at all.[80]

Thus, "the creation of *un estado de las autonomías* took place in an ad hoc, piecemeal, and uncoordinated manner" rather than through a thoughtful, precise plan.[81] This process produced an incentive for the Autonomous Communities to engage in identity building in order to prove a need for quicker autonomy. We will return to this issue in the following section.

After the failed coup attempt of 1981, Spain consolidated its constitutional rule. Central to this process was the LOAPA (*Ley Orgánica de Armonización del Proceso Autonómico*, "the Organic Law on the Harmonization of the Autonomy Process"), which sought to harmonize and limit the various powers and competencies of the regions. The Cortes enacted LOAPA in an attempt to make regional government authority more uniform. One of LOAPA's more notorious terms was that central state law was always to prevail when in conflict with regional law, even law in the regions of the historic minorities.[82] Catalan and Basque nationalists appealed against LOAPA in 1983, claiming that it led to government regulation of practices (e.g., the *fueros*, the set of common laws, and charters of the Basque Country) that are native to a region. In particular, the Basques and the Catalans claimed that LOAPA sought to remove their national identity.[83] Both the masses and the elite in Catalonia and the Basque Country opposed LOAPA on the grounds that it would limit regional autonomy. One PNV official claimed, "The extension of the [autonomy] process to other communities [under LOAPA], many of them fictitious, and especially the creation of uniprovincial communities have a very clear meaning—the weakening of our claims which derive from the historic tradition of the Basques and the Catalans."[84]

In the same year the Constitutional Court ruled that while the principle behind LOAPA was a good one (i.e., that all regions and groups within Spain should be considered equal) institutional conformity was not compatible with the autonomous process.[85] From 1983 to 1993 LOAPA was abandoned and the Constitutional Court handled decisions on the autonomous powers and conflicts between them and the national powers. Due to a reconsideration of the power of the Spanish Senate in the 1990s, authority to resolve disputes over autonomous powers moved out of the Constitutional Court. From 1994 to the present the General Committee for the Autonomous Communities in the Senate handles such issues. Thus, despite twenty years of democracy, Basque and Catalan nationalists have still found that their calls for nationalist recognition have gone unheeded. Moreover, it is clear that conflict over center-periphery issues has not receded. All federal arrangements lead to a certain low degree of continual conflict between the central power and the regional powers (e.g., the ever present tension in the American or German systems between the federal government and the states). However, Spain is different in one major aspect: it does not have a blueprint for the orderly transformation of the old Francoist, centralized Spanish state to the new post-Franco, federal Spanish state.[86]

The lack of a blueprint allows the latent center-periphery divide to continue without any firm resolution or even an anticipation of a resolution. Thus, latent nationalist or periphery demands may reemerge as potent and salient issues. One author claims that the "peripheral nationalisms of the Catalans and Basques have become the strongest stateless nationalisms in Western Europe."[87] In the 1998 Declaration of Barcelona the main nationalist parties of Catalonia, the Basque Country, and Galicia signed a joint declaration demanding a multicultural and multinational definition of Spain. The goal was to signal their preference for a more asymmetrical decentralization. The Barcelona Declaration seeks something akin to the current wave of devolution occurring in Britain where Scotland and Wales have gained differing degrees of political autonomy mirroring their intensity of nationalist aspirations.[88] To summarize, the parties to the Declaration seek the recognition of their communities as nations and not as regions. They seek greater self-determination within a less unitary Spain, their goal for many centuries. In the next section we examine the continuing salience of identity and nation in Spain. We show that federalism exacerbates the building of exclusive identities, leading to a destabilization of Spanish politics.

Identity-Building: Institutions, Nation, and Nationalism in Spain

Our central hypothesis is inherently constructivist: institutions can promote identity formation, identities are malleable, and individuals can possess multiple identities. Institutions can promote either inclusive, overlapping identities or an exclusive identity. We argued in chapter 1 that institutions that promote overlapping identities provide the groundwork for conflict reduction. The opposite is also true: institutions that promote an exclusive identity provide the foundation for increased conflict. In this section we show how the federal state in Spain promotes the formation of exclusive identities. In brief, the pattern of causation is as follows. Federalism allows for greater regional autonomy. Regional parliaments emerge in order to administer autonomous competencies. Nationalist and regional political parties contest elections and eventually win the power to govern the regional parliaments. The nationalist/regional parties base their appeals on the promotion of nationalist/regional identity. National identities, rather than an overarching state identity, gain in prominence and center-periphery conflict increases.

Spain is of interest because of the two historical attempts (Castilian Empire and Franco regime) at creating a central state. The centralization of the state did produce by the eighteenth century the development of a Spanish identity. Also, the Franco regime was somewhat effective in its process of *españolización*. However, alongside this "national" identity, the regional identities also developed.[89] Non-Castilian nationalities retreated during periods of intense Spanish centralization, but they neither vanished nor merged with the dominant culture. The regional nationalities, especially Catalan and Basque, form a coherent periphery cleavage, as discussed previously, which has been latent at times, but that now is becoming more and more manifest.

The link between institutions and national identity formation is clear: cultural, social, and political institutions in the nations can either promote identities inclusive of a Spanish identity or promote an exclusive identity. The difference in institutional structure of each nation provides for the difference in the current pattern of nationalism. In particular, the Catalan identity is more inclusive of a Spanish identity while the Basque identity is primarily exclusive of all other identities. This difference can be traced to three elements: a difference in the main forms of acceptable political participation, a difference in the salience of language, and the impact of modernization.

Juan Díez Medrano argues that identity and nationalism in Catalonia and the Basque Country developed in different ways: the former inclusive and the latter exclusive. Moreover, he seeks to explain why the Basque nationalist movement developed a radical flavor while the Catalan nationalist did not.[90] Díez Medrano rejects the theory that Basque radicalism is solely the product of repression by the central state, as advanced by some earlier authors.[91] The repression theory claims that the violence inflicted against the Basques by the Franco regime forced the Basque nationalists to resort to the use of violence. This led to the shifting of the nationalist focus from the PNV to ETA. The emergence of ETA in 1959 was the direct result of the inactivity of the PNV in opposing Franco. Díez Medrano rejects this theory (as does Danicle Conversi in the next section) on the grounds that Catalonia also suffered repression but did not develop any substantial radical militant nationalists. The repression theory also has difficulty explaining the continuance of ETA in the 1980s and 1990s under democratic g-overnance.[92]

Díez Medrano advances a "structural conduciveness" theory to explain the differences in nationalism. The structures of political mobilization in each community dictate the forms of political activity by which nationalism expresses itself. If there exists a large number and/or broad distribution of social, cultural, and economic institutions to promote political mobilization, the resulting nationalist activity encompasses a wide range of action, thought, and ideology. This produces a nationalist movement that can seek compromise and can accommodate inclusion of others. Díez Medrano argues that the diversity of the Catalan societal institutions promotes a broad nationalist movement that incorporates both moderate and extreme forms of nationalism. He points to the role of the middle class, intelligentsia, universities, and others in seeking relative consensus.[93]

Díez Medrano posits that the socioeconomic institutions in the Basque region are more dependent on the central Spanish economy. Moreover, Basque society, with its domination by the Church, is conservative and reactionary. Basque nationalism developed in a more radical manner. Under the threats of modernization and urbanization, the Basque institutions could not find ways to accommodate the changes. ETA and others turned to Marxist ideology and to extreme pronationalist forms of activity. Thus, the "radicalization of Basque nationalism can be explained not so much by Spanish oppression . . . as by the persistence of an older anticapitalist political culture whose youthful militants experienced the full effects of the crisis of late modernity."[94] Therefore, Díez Medrano qualifies and perhaps clarifies the repression theory.

Conversi agrees that the Catalan nationalism is more inclusive. He outlines six elements that contribute to differences in Basque and Catalan nationalism: class, culture, economics, politics, history, and anthropology. His primary focus is on the linguistic differences between the two communities and the salience of language to each. As Stanley Payne points out, Conversi's "economic and class explanations parallel those of Díez Medrano"[95] so it is Conversi's emphasis on language that distinguishes the two authors. Also, both distinguish themselves from previous authors who focus primarily on Basque culture as the source of Basque radicalism.[96]

Conversi argues that one of the primary ingredients of Catalan nationalism and identity is language.[97] The ubiquitous nature of the Catalan language allows it to persist as an important foundation of Catalan nationalism. Kathryn A. Woolard explains that four possible popular definitions of Catalan identity (i.e., birthplace, descent, sentiment/behavior, and language) exist. Of these "language . . . is both the most commonly used and the most powerful."[98] Language is the foundation of Catalan identity, providing the focus for inclusion into the Catalan community.

The central importance of language as the definition of Catalan identity unites political and cultural nationalism. Language is a unifying national symbol. Conversi argues that this unity gives Catalan nationalism its particular strength, stability, and inclusiveness. Immigrants to Catalonia were never resented, but rather welcomed and assimilated. Jordi Pujol, a nationalist leader and thinker, expressed the integration of immigrants into the Catalan nationality in a succinct manner:

> The basic objective is to build up a community valid for all
> Catalans. And I would add that by Catalan I mean every-
> body who lives and works in Catalonia, and who makes
> Catalonia his/her own home and country, with which
> he/she incorporates and identifies. . . . Language is the
> decisive factor in integration. It is the most definitive. A
> man who speaks Catalan and who speaks Catalan to his
> children, is already a Catalan at heart.[99]

Conversi posits that the widespread use of the Catalan language
and its similarity to Spanish make it more essential to
(im)migrants for employment and easier for Spanish migrants to
learn.[100]

Evidence of this assimilation exists. Immigrants to Catalonia
and to the Basque Country do identify themselves as possessing
multiple identities. Immigrants who expressed only a Spanish
identity fell by one-half and one-third from 1979 to 1991, respectively in Catalonia and in the Basque Country.[101] Moreover, a
growing acceptance of the compatibility of Spanish and a Basque or
Catalan identity is evident even among natives of the nationalist
regions. Only 47.6% of natives in the Basque Country saw themselves as exclusively Basque or Spanish, as compared to 60.3% in
1979. Likewise, exclusivity among natives in Catalonia dropped
from 37.1% to 27.9%.[102] Taking immigrants and natives together,
there is mild evidence that overlapping identities are emerging.
Gary Marks compares self-identification in the nationalist regions
from 1979 to 1994.[103] He finds that the percentage of respondents
identifying themselves as having multiple identities increases by
12% (44% to 56%) in the Basque Country and 17% (50% to 67%) in
Catalonia.[104] The percent of immigrants in Catalonia who self-
identify as only Spanish has dropped from 63.8% to 32.0% from
1979 to 1991. In 1991 more than half of all immigrants in Catalan
see themselves as more Catalan than Spanish or at least as Catalan as Spanish.[105]

The ability of immigrants to understand the Basque language
(Euskera) can provide evidence for or against assimilation. The
Basque language is divided into a number of dialects, is very difficult to learn, being a remnant of a pre-Indo-European language,
and is spoken by few Basques themselves. Whereas 86% of the population in Catalonia understand Catalan, over 64% can either speak
or read it, and 31% can write it, and only 28% of the Basque population can understand Euskera with about the same number who can

speak, read, or write it.[106] The number of Euskera speakers is roughly 400,000 to 500,00; a figure that has remained fairly constant since the middle of the nineteenth century.[107] However, as a percent of the population of the Basque regions, Euskera speakers have declined over this same time period from over 50% of the population to certainly less than 30% and maybe even less than 20%.[108]

However, if we look at the post-Franco period we see a resurgence in spoken Basque. The number of Euskera speakers has increased dramatically from roughly 450,000 in 1981 to 540,000 in 1991.[109] Correspondingly, the percent of the population in the Basque regions who speak Euskera increased from 21.5% to 26.27% over the same time period. The continuation of this trend into the future looks bright. The number of students educated in Euskera has advanced 50% since 1981.[110]

In contrast to the assimilative nature of Catalan nationalism and its use of language, Basque nationalism uses language as an ethnic barrier. Basque nationalist Sabino Arana, who himself did not speak Euskara as a child, but rather learned it as an adult, commented that the "difference between languages . . . is a great means of preserving ourselves from the contagion of the Spaniards . . . if our invaders were to learn Euskera, we would have to abandon it."[111] To this end, Arana sought to "utilize the language . . . as an instrument of political mobilization."[112] The language could be used to spur Basque nationalism among the Basque people.

Arana was not successful in his attempt primarily because the inhabitants of the larger cities (e.g., Bilbao) did not speak the language and did not care to learn. Furthermore, "some Basques, uninterested in or disenchanted with the nationalist struggle, have reacted against the language movement as part of their rejection of politically motivated Basque patriotism."[113] Predictably, the "politicization" of the Basque language reduces its usage among non-Basques in the Basque regions.

The exclusivity of the Basque national identity is a way to keep the Basque people from mixing with immigrants to the Basque Country or foreigners (*maketos*). Basque nationalism relies on the concept of a collective nobility (*hidalguía colectiva*) of the Basque people. The Basques think of themselves as possessing an ethnic uniqueness.[114] Foreign immigration into the Basque Country threatens and possibly dilutes this uniqueness.

This difference in the use of language as a national symbol contributes to the difference in the nature of nationalism: inclusive in Catalonia and exclusive in the Basque Country.[115] As we mentioned earlier, Ole Waever elucidates the distinction between civic/political identity and ethno-cultural identity.[116] It is clear that Catalan nationalism defines itself by the former and Basque nationalism by the latter. While Catalan nationalism is centered on a widespread use of the language, Basque nationalism must develop the language in order to produce a more widespread nationalism.

Moreover, the differing nature produces differing methods of achieving nationalist goals: political negotiation by Catalan nationalists and militancy by Basque nationalists. Since the early 1960s, the Basque separatist group, ETA, has waged a campaign of violence and terrorism against the Spanish state. Journalists report that over 800 people have died from ETA actions.[117]

The activity of ETA elicits a novel definition of Basque identity. Many ETA activists are sons of immigrants or even immigrants themselves. Their active participation, not their ethnicity, defined them as Basques. Action became important as a designator of identity. Anyone willing to take action for the cause of Basque nationalism is a Basque.[118] Thus, in the last two decades, the Basque identity has become less exclusive, but the barrier to inclusion is still quite high.

To return to a concept that we mentioned earlier, another way to understand the differences between Basque and Catalan nationalism is to focus on modernization. While both regions possessed wealth, Catalonia was already urbanized and a strong middle class was present. The Basque region was not urbanized nor industrialized. Therefore, "the tone of the two nationalisms was vastly different. Catalanism was solidly based on the modernizing Catalan bourgeoisie and propounded regional autonomy within a more modern, reformist and progressive Spanish system, within which the Catalanists hoped to play an even more leading role in the future."[119] To the contrary, "Basque nationalism developed as a kind of reaction against the beginning of rapid industrialization."[120] Basque nationalism refused to assimilate with the Spanish nation.

This difference in economic modernization also provides a plausible explanation for the differences in nationalism in the 1960s to the present. As we already mentioned, migration into the Basque and Catalan regions intensified in the late twentieth century. Migration from other parts of Spain into the Basque Country jumped dramatically in the period from 1951 to 1970. Estimates place the figure between 300,000 and 400,000 migrants. Likewise, over 1.1 million persons migrated into Catalonia during the same period. The result of such a high level of migration is predictable. By 1981 one-third of the population of the Basque Country and Catalonia were born in other areas of Spain.[121] Franco's economic policies led to a growth in heavy industry in both Catalonia and the Basque Country. Migration into these areas added lower-class workers to both societies. Catalan society was already "sophisticated and secularized" and could absorb the psychological impact of the recent arrivals and their customs.[122] In the Basque regions the expansion of industrialization and urbanization "engulfed more of the remaining culturally semitraditionalist countryside."[123] Consequently, the Basques suffered a greater sense of cultural shock from migration than the Catalans.[124]

Federalism and its Impact on Nationalism and Identity

Structural factors have played a more recent part in the development of nationalism and identity in Catalonia and in the Basque Country. We argue that the failure of federalism in constructing overlapping identities has exacerbated nationalist tendencies in the periphery. Regional autonomy has neither satisfied the nationalist movements nor promoted a sense of Spanish identity among the Catalans or Basques. In both Catalan and the Basque Country, the percent of natives who self-identified themselves as being at least "as Spanish as Catalan/Basque" has steadily declined since 1979.[125] This trend is most noticeable in Catalonia where 63.9% of natives self-identified as at least "as Spanish as Catalan" in 1979, but only 39.9% did in 1991. Federalism has not promoted a larger Spanish identity among natives in the nationalist regions. Kenneth Bollen and Díez Medrano argue that federalism and decentralization provide Spanish citizens with competing sources of identity.[126] For the historical minorities (e.g., Basques and Catalans), federalism allows them to express their belief in their cultural difference from the Castilian norm.

As we mentioned in the previous section, federalism provides a means for non-historical autonomous communities to seek equality with the historical minorities through the creation of new identities. The perceived inequality of the non-historical minorities has many roots. The first is the slower route to autonomy that the non-historical regions must pursue, according to the 1978 Constitution. The "normal" (or Grade Two) route in Article 143 "required [non-historical] regions to follow a lengthy process of consultation before making a formal application and subject to a transitional period of five years prior to their being granted the option of seeking a level of autonomy similar to that enjoyed by the privileged regions."[127] The second is the lower level of autonomous powers granted to these regions.[128] The last is the economic differences between the Autonomous Communities. When we compare the rank of each Autonomous Community versus the self-perceived discrimination of that region's residents by other Spaniards, we find a clear connection. Residents of the poorer regions claim greater regional group discrimination. The six regions that felt the greatest discrimination are also six of the seven poorest regions (in order starting from the poorest): Extremadura, Castile-La Mancha, Andalucía, Castile y Leon, Galicia, and the Canary Islands.[129] In a 1982 survey, 76% of respondents in Andalucía expressed a self-perceived discrimination. A 1979 study finds that "invariably, Basques and Catalans were regarded the most negatively by other Spaniards."[130] The study also provides a link between perceived differences and the economy, "in a number of interviews, regional party leaders accused Euskadi (the Basque Country) and Catalonia of lacking a sense of economic solidarity with the less developed areas of the country."[131] Furthermore, the process of developing *el estado de las autonomías* "had exacerbated, if not created, feelings of relative deprivation and of discrimination among the poorer regional populations."[132]

Federalism also creates new national identities where none existed previously. We find evidence of new identities in the emergence of new regional parties following the transition to democracy. Regional and nationalist parties contest elections and hold seats in many regional parliaments. Other than the expected strong showings of regional parties in the Basque regions and Catalonia, strong regional parties exist in Andalucía, Aragon, Galicia, Valencia, and the Canary Islands.[133] In the March 2000 election to the Spanish Congress of Deputies, regional parties obtained 34 of the 350 seats, or 9.7%. Although the Catalan nationalists represent 17 seats and the Basque nationalists 8 seats, other regional parties control the remaining 9 seats.[134]

Spanish activity in the European Union (EU) provides another element in constructing and promoting identity in the nationalist regions. Spanish entry into the European Community (EC) in 1986 paved the way for supranationalism, or the development of a larger pan-European identity, at the same time that regional nationalism was expanding.

Supranationalism and regionalism pull the construction of identity in two separate directions: outward toward the larger community of Europe and inward toward the small national community. Therefore, localist and universalist tendencies reside alongside each other. What is different in modern times is that these tendencies are not solely the domain of the nation and the state. Member states of the EU have three layers of "national" government, for want of a better word: region/state, member state, and EU institutions. Through the dual process of devolution and European integration, sovereignty moves from the nation-state in both directions. The regions and the EU take sovereignty from the national government. In a strange relationship, the processes of localism and globalism have a similar effect: a diminishing of the authority and sovereignty of the nation-state.

The participation of Spain in the EU has had a significant impact upon the nationalist regions. Because Spain is a decentralized, federalist state, the transfer of sovereignty to the EU diminishes the competencies of the regions. Spain participates directly in EU decision making, while the regions do not. Thus, the federal government helps create laws, makes treaties, and enters into compacts that are binding in the regions, but are not necessarily acceptable to the regions.[135] This arrangement does cut both ways. The effect of an EU directive may lead to regional implementation when the policy area lies under the constitutional authority of the regions (e.g., education). Therefore, there exists an incentive structure for the regions to gain direct participation in the decision-making structure of the EU. The governing institutions of the EU are an avenue by which the regions can attempt to rectify perceived inequality.

The nationalist regions have established regular contact with the EU.[136] Likewise, the European Commission already possesses a number of consultative mechanisms to coordinate policy with regional governments. Almost all of Spain's Autonomous Communities (the exceptions are Navarre and Castilla-La Mancha) are members of the Assembly of European Regions. Catalonia and the Basque Country are also members of the Consultative Council of Regional and Local Authorities.[137] A number of regional governments, including the Basque Country, have established offices in Brussels in order to lobby the EU. The EU's establishment of the

Committee of the Regions (COR) in 1994 highlights the role of the non-Spanish nationalities on the European stage. Of Spain's 21 members of COR, 17 are from the regions. Two prominent members of the COR are Jordi Pujol and Pascal Maragall of Catalonia.

The transfer of receipts from the EU to the poorer regions of Spain occurs through the European Regional and Development Fund (ERDF). These "structural" funds provide a means to build infrastructure (e.g., roads, energy plants, and communication facilities) in the lesser-developed regions of the EU.[138] Spain received roughly 12 billion ecu from 1989 to 1993 and another 26.3 billion ecu from 1994 to 1999. This expenditure is roughly 1.5% of the Spanish GDP (Gross Domestic Product) and over 20% of EU structural expenditure.[139] Over 3 billion ecu went to Andalucía alone. With the assistance of the EU (then EC), regional authorities established the *Instituto de Fomento de Andalucía* to promote the region's productive resources and to coordinate the distribution of EU funds.

Some authors describe the phenomenon of increasing, institutionalized contact between regions in Europe and the EU as the "Europe of the Regions."[140] With the growing EU emphasis on cohesion policy and structural adjustment in the poorer regions, these regions have emerged as important actors. Moreover, the regions see allies in each other. These "periphery" nations can band together in the EU and sidestep the authority of their central governments. Thus, the EU provides another forum for the representation of the nations and their national interests. A 1989 survey shows that regional elites in Andalusia, Catalonia, Galicia, and Valencia perceive benefits from the participation of the regions in the EU decision-making framework. Moreover, these elites express positive attitudes toward the EU and toward the process of Europeanization.[141] Among the citizens of Spain, support for EU membership is as high as 64%, up 9% from the start of 1999.[142] Those who say that Spain has "benefited" from EU membership is at an all-time high of 61%.[143] In 2002 the number of Spaniards who had a sense of European identity rose to 65%.[144] Of this 65%, 4% replied that they have only a European identity, while 5% said that their identity was more European than Spanish.

Thus, it appears that at the same time that regionalism is constructing sub-national identities, Europeanism may be producing a supranational identity. This finding is consistent with that of other works. As we mentioned in chapter 1, Marilynn B. Brewer identifies federal divisions as important in creating optimal distinctiveness for ethnic groups. We have argued in both chapters 1 and 2 that federalism may exacerbate ethnic security dilemmas and promote sub-nationalism. Maria Ros, Carmen Huic, and Angel Gomez point out that the relationship is indeed as complex as the preceding paragraph portrays it. They claim that "In the Spanish context an important distinction is possible between groups that identify to some extent with the Autonomous Communities and with Spain . . . and groups whose identification with the Autonomous Communities reduces identification with Spain."[145] They also claim that the survey work of Jose Luis Garcia Sangrador tends to support this claim.[146]

Conclusion

In conclusion, federalism in Spain does not appear to be solving all of the nationalist demands. The end of the Franco regime was not a panacea for all the ills of the multinational Spanish state. The 1978 Constitution embraced asymmetrical federalism through the creation of the Autonomous Communities. In a sense, the Constitution recognized the historical nationalities, but in a sense it made them indistinguishable from the non-nationalist communities. Scholars emphasize that the Constitution is ambiguous on key points regarding the structure of the Spanish state and its relation to the Autonomous Communities.[147] Thus, the centralizing and normalizing tendencies of the Franco regime (and before that the Spanish Monarchy over the Kingdom of Castille and Aragon) gave way to regional administration, but not entirely. Nationalist sentiments that Franco pushed into latency became manifest with the liberalization of society following democratization.

In a comparative perspective, the democratic Constitution and asymmetrical federal arrangement has done more to assuage Catalan demands than Basque demands. Catalan nationalism has reconciled itself under the Spanish state to no longer seek "the highest number of instrumental 'state' competences" but rather to "achieve the highest level of democratic self-government."[148] The bleaker picture is that Basque nationalism continues almost unabated. It emerged from Francoist rule in a more radical and violent form than Catalan nationalism. The 2002 banning of *Batasuna* (the more recent incarnation of *Herri Batasuna*) by the Spanish parliament is evidence of the continuing tension between the center and periphery.

Asymmetrical federalism is also not contributing to the construction of overlapping identities among national groups in the nationalist regions. First, national groups do not display any clear movement toward replacing their national languages with Spanish. Most evidence points to the contrary as cultural and social movements attempt to revive interest in the national tongue. Second, while migration into Catalonia and the Basque Country appears to create overlapping identities among the immigrants, these immigrants are developing new, sub-national identities that may be hostile to the nation-state. Both trends are certainly more prevalent in the Basque Country than in the Catalan-speaking areas. Both promote a furthering of mistrust between the regional and central governments and the building of enemy images that portray the other in a negative light.

On the positive side of things, we have shown that Spanish involvement in the EU, and particularly the involvement of the nationalist regions, provides a forum for the representation of nationalist concerns. This has led to the beginning of a European identity among the nationalist elite. Moreover, the nationalist movements have organized in an attempt to lobby the EU for policy favorable to their regions. In chapter 3 we examine the role of institutions in the EU and their potential to construct a European identity. We highlight how a European identity is emerging slowly.

3

Integrating Strong National Identities
in the European Union

*If... the victors and the vanquished agreed to exercise joint
sovereignty over part of their joint resources ... then a solid
link would be forged between them, the way would be wide
open for further collective action, and a great example would
be given to other nations of Europe.*

—Jean Monnet, director, French Modernization Plan
As quoted in Carolyn Rhodes, *Pivotal Decisions: Selected
Cases in Twentieth-Century International Politics*

*The success of various symbolic initiatives has demonstrated
that Europe's cultural dimension is there in the collective
consciousness of its people; their values are a joint cultural
asset, characterised by a pluralist humanism based on
democracy, justice and liberty. The European Union which
is being constructed cannot have economic and social objec-
tives as its only aim. It also involves new kinds of solidarity
based on belonging to European Culture.*

—Commission of the European Communities, 1988
As quoted in Chris Shore, "Transcending the Nation-State?:
The European Commission and the (Re)Discovery of
Europe"

Identity and Institutions in the European Union

The member states of the European Union (EU) are not engaged in
nationalist or ethnic conflicts between themselves. Yet we examine

the case of the EU as it provides an interesting illustration of the relationship between overlapping identities and representative institutions as a means to promote cooperation between states previously in conflict. Germany and France, at odds for much of their history over the last several centuries, came together after World War II to cooperate over a source of continuing tension in their relations: coal and iron. They established, along with four other countries, the European Coal and Steel Community, which over time, became the EU of today.

The challenge for the EU, as it has evolved and become further integrated, has been to foster a European identity while faced with the strong national identities of the member states. In this challenge, the EU confronts the issue of defining a European identity that differs from, yet complements, national identities.[1] There is evidence of the existence of overlapping identities of national identities and a European identity. Recent *Eurobarometer* (EB) surveys on the question of identity of the current fifteen EU member states indicates, on average, that 52% of those polled feel *both* a European and national identity (with an additional 4% "feeling European only").[2] Moreover, while people feel more attached to their country (89%), town/village (85%), and region (83%), more than half (58%) also feel attached to Europe.[3]

In addition, EU citizens are able to pool sovereignty among different layers of representative institutions as they are able to elect directly members of the European Parliament (EP) as well as their national governmental bodies. Parties from the member states work together in transnational party groups at the supranational level in the EP.[4] Domestic actors can also appeal to the European Court of Justice for "rulings, based on EU law, that are enforceable against their own governments."[5] Regional groups exist, through the EU's Committee on the Regions, which can promote areas of common interest. In fact, overlapping authority for the EU member states is present at the EU, interstate, state, and regional levels[6] and hence, there's the opportunity for overlapping, or multiple, identities.

This chapter discusses the efforts of the EU to promote (and in some sense construct) a European identity through the concept of the "Citizen of Europe," in large part, through the various institutions (i.e., European Parliament [EP] and transnational political parties) and symbols of identity (i.e., EU flag, anthem, passport, and currency). We argue in this chapter that the EU has been quite successful in promoting a European identity (and citizenship) that links to increasing representation through its institutions at several levels (supranational, national, regional, and local). While we readily acknowledge that there are differences in levels of "feeling" a European identity in the various member states, the trend, as indicated by the biannual *Eurobarometer* surveys, indicates that large numbers of people in the EU do feel both a European as well as national identity. Importantly, as the EU has become more institutionalized over time, people have become more inclined to see themselves as European as well as their own nationality. In fact, a previous *Eurobarometer* survey showed that "it is in the six founder Member States that we find the highest proportion of respondents saying they see themselves most of the time in addition to their nationality as 'Europeans.' 'In the near future': two out of three in the 'old six' Member States identify themselves as 'Europeans' as well as their own nationality."[7]

The first section of this chapter briefly discusses the historical developments, from the original European Coal and Steel Community to the present-day EU. This historical background is useful for understanding the evolutionary process of the organization, particularly the recognition of its member states of the need to deepen integration as well as the need to develop a European identity (and citizenship) in order to address the "democratic deficit." The "democratic deficit" refers to the "perceived lack of democratic participation in and control over the decision-making institutions of the EC."[8] The second section examines the development of a European identity (and citizenship) through the actions of elites in the member states. For the first few decades of its existence, the EU focused on furthering economic integration. Only in the 1970s, but more so in the 1980s and 1990s, did the organization actively seek to promote and construct a European identity.

The third section examines the various institutions of the EU, particularly the European Commission, Council of Ministers, and European Parliament, as well as transnational parties and regional organizations. These institutions provide different layers of representation, whether at the supranational, national, regional, and local levels, through pooled sovereignty. These levels of representation enhance cooperation among entities of the EU member states, while also providing a mechanism to promote a European identity. However, the EU faces the "democratic deficit" and thus the challenge for the EU is to make these institutions even more representative of the citizens of Europe. For example, by "providing the European Parliament with more effective authority over the

Commission, and reducing the influence of the Council of Ministers and the national governments," the EU can overcome the "democratic deficit."[9] Only through increased representation can the EU succeed in developing perceptions of citizenship and an overlapping European identity.

The final section addresses the trends for the future of European identity and pooled sovereignty. We argue that there is a positive trend toward the inculcation and deepening of a European identity. We also acknowledge that the development of a European identity is a slow process as such an identity is sometimes viewed at odds with national identities. Identities are salient, but also malleable, as discussed in chapter 1 that dealt with social constructivism. Importantly, we argue that such a European identity will flourish as long as people are able to maintain overlapping, or multiple, identities. Moreover, these overlapping identities, be they European, national, regional, and/or local, related to representative institutions will likely lead to further cooperation and integration between the member states.

The Origins of the European Union

When the European Community (EC) first formed as a result of the merger of the European Coal and Steel Community (ECSC), the European Economic Community, and the European Atomic Energy Community in 1967, the organization sought to foster economic integration, with less attention paid toward the issue of European citizenship and identity. Only in the 1970s did the EC move toward promoting a European identity. Importantly, however, was the increased integration of the organization over time that then provided the opportunity for the promotion of such an identity.

Before examining the development of a European identity, a discussion of the EU's history is necessary as it provides the background necessary for understanding the link between institutions and identity as a means to reduce conflicts between states or groups. This section examines the origins and evolution of an organization formed in response to the historical conflicts in Europe, namely between France and Germany, which would promote cooperation through membership in institutions.

Continual conflict over territory in the region, particularly between France and Germany, involved control over iron and coal resources. Consequently, the experience of World War II led France to seek to prevent Germany from being able to acquire those resources for militarization and territorial expansion at the expense of France. France also recognized the need for these resources for its own development following the devastation from the war. As a result, the French government sought to ensure supplies of coal.[10] While others, both in the United States and Europe, spoke of the need for integration and union among the European states, a particular individual stands out. Jean Monnet, director of the French Modernization Plan, took the mantle and promoted the idea of a "supranational authority for overseeing French and [West] German coal and steel production in such a way as to guarantee French competitiveness while at the same time provide Germany with legitimacy in its return to international industrial competition."[11] Monnet had come to his ideas about the role of economic integration in order to prevent conflict in Europe during the world war. He believed that cooperation in one sphere would have spillover effects in other areas.[12] In August 1943 he wrote to the French Committee of National Liberation in Algiers that peace in Europe could only come about if "the States of Europe . . . form a federation or a 'European entity,' which will make them a single economic entity."[13] In 1950 he "sent his proposal for a coal and steel community" to French Foreign Minister Robert Schuman and Prime Minister Rene Pleven. As Pleven did not respond to his proposal immediately, Schuman became the individual charged with promoting the idea of such a community. The Schuman Plan was presented to the United States and West Germany for their reaction. Both countries indicated their support for the plan.[14] The West German chancellor, Konrad Adenauer, enthusiastically supported the idea, recognizing that Germany's legitimacy as an international actor was crucial, particularly given Germany's role in the outbreak of World War II. The draft treaty called for a common market under the High Authority of a supranational body, which eventually became the Council of Ministers.[15]

In 1951 six countries signed the Treaty of Paris—Belgium, France, Germany, Italy, Luxembourg, and the Netherlands—that created the European Coal and Steel Community. The treaty, ratified by all six, came into being a year later. Monnet became first high commissioner of the new organization. Interestingly, the preamble of the treaty stated that the members "resolved to substitute for age-old rivalries the merging of their essential interests; to create, by establishing an economic community, the basis for a broader and deeper community among peoples long divided by bloody conflicts; and to lay the foundations for institutions which will give direction to a destiny henceforward shared. . . ."[16] Thus, the EU was born.

Not to be limited only to coal and steel, the six states of the ECSC sought to work together in other areas of common interest, namely nuclear power and a customs union. In 1957 the Treaty of Rome created two organizations to deal with these two areas, Euratom and the European Economic Community (EEC), respectively. Euratom focused on developing and regulating nuclear power in an integrated manner, while the EEC promoted a "customs union and integrated common market." Specifically, the EEC comprised three major policies: common external tariff, free trade area, and a Common Agricultural Policy (CAP) that would set minimum price levels.[17] As Carolyn Rhodes notes, during the 1960s, "member states accustomed themselves to, and came to rely upon, the institutions of the three communities (ECSC, Euratom, and EEC) to negotiate and regulate trade with third countries and to encourage deeper cooperation and management of intracommunity trade."[18]

However, all was not well for continued integration. French President Charles de Gaulle desired a "Union of States," a European security community, which would enable Europe to resist domination by the United States and the bipolar structure of the international system.[19] In fact, the members of the ECSC proposed a European Defense Community (EDC) as a means "to provide a supranational defense structure based on an integrated European army under a permanent European command." Importantly, these countries worried about German rearmament, and for the French, the United States' role in military affairs in Europe. The EDC failed, however, in 1954, as a result of national loyalties and identities superceding those of Europe, as well as "suspicions, and fears of other nations, especially the fear of Germany."[20] The French National Assembly refused to ratify the EDC treaty, and the government chose to focus on a national nuclear deterrent rather than European unification of defense and foreign policy.[21]

De Gaulle became concerned about the impact of the three European communities on French sovereignty, particularly the EEC's executive body, the European Commission, and the EP. As a result of his concerns about sovereignty, in 1966, de Gaulle successfully negotiated the Luxembourg Compromise, which enabled any member to veto an item considered a "threat to its vital interests."

Thus, unanimity was necessary for controversial items, which further hindered the development of full integration.[22]

And yet, integration would not be halted entirely, particularly given the high rates of economic growth in Western Europe in the late 1950s and early 1960s. In 1967 the three communities merged to form the EC with the conclusion of the Merger Treaty.[23] Five years later, the declaration of the 1972 Paris summit stated that "The member states of the Community, the driving force of European construction, affirm their intention before the end of the present decade to transform the whole complex of their relations into a European Union." Unclear as to what "European Union" meant exactly, the declaration of the concept pressured the member states to push for further integration, or deepening.[24]

During the next two decades much of the EC's activities focused on enlargement of its membership. In 1973, Britain, Denmark, and Ireland became members, followed by Greece in 1981, and Spain and Portugal in 1986. The 1980s also witnessed a desire for further integration and strengthening of the community as a more unified entity. In 1986, the Single European Act (SEA) was concluded in order to create a single market (targeted date: 1992), as noted in Article 8a: "an area without internal frontiers in which the free movement of goods, persons, services, and capital is ensured."[25] Importantly, a free internal market benefited not just those in business, but ordinary citizens as well. "The idea that the credentials of lawyers, medical doctors, and other licensed professionals from one country of the EC would be recognized in all the other countries of the EC was an attractive one."[26] In addition to the free internal market, the SEA also included the goal of monetary union. Member states recognized that while a single commercial market was important for free trade, so too was monetary union as a solution for problems related to fluctuating currencies exchange rates.[27] According to Desmond Dinan, "the SEA was more than a device to launch the single market program. It was a complex bargain to improve decisionmaking, increase efficiency, achieve market liberalization, and at the same time promote cohesion."[28] The components of the SEA permitted movement to qualified majority voting from unanimity as a means to ease the decision-making process as well as overcoming the "democratic deficit" by increasing the power of the EP.[29]

Demands by some members of the community and international events in the late 1980s and early 1990s (e.g., the collapse of the Soviet Union and the fall of the Berlin Wall) led to pressure for further integration.[30] The result: the Maastricht Treaty of 1991 (Treaty on European Union, TEU, which entered into force in November 1993) and the creation of the EU. The Maastricht Treaty sought to unify economic policy among the member states even further, including the creation of a European Monetary Union (EMU) with a single currency (ECU, European Currency Unit, later replaced by the "Euro") by 2000, a European Central Bank, and the opening of internal borders.[31] Besides economic union, the Maastricht Treaty also included elements of political union, including two intergovernmental bodies, the Common Foreign and Security Policy (CFSP) and Justice and Home Affairs (JHA).[32] Importantly, for this project, the Maastricht Treaty extended the rights of citizens in the EU by establishing "the foundations for a Union citizenship which will complement national citizenship without replacing it."[33]

During the 1990s, the EU focused on enlargement, with three countries gaining entry in 1995: Austria, Finland, and Sweden. In addition to considerations of enlargement, the EU concluded another treaty, the Treaty of Amsterdam in 1997, to address issues of institutional reform. Though scholars argue that the treaty is not likely to increase the efficiency of the EU's institutions as related to questions about their size, the increased power for the EP and more use of the qualified majority voting are two positive aspects of the treaty. Importantly, the treaty deals with issues related to freedom, security, and justice—external border control, immigration and asylum policy, and cooperation among the various national judiciaries. While these areas historically are under the purview of national governments, "most Europeans want to see more effective transnational cooperation."[34] In 2000, the EU concluded the Treaty of Nice that further addresses the issues of enlargement and amendments to the Maastricht Treaty. Finally, in 2003, ten additional countries, including Malta, Cyprus, and Slovenia, signed a Treaty of Accession, which will enable them to join the EU in 2004.

European Identity in the Making

As the previous section demonstrates, the first two decades of the EU's existence focused on furthering economic integration, with the added issue of enlargement of its membership, not the promotion of a European identity. And yet, in the background the rumblings of the movement of integration from the economic sphere into the political and cultural sphere existed. Elites in the member states recognized the connection between continued integration and the need for more citizen representation, and thus the desire to promote a European identity that complemented national identities. However, this section will show that it was not until the early 1990s that the EU took steps to institutionalize (and thus legalize) the concept of European identity (and citizenship).[35]

The final communiqué of the 1972 Paris summit declared that "the Member States of the Community, the driving force of European construction, affirm their intention before the end of the present decade to transform the whole complex of their relations into a European Union."[36] Following the Paris summit, in 1973 the official and formal concept of a European identity was brought to the fore with the "Copenhagen Declaration on the European Identity." The Declaration stipulated the components of the European identity: representative democracy, social justice, rule of law, and human rights. Linked to these political components, of course, were the economic ones, such as a common market and EC/EU common policies.[37] The Declaration, signed by the then nine member states, noted that they "shared 'the same attitudes to life, based on a determination to build a society which measures up to the needs of the individual,'" "to defend the principles of representative democracy, the rule of law," "social justice . . . and respect for human rights."[38] These shared attitudes formed the basis of a European identity and citizenship. Thus, at the 1974 Paris summit, the final communiqué focused on the idea of European citizens as it "proclaimed the creation of a Passport Union and the establishment of special rights for citizens of the [then] nine Member States respectively."[39]

Building on the Copenhagen Declaration and the 1974 Paris communiqué, in 1975, the Tindemans' "Report on European Union" introduced the term *Citizen's Europe*.[40] In addition, the report recommended a common foreign policy as well as a popularly elected legislative body.[41] This and other documents, such as the 1983 Solemn Declaration on European Union, pushed for cooperation beyond economics into the cultural and political spheres as a means to foster a sense of belonging.[42] As Ulrich K. Preuss notes, "the concept of citizenship is a social construction which is not only constitutive of the identity of a particular—political—community, but which at the same time defines the social identity of the individuals who in their quality as members replace their family, clan or tribal affiliation with their status in a more abstract community, the polity."[43] In this sense, the community tied the idea of citizenship with identity—the construction of a political identity at the European (supranational) level.

As a result of the low voter turnout in the 1984 EP elections, the EC/EU began an active and conscious campaign to promote a European identity with the formation of the Adonnino Committee ("Committee for a People's Europe") in 1984.[44] The Committee's mandate, produced in two reports (the proposals were adopted by the Council in 1985), included formulating recommendations to bolster the European identity and suggesting procedures to increase the involvement of citizens in the EC.[45] The Committee's report asserted, "through action in the areas of culture and communication, which are essential to European identity and the Community's image in the minds of its people, that support for the advancement of Europe can and must be sought."[46] As noted by Chris Shore, in order to foster a European identity, the report made several suggestions, such as the creation of a Europe-wide "multilingual television channel 'in order to bring the peoples of Europe closer together.'" The report also recommended the creation of a European Academy of Science ("to highlight the achievements of European science and the originality of European civilisation in all its wealth and diversity"), educational exchange programs, and European sports teams. In addition, the report encouraged the community to provide information about its policies and their importance for its citizens, "including 'the historical events which led to the construction of the Community and which inspire its further development in freedom, peace and security and its achievements and potential in the economic and social field.'"[47] Importantly, the Committee recommended that symbols of identity, much like those for states, also be introduced: EC emblem and flag, passport, driver's license, May 9 as Europe Day (date of the Schuman Declaration), and an anthem (Beethoven's Ninth Symphony, "Ode to Joy"). The Committee reinforced the importance of symbols for transforming the organization into a "People's Europe": "symbols play a key role in consciousness-raising but there is also a need to make the European citizen aware of the different elements that go to make up his European identity, of our cultural unity with all its diversity of expression, and of the historical ties which link the nations of Europe."[48]

All these recommendations were designed to promote an overlapping European identity that unified the various people of the

EC/EU, in other words, promoting a sense of belonging through symbols as well as through economic and political participation.[49] As Brigid Laffan notes, "[t]he objective of the package of policies that flowed from the Adonnino Committee is gradually to change people's consciousness of political realities and the political domain to which they belong. This is a deliberate process of manufacturing and legitimizing a European identity from the 'top down.'"[50] In essence, constructing an overlapping identity. Three aspects of policy are meant to promote the idea of a "people's Europe" connecting identity with representation for Europe's citizens: "move from consumer to citizen"; "politics of identity and symbols"; and "creation of non-economic cross-national networks."[51] Examples abound of the impact of the Adonnino Committee's recommendations regarding symbols of identity: the EU flag is "flown from public buildings, industrial enterprises and even on beaches that conform to EU environmental standards. In many regions and towns throughout Europe, the name of the region or commune is contained within the 12 stars of the Union. Individual travelers [sic] arriving at airports or ports are reminded of their status as *Cives Comunitatis Europeae* or 'EC [EU] Nationals.'"[52]

Several years after the Adonnino Committee's report, in 1988 the Council "decided to introduce a European dimension into school subjects such as literature, history, civics, geography, languages, and music. Legitimacy for future integration is being created by invoking a common history and cultural heritage."[53] Moreover, the EU initiated "public awareness" campaigns such as funding the "European literature prize" as well as the "Jean Monnet Awards" for the creation of courses in universities that focused on European integration studies.[54] Thus, the 1980s witnessed an overt attempt by the Community to promote and foster a European identity.

The further promotion and institutionalization of European citizenship occurred in the 1990s with the signing of the Maastricht Treaty when the EU pushed to link economic/market integration and political integration. With the "Citizens of Europe," the Maastricht Treaty focused primarily on economic issues in the understanding of European citizenship, such as the free movement of people across member state borders and the completion of EMU through a common currency. Besides the economic aspect of citizenship, Maastricht's Article 8b gives "every citizen of the EU residing in a member state of which she or he is not a national, the right to vote and stand as a candidate in municipal elections."[55] As Christine Lemke notes, the treaty widened citizenship rights (and hence participation and representation) within the EU with the voting rights—"one of the most salient features of national power."[56] In addition, ratification of Maastricht meant changes in the constitutions of member states that removed their exclusive national sovereignty, thus pooling sovereignty among the member states.[57] For example, France's Constitution acknowledges "that some competencies are not the exclusive domain of the French state, but rather are exercised jointly with other states in the EU."[58]

Moreover, the treaty made explicit that the EU "[s]hall contribute to the flowering of the cultures of the Member States, while respecting their national and regional diversity and at the same time bringing the common cultural heritage to the fore."[59] Importantly, "the TEU marks an important shift from EU consumer to EU citizen."[60] Article 8 of the TEU stated that "every person holding the nationality of a Member State shall be a citizen of the Union."[61] Thus, the Maastricht Treaty established "legal ties of belonging." As Antje Wiener notes, "The legal ties were not only important for defining the relation between citizens and the Community anew, they also raised questions about the political content of nationality." Thus, because of the different rights citizens were given at the supranational level, "it became increasingly difficult to define citizenship practice as based on nationality."[62]

The 1997 Treaty of Amsterdam (which entered into force in May 1999) further integrated the rights of EU citizens, including voting rights, freedom of movement within the EU (right to reside and establish a business in any member state), social rights, and the role of the European Parliament (EP).[63] Importantly, the treaty recognized the notion of multiple citizenship or nationality, and thus identity: "Citizenship of the Union shall complement and not replace national citizenship."[64]

Some scholars have argued, however, that both the Maastricht and Amsterdam treaties have not gone far enough in pushing for a European identity and citizenship. As Jeffrey Checkel notes, "despite persistent agenda-setting efforts by the Commission and the EP, the member states maintained firm control over development of the TEU's citizenship provisions—perhaps not surprising given how national conceptions of citizenship are such a deeply rooted part of state identity in contemporary Europe." Moreover, he argues that the Maastricht citizenship provisions "are a list of minimal rights and information, which essentially codify (but do not further develop) what was already extent in Community law."[65]

Yet, as Preuss argues, "to be a citizen of a supranational entity is a major innovation in the history of political membership."[66]

In fact, the EU did recognize the importance of belonging and citizenship following the Maastricht Treaty, particularly in the area of culture. In February 2000, the EP and the Council of Ministers established the "Culture 2000" program (the first framework program from 2000 to 2004), "to encourage creative activity and the knowledge and dissemination of the culture of the European peoples." According to the official site, "Culture 2000 recognizes the role of culture as an economic factor and as a factor in social integration and citizenship."[67] The intent is to strengthen "the feeling of belonging to the European Union, while respecting the diversity of national and regional traditions and cultures." The EU readily recognizes that "culture must contribute to European citizenship, . . . to economic and social cohesion among Member States . . . and generally to enriching the quality of life in Europe."[68]

In addition to the formal treaties and proposals addressing the issues of European citizen and identity, the European Commission (to be discussed in greater detail in the next section) has taken measures to foster relations between individuals, groups, and regions within the member states. For example, the European Community Action Scheme for the Mobility of University Students (Erasmus), created in 1987, promotes faculty and student exchanges at the university level, as well as offering grants for curriculum development. The Action Program to Promote Foreign Language Competence in the European Community (Lingua) provides money for learning a second or third language.[69]

Thus, through the deepening of economic and political integration through formal treaties and other measures, the EU has expanded and promoted, and continues to do so, the conception of EU citizen (legal belonging) and European identity (cultural).[70] Evidence of this expansion of European identity and citizenship at the mass level can be found in the data from the *Eurobarometer* surveys conducted biannually by the EU. From 1982 to 2003, for the EU average, respondents indicated that they do feel European and nationality (or European only) *more so* than "nationality only" (or never feeling European).[71] Figure 3.1 displays data supporting this claim.

Importantly, since 1992 (which coincides with the Maastricht Treaty's ratification process and the expansion of EU citizenship rights), more than half of the respondents claim to feel *both* a

Figure 3.1. National and European Identity

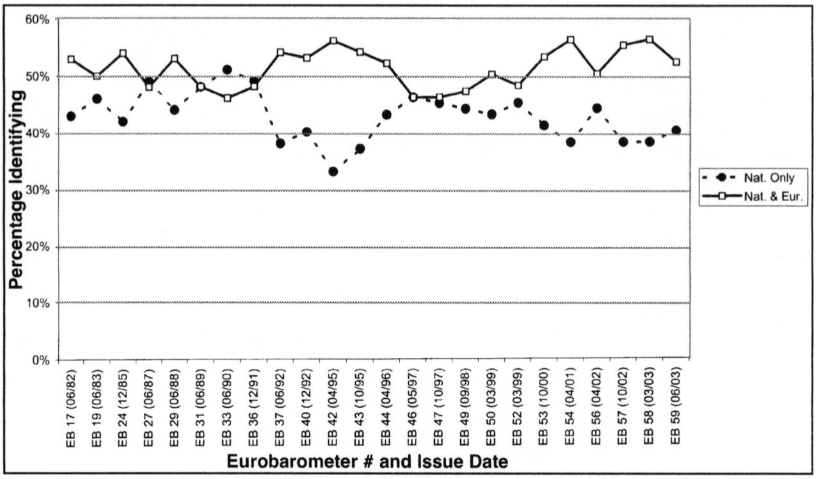

Source: Commission of the European Union, *Eurobarometer Reports* (Brussels: European Commission).

European and national identity (and European only). The most recent *Eurobarometer* survey on identity of the EU average shows that 56% of the respondents feel both a European and national identity (of which 4% feel European only), with 40% feeling nationality only.[72]

Moreover, people in the member states seem to agree with the elites that a European identity is compatible with national identities (thus, multiple identities). For example, in 1992 (prior to the change from EC to EU) the *Eurobarometer* survey asked two questions that related to the compatibility of a European identity with national identity, and whether "a real European Union" would protect national identities. In terms of the compatibility of a European identity with national identity, the question asked: "If all countries of the European Community come together in a European Union, do you think that the sense of national identity will end up disappearing and being replaced by a sense of European identity or can one have a national sense of identity and a European sense of identity at the same time?"[73] "By a proportion of almost three-to-one (62:32), EC citizens believe that a national and European identity are compatible. Absolute majorities everywhere see compatibility possible, from a high of 71% for Italy and 69% for the Netherlands to a low of 52% for the United Kingdom and 50% for Ireland."[74] In terms of protecting European identities, 46% responded that "if a real European Union came about" it would protect national identities, 14% said "in between," and 30% responded that such a union would end national identities.[75]

Finally, evidence does show that people do see themselves as European and have a positive feeling about that identity. In a recent *Eurobarometer* survey, for the first time, people were asked, "Would you say you are very proud, fairly proud, not very proud, or not at all proud to be European?" For the EU average, more than half of the respondents (62%) claimed they were "very" or "fairly" proud of being European. Interestingly, in the two countries with the lowest percentage of pride in being European of all fifteen states, Germany and the United Kingdom, "people who feel proud outnumber those who do not feel proud."[76]

As we have demonstrated in the previous section, the EU has actively promoted and fostered the concept of a European identity and citizenship that connects to representation and rights. While the organization began as one that focused on economic integration, the EU has expanded its goals to include political and cultural integration. Importantly, the leaders of the EU continue to recognize that a European identity cannot replace national identities (nor do they claim that such supranational identities should do so), but hope that with continued integration the overlapping European identity will bring the peoples of Europe closer together. Interestingly, the people seem to agree. In *Eurobarometer* surveys conducted in 2002 and 2003, nearly three fourths of Europeans consider "getting closer to EU citizens" a priority.[77] The next section examines the various EU institutions that pool sovereignty and, thus, increase representation of EU citizens—and provides the link to an overlapping European identity.

Representation in the EU: Pooling Sovereignty as a Means to Overcome Inequality

The previous section traced the efforts of the EU to promote a European identity through the expansion of economic and political rights (citizenship), particularly in the Maastricht Treaty. The expansion of voting rights (a means for citizens to get their voices heard) relates directly to representation in the political institutions of the EU across various levels. The main bodies of the EU are the European Commission, Council of Ministers,[78] and the EP. In addition, transnational political parties and regional organizations are also important. This section examines the various institutions of the EU because, together, these institutions provide mechanisms for representation through pooled sovereignty, and hence, promote an overlapping European identity, and in turn enhance cooperation among the EU members that is often challenged by perceptions of inequality among the member states.

Council of Ministers and the European Commission

The Council of Ministers and European Commission have shared decision-making authority in the EU. EU citizens do not elect members to either body, but because these two bodies tend to focus on EU interests rather than on national ones,[79] they do provide an opportunity to promote an overlapping European identity. For example, the Council, representing the national governments of member states, acts "according to E.U. interests, just as parliamentarians in most countries, although representing specific constituencies, come together in the capital to discuss the interests of the nation as a whole."[80]

The Council adopts proposals and legislates for the EU on a wide range of policy areas. The foreign minister of one of the member states heads the Council for a rotating six-month term.[81] The importance of the presidency has increased over time as a result of deepening integration, increased political importance of the Council, expanding influence of the European Council, as well as the growth of working groups in the Council. With the increased importance, so too have the responsibilities of the presidency, which include "arranging and chairing meetings of the European Council (summits)," "preparing and chairing meetings of the Council and its subcommittees," "representing the EU internationally," and "acting as an EU spokesperson."[82]

Importantly, the state holding the presidency must engage in a delicate balancing act: advancing their own country's positions as well as acting impartially. Interestingly, presidents sometimes find it "necessary to subsume national under presidential interests."[83] In addition to balancing between national and presidential interests, the presidency also works to establish and maintain positive relations with the other institutions of the EU. In its workings with the Commission, the presidency can contribute to effectual decision making. In working with the EP, the Council is colegislator.[84]

However, as noted previously, the Council is not a fully democratic body. It meets in secret and is not collectively accountable at the EU level, and delegated, not elected, officials make the majority of decisions.[85] The fact that it deliberates behind closed doors has contributed to the "democratic deficit." As a result, many have called for more openness in the deliberation process of the institution and access to the meetings of the Council members. The Council permits media representatives and members of the public to view some, but not many, "public ministerial debates" in Brussels (or "Luxembourg if the Council meets there"), but they must obtain permission beforehand. The Commission sometimes broadcasts the debates by the "Europe by Satellite" information service. The problem is that very few people can go to Brussels or Luxembourg to view the debates in person and the "Europe by Satellite" is not available everywhere.[86] Thus, the citizens of Europe may not feel connected to this particular institution, as representing their interests.

The Council has tried to address some of these concerns, namely making more documents of its proceedings available and permitting access to some debates, albeit on a limited basis, to the media and public at large. Moreover, because the Council also has representatives from sub-national governments, citizens' interests may be heard and represented at the supranational level. Two federal states, Germany and Belgium, were able to push for such a change with the Maastricht Treaty to include regional representatives. "Members of regional governments had insisted on representation in the Council when the Council discussed issues that, in their own countries, were the responsibility of regional rather than federal government."[87]

Yet, in the end, the Council still suffers from lack of direct involvement by the citizens of Europe, and therefore contributes to the perceived "democratic deficit." In fact, one of the most recent *Eurobarometer* surveys (2003) asked respondents whether ten EU institutions and bodies played "an important role or not in the life of the European Union." For the EU average, the Council of Ministers ranked fifth at 58% (preceded by the EP [78%], European Commission [69%], European Central Bank [66%], and Court of Justice [65%]) in terms of a perceived important role.[88] Moreover, in terms of *trust* of the same ten institutions and bodies, the Council ranked fifth (preceded by the EP, Court of Justice, European Commission, and the European Central Bank). On an individual country basis, only for Denmark and Spain did the Council of Ministers rank in the top three.[89] Thus, these overall results suggest that the citizens of Europe do not view this institution in terms of trust and importance very highly relative to other EU institutions, further contributing to the argument that the Council contributes to the perception of the "democratic deficit."

The European Commission, which implements EU policy, also has no direct democratic requirement although it is held accountable by the EP.[90] The Commission also represents the EU in some international organizations and trade negotiations with non-EU states. Each commissioner swears an oath of loyalty to the EU.[91] Importantly, the Commission's members are nominated by their national governments (and appointed by the Council) but are obligated to act in the interests of the EU—an overlapping membership in a supranational body. The commissioners tend to have held elected office in their individual countries, "an unofficial criterion for appointment to the Commission in order to enhance vicariously the Commission's democratic legitimacy."[92] As such, according to Dinan, "the Commission epitomizes supranationalism and lies at the center of the EU system."[93] The Commission president's responsibilities include "launching major EU policy initiatives," "representing the Commission in meetings of the European Council," and "representing the Commission in meetings of the General Affairs Council (of foreign ministers)."[94]

Besides the "unofficial criterion" of having held elected office prior to becoming a commissioner, other aspects of the workings of the EU provide legitimacy for the Commission. As mentioned previously, because the Commission is held accountable to the EP, the EP can affect the perception of legitimacy when it threatens censure of the Commission, thereby demonstrating its desire to increase its influence over the non-elected body. For example, in 1998 the EP threatened censure, claiming that the Commission had mismanaged the EU budget.[95] In this way, the Commission's legitimacy as an institution representing the interests of the EU as a whole may increase.

Another avenue for increasing the legitimacy of the Commission is related to the role that the Commission plays in proposing EU legislation. Both external and internal committees provide support for the Commission and for its legislation. Internal committees coordinate parts of the Commission and commissioners. External committees are comprised of expert committees and consultative committees, both of which consist of specialists in and out of government as well as interest group and professional organization representatives. "Consultative committees are also valued for their technical advice and help the Commission keep in tune with the real world of business and commerce."[96]

While this section maintains that the Council and Commission are not democratically elected bodies, their EU focus demonstrates the overlapping membership (and perhaps identity) of member states at the European, supranational level. By providing a means for national governments to coordinate interests in common areas, governments influenced by their own citizens, the citizens of Europe have a voice in the formulation of EU policy. The challenge for both bodies is to overcome the perceived democratic deficit and to address the issue of legitimacy.

European Parliament and Transnational Party Groups

The third official institution of importance in the EU structure is the EP (comprised of 626 members from the member states), which participates in the legislative and budgetary process of the EU.[97] Since 1979, the EP is the only institution in which EU citizens directly elect their representatives, the Members of the European Parliament (MEPs). The 1987 Single European Act set up a means for cooperation between the EP and the Council of Ministers, thereby increasing the relationship between the various EU institutions.[98] Moreover, the Maastricht Treaty expanded the cooperation with the Council to other areas and granted the EP "a limited form of legislative codecision with the Council."[99]

Importantly, the transnational party-groups in the European Parliament provide the arena for direct representation of EU citizens and for promotion of a European (overlapping) identity. These transnational parties form political groups of ideologically similar national parties. For example, the two largest transnational parties, the Party of the European Socialists (PES) and the European People's Party (EPP) are composed of members from the Social Democratic parties and Christian Democratic/Conservative parties in all the member states, respectively.[100] As Robert Ladrech asserts, transnational political parties and federations (e.g., European People's Party and Green/Ecologist) at the European level formed as a means to increase their power at the supranational level (and thus, have influence from within the EU) and to further common goals. For example, the British Labour Party and Danish Social Democrats objected to coordinating policies at the EU level with their counterparts from other member states. However, by the late 1980s, these two parties ended their opposition and "began to participate in some transnational initiatives."[101] In 1992, the Socialist Party federation renamed itself the Party of European Socialists, whose membership is "based on national party affiliation" with its budget from national party contributions.[102] Importantly, since 1989 the PES has the largest political group in the EP and its national parties comprise a majority of the governments of the member states.[103]

While the PES is thus dependent on the national parties, it plays an important role as a conduit of information from the European level (EP Socialist group) to the national parties, fostering "increased transnational contacts among national parties."[104] For example, the Swedish Labour Party (SAP), at the request of PES party leaders, produced a report on unemployment. Input from representatives from the European Commission, the EP Socialist group, and the European Trade Union Confederation—the top levels of party and national governments—demonstrates the transnational aspect of the report. The PES party-group leaders submitted the SAP's report ("The European Employment Initiative") to the European Council summit meeting in December 1993. Additionally, national parties receive benefits for those that belong to these larger transnational parties, including committee chair appointments.[105]

In addition to the transnational party groups that coincide with national parties based on ideology, there are "intergroups," or cross-party groups, comprised of MEPs from different party groups with a common interest on issues, such as disarmament and gay and lesbian rights. The role of such intergroups is to "build broad support for important initiatives and proposals."[106]

These transnational parties, in essence, foster a European party identity that is important *both* for those engaged in policy making and for EU citizens who are members of their respective national parties. Article 138a of the Maastricht Treaty explicitly notes, "parties at the European level," thus recognizing the pooled sovereignty across national lines at the supranational level.[107] The treaty further states that these European level political parties "are important as a factor for integration within the Union. They contribute to forming a European awareness and to expressing the political will of the citizens of the Union."[108]

As a result of criticisms about the democratic deficit and the perception that the EU decision-making process kept national parliaments out of the loop, the Maastricht Treaty included declarations directly addressing the role of national parliaments. Importantly, one declaration stressed that member state governments would submit to their national parliaments "proposals for (EU) legislation in good time for information or possible examination." In this way, the intention of the declaration was to push for contact between members of the national parliaments and MEPs. The 1997 Amsterdam Treaty further addressed the national parliament demands for greater influence in the EU through a protocol on ways for the national parliaments to obtain information on EU developments. The treaty protocol further called for the Conference of European Affairs Committees (CEAC) of the National Parliaments and the EP to have input on matters they consider important for the EU institutions to address.[109]

As the body most representative of EU citizens, the interesting question arises as to how people view the EP. While, on average, almost two-thirds of people regard the EP as very important/important, voter turnout is low compared to national elections. In the most recent elections, held in June 1999, only 55% of EU citizens voted.[110] In fact, voter turnout has continuously declined from the high of 63% with the first direct election in 1979 (EP UK Office). EP elections are regarded as competitions between national political parties that focus on domestic, rather than European, issues.[111] Thus, as Laffan notes, "[r]epresentative politics is still largely national which constitutes a barrier to the emergence of a genuinely European political realm. The public space remains fragmented into national units."[112]

Moreover, the question arises as to how people perceive the impact of the EP in comparison to their national parliaments. For the first time, a *Eurobarometer* survey, conducted in 2000, examined the extent people feel that the EP and national parliaments impact their lives. The positive impact of national parliaments exceeds that of the EP. For the national parliaments (EU average), 20% felt that there was very little impact, 46% considerable impact, and 26% major impact. For the EP, 33% felt there was very little impact, 46% considerable impact, and 10% major impact.[113] In a *Eurobarometer* survey conducted in 2003, the question was changed slightly, asking "people's perception of the effects" of the decisions and activities of the EP and national parliament (as well as the EU as a whole, regional/local government, and national government). For the EU average, 17% said the EP had "great effect," 47% "some effect," and 22% "no effect." For the national parliaments, 43% said they had "great effect," 40% "some effect," and 12% "no effect."[114] Thus, the view that national parliaments have a greater impact (or effect) on people's daily lives relative to the EP may explain the low voter turnout for EP elections—and also affect the development of a deepening European identity. (Interestingly, the same *Eurobarometer* survey [EB 59] found that 65% of respondents thought that EP elections are "really important.")[115]

Consequently, the gap between perceptions that the EP is considered to be "very important" or "important," low voter turnout, and the perception that the EP has less impact on daily life than national parliaments may explain the fact that only slightly more than half of EU citizens feel both a European identity and national identity—particularly as long as people view the elections in national terms. In fact, of those that voted in June 1999, the most frequent (and seemingly overwhelming) reason for voting (64%, EU average) was "civic duty," followed by "to protect national interest" (16%) and "to support a particular party" (16%) in distant second place.[116]

Yet, at the same time, those who voted expressed high levels of *trust* for EU institutions, first and foremost, the EP (74%), and want the EP to play a more important role (69%).[117] Of *all* those surveyed (voters and non-voters), trust for all bodies of the EU increased, with the public most likely to trust the EP (53%).[118] Interestingly, 67% of those polled stated that they intended to vote in the 2004 EP elections.[119]

Thus, as this section demonstrates, the existence of transnational parties at the EP level permits the promotion of overlapping and multiple memberships, of their national governments as well as at the European level. Moreover, these multiple memberships permit the promotion of a European identity as these MEPs advocate at the supranational level while also consulting with representatives from their national governments. Importantly, citizens of the member states, who vote for both MEPs and national parliamentarians, gain representation at both the national and supranational level. Consequently, in line with our argument, as more EU citizens participate in EP elections (thus a means of representation) and continue to trust EU institutions, multiple identities— European *and* national identity—are likely to become more salient and enable further cooperation (rather than conflict) between member states. The ability to have representation at these levels, national and European, are the first steps at rectifying the democratic deficit and at promoting an overlapping identity at the supranational level.

Regional Representation

At the regional level, EU citizens are able to express a European, national, and regional identity (and thus transnational linkages) through various regional institutions that have increased in number over the years (e.g., regional representative offices increased from two in 1985 to fifty in 1994).[120] These offices, such as the Association of European Regions, the Council of European Municipalities and Regions, and the Conference of Peripheral and Maritime Regions have a transnational focus for both regional and local communities.[121] Of particular importance for pooled sovereignty, the Maastricht Treaty established the Committee of the Regions (CoR), with representatives from regional and local bodies such as federal states, towns, and municipalities.[122] Following the entry into force of the Treaty of Amsterdam in 1999, the Committee of the Regions became a consultative body to (and hence a degree of representation in) the EP in areas such as economic and social cohesion, education, and culture as well as trans-European infrastructure networks. The consultative role of the Committee enables involvement in the making of EU policies that affect these regional and local bodies.[123] For example, according to the mission statement of the EPP Group in the Committee of the Regions,

> Via the political groups the CoR members can effectively represent local and regional interests by getting their voices heard in the political concert. As is the case with the European Parliament, the political parties in the CoR want to contribute more to political opinion-forming. They intend to contribute to a more efficient and influential work of the CoR with a view to becoming a political body which represents the interests of the citizens in the regions and municipalities in the best possible way.[124]

Moreover, according to the Party of European Socialists (PES) group in the CoR, the CoR provides an excellent opportunity for "closeness to the citizen" and a means to overcome the EU's democratic deficit: "European integration must be explained at grassroots level. This is the only way to avoid democratic deficit. The CoR strengthens the democratic legitimacy of the Union."[125]

Additionally, these many sub-state regions in Europe "established missions to the EU in Brussels." Such sub-state regions are able to "bypass the state . . . becoming increasingly important voices in European affairs."[126] As Alexander Murphy notes, "[m]any of the lobbyists are bypassing the state and going directly to Brussels because they see in the EU a viable alternative to the state as a focus for the organization of cultural, social, and political life." For those regions that are poor, focusing on a European "posture" may be more beneficial in meeting their demands, than is the case for appealing to their state governments. "The pursuit of such strategies fosters structures and arrangements that lend credence to the idea that Europe does indeed matter."[127] A clear example of how sub-state regions are linked to a conception of European identity can be found in the actions of nationalists in Wales who have looked to the EU in order to push for enhancing their regional status relative to the United Kingdom, but not quite a state either. The former leader of Plaid Cymru, the Welsh nationalist political party, stated that "one day Wales may be able to be a region within a unified Europe without having to apply for UN membership."[128] In another example, as discussed in chapter 2, the Basques have looked to the EU as a means of promoting their interests, in essence, leapfrogging over the Spanish national government for representation.

The importance of such regional bodies as related to identity and citizenship can be found in the levels of attachment people feel toward their region, town/village, country, and the EU. According to a 2003 *Eurobarometer* survey, 90% feel "very" or "fairly attached" to their country, 87% to their town or village, 86% to their region, and 45% to the EU (52% did not feel very or not all attached).[129] The problem, however, is that of ten EU institutions, the Committee of the Regions recently ranked last in people's awareness of the institution (26%), whereas the EP ranked first at 91%.[130]

In summary, this section demonstrates that EU-level institutions, with EU interests (Council, Commission, and EP) as well as national interests, the transnational links through transnational parties at the EP level, and representatives at the regional level provide avenues for representation at different levels. As Ladrech notes, "[a]lthough national governments continue to play a dominant role in the decision-making process, they are themselves more deeply enmeshed in the EU system; therefore, bargaining is affected by dynamics inside states, among states, and above states."[131] Thus, the EU decision-making process at the various levels provides an opportunity for the expression of multiple, and even overlapping European and regional, identities of the member states.

Trends for the Future of European Identity and Pooled Sovereignty

While the EU has actively sought to promote, and perhaps construct, a European identity through both the symbols of identity (flag, anthem, passport, etc.) and representation (EP, transnational party-groups, and regional associations), the institution does face challenges from the salience of national identities and from the issue of the democratic deficit. As Lemke asserts, for democratic participation, whether at the national or supranational level, three components of citizenship are important: identity, rights, and political participation.[132]

In terms of the democratic deficit, *Eurobarometer* surveys indicate that those surveyed are more satisfied with national democracy than with the way democracy works in the EU. In 2003, the EU 15 average was as follows: 58% are "very satisfied + fairly satisfied," with 40% "not very satisfied + not at all satisfied" with their national democracy. In comparison, 46% are "satisfied . . . with the way democracy works in the European Union," and 38% "are not very" or "not at all satisfied."[133] The fact that slightly less than half of those surveyed are satisfied with democracy in the EU is a challenge for the EU as a supranational level organization representing its citizens. Yet, interestingly, in a list of 27 policy areas in which the EU can make decisions (e.g., information about the EU, foreign policy, humanitarian aid, support for regions in economic difficulty, and currency), 18 of those areas had majorities that "support joint EU decision-making in these policy areas." Large majorities supported European level decision making for several of these areas, including, the "fight against international terrorism" (85%), trade/exploitation of humans (80%), information about the EU (74%), foreign policy (73%), and humanitarian aid (72%).[134]

In terms of salience of national identities, for example, in a recent study comparing British and Italian attitudes, Marco Cinnirella found that most British people feel more British than European in that they had "no sense of common culture ties within Europe, which might have allowed for a sentimental/symbolic attachment." In comparison, Italians "often felt their cultural and

historical heritage to be intimately bound-up with that of Europe."
Interestingly, Cinnirella argues that the difference relates to the
perception of Europe's future. British people worried that further
integration in Europe threatened their national identity. In contrast, Italians saw the future as more positive for Europe and thus
for the possibility of a European identity.[135]

In addition, the EU faces the question of how to define a European identity, particularly as more states are admitted into the EU
(and those waiting in the wings for admission) with their different
histories. Moreover, the member states may face a challenge from
immigration on the conception of a European identity.[136] Finally,
what of the other—the out-group that is so much a part of social
identity theory? To whom are the "others" that Europeans will compare themselves? During the Cold War, the other was the Soviet
Union and the Eastern European bloc. However, many of these
countries have applied for admission to the EU. In the post-Cold
War period, who are the new others that Europe will compare
themselves to, given the need for comparison as argued by social
identity theory? Will it be the United States or perhaps the Third
World?[137]

Yet, as Anthony D. Smith notes, these states do share some
political and civic traditions and heritage, such as Roman law,
political democracy, parliamentary institutions, and Judeo-Christ-
ian ethics. They also share a cultural heritage: Renaissance
humanism, rationalism, romanticism, and classicism—in essence,
a "family of cultures."[138] Thus, to reconcile national and European
identities, Ole Waever argues that the EU should promote a European citizenship based on civic and political identity, rather than
on an ethno-cultural identity. In this way, the political identity for
Europe does not supplant national or state identities, rather a
"fusion of national and European identities, and more specifically,
the importance of Europe *in* national identities."[139] As Waever further notes, "[a]n identity basis for Europe is probably only possible
if it penetrates, rather than confronts, national identities, giving
European and national identities an interdependent relationship,
where each is mutually present in the other's identity." Moreover,
in the case of immigrants, the civic and political identity is inclusive, allowing them to become "European."[140]

In the end, a shared European identity may only be possible if
based on the idea of multiple, or overlapping, identities.[141] As the
social psychological theories discussed in chapter 1 indicated,

Figure 3.2. EU Membership Benefits and the Member-States (EU Member Average)

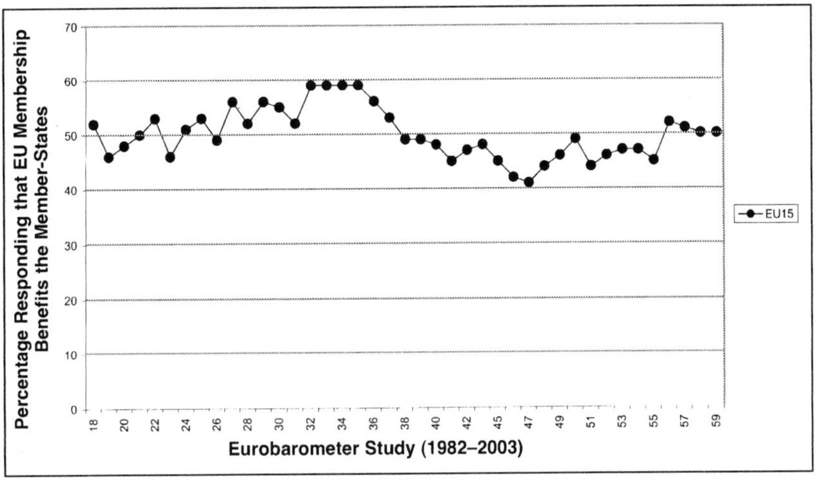

Source: Commission of the European Union, *Eurobarometer Reports* (Brussels: European Commission).

people do hold multiple identities. As the *Eurobarometer* surveys indicate, a majority of EU citizens do feel *both* a European and national identity. In addition, significant numbers of people trust the EP—the only institution directly elected by EU citizens and also influenced by transnational political parties acting at the supranational level. Moreover, the evidence indicates that there is a connection between support for EU membership and the perception that membership in the institution is beneficial.

Figure 3.2 shows the rate at which citizens of the EU member states think that EU membership benefits their nation. In *Eurobarometer* surveys, the average response (EU15) has held fairly steady near 50 percent. Some member states have seen a dramatic increase (e.g., Spain and Ireland); others declined with time (e.g., Germany); and others have been persistently low (e.g., the UK). It is clear that the states that have benefited from direct transfers from the European Regional and Development Fund (ERDF), such as Spain and Ireland, have citizens who believe that membership in the EU benefits their nation. On the other hand, in member states that give large sums of money to the EU but receive very little from the ERDF their citizens do not see the direct benefit of membership.

Thus, as we argue, the relationship between representation in institutions at various levels (local, national, regional, and EU) and promotion of an overlapping European identity not in opposition to national identities, will likely lead to further cooperation, support, and integration between the member states of the EU. As Martin Marcussen and his colleagues note, "In a certain sense, multiple European and nation state identities might actually be appropriate for a multi-level system of governance, such as the EU."[142]

4

Protestants, Catholics, and the Good Friday Peace Agreement in Northern Ireland

The fact that we agree to negotiate at all on any basis was possibly the primary cause of our down fall. Certainly it was the first milestone on the road to disaster.
Robert Barton, Irish negotiator who signed but later rejected the 1920 Government of Ireland Act

—Robert Barton, *Notes for a Lecture*

But why should words my frenzy whet
Unless we are able to strike
Our despot lords who fear no threat
But reverence the pike
Oh, do be wise, leave moral force
The strength of thought and pen
And all the value of discourse
To lily-livered men.

Popular ballad of IRA men during the Irish Civil War

—Tim Pat Coogan and George Morrison,
The Irish Civil War

The people of Ireland are sick of war. They are sick of sectarian killings and random bombings. They are sick of the sad elegance of funerals, especially those involving the small white coffins of children, prematurely laid into the rolling green fields of the Irish countryside. They want peace.

—George J. Mitchell, *Making Peace*

Struggle without End in Northern Ireland

The Chief Constable's Office in Northern Ireland reports that from the years 1969 to 1996 there were 3,212 fatal casualties from sectarian violence in Northern Ireland.[1] Roughly two-thirds of these fatalities were civilians. The greater part of the violence occurred from 1972 through 1976, or during the time of the "Troubles" in Northern Ireland. An average of over 200 civilians and more than 60 security officers (both military and police) lost their lives each year during this time. Brendan O'Leary and John McGarry figure that the responsibility for deaths from 1969 to 1989 can be distributed in the following manner: republican paramilitaries, 57.7%; loyalist paramilitaries, 25.3%; and security forces, 11.8%.[2] Malcolm Sutton lists every fatality from the violence, including those killed in Britain, Ireland, and elsewhere in Europe and arrives at a fairly similar distribution of responsibility.[3]

The enormous violence in Northern Ireland led eventually to the negotiating table. The Irish Republican Army (IRA) and Loyalist paramilitaries declared a joint cease-fire in 1994 that led to the British government initiating inclusive, all-party talks about the future of Northern Ireland. Despite a resumption of IRA bombing in 1996, and the removal of Sinn Fein from the negotiating table, the talks moved forward with the participation of the British government, Irish government, and former senator George Mitchell as mediator. The talks also survived the IRA's new cease-fire in 1997, the reinclusion of Sinn Fein, and the withdrawal of the Democratic Unionist Party. Eventually on April 10, 1998, the British-Irish Peace Agreement (or Good Friday Agreement) was signed by all parties.

The Good Friday Agreement signals a new approach to solving the regional conflict that has gripped the six northern counties since the partition of Ireland in 1920. Unlike previous agreements, the Agreement emphasizes the role of international parliamentary institutions, as embodied in the proposed cross-border councils. We argue that the institutions (councils) established by the Agreement can contribute to a resolution of the conflict. These institutions promote overlapping identities and multiple layers of representation, and pool sovereignty that can, in turn, reduce threat perception, establish trust, and reduce the ethnic security dilemma that exists between the Catholic and Protestant communities.

The new international councils provide three tangible methods to reduce conflict in the region and to encourage reconciliation by promoting overlapping identities and multiple layers of representation of the parties involved. First, these institutions give the Protestant majority an alternative source of security other than direct British rule or intervention. Second, they allow both communities (and even divisions within the communities) access to policy making and representational forums at several levels. Last, they allow for a qualitative change in British involvement in the region. Britain's recent approach to the conflict views it as an "island-wide" problem, not just as an internal "British" problem. This new approach led to increased involvement by the Government of the Republic of Ireland, particularly its inclusion in many of the proposed new councils. In turn, the "pooling of sovereignty" by the British and Irish governments regarding Northern Ireland has increased the security of Britain. No longer will both Northern Protestants and Northern Catholics blame the British government for a breakdown in peace. Moreover, the British government would no longer be obligated to intervene in Northern Ireland. Reciprocally, the Unionist parties would no longer be able to take for granted British assistance.[4]

This new institutional arrangement is certainly a tightrope walk. The Northern Protestants must feel secure that their power as the majority is respected. The Protestants have relied historically upon British assurances of that power, while at the same time the Protestant dominance of the region has eroded in the face of demographic changes and economic growth in the Catholic community. Under the new agreement, the Protestant community cannot take for granted any assistance from the government in London. The dilemma for the British government is how to reconcile two competing aims: the desire of the British mainland to extricate itself from the Irish Island while at the same time establishing a means to ensure the security of the Protestant majority.

This chapter demonstrates how the new international parliamentary institutions can provide a solution to this dilemma. The first section describes how friendly and enemy images develop from processes both internal to Northern Ireland and external to it. This section highlights the international nature of the conflict. Specifically, it shows how the communities in Northern Ireland are linked to national communities in both Britain and the Republic of Ireland. Identity in Northern Ireland is the product of shared community with other nations and of constructed identity in Northern Ireland, primarily based on the externally derived identities.

We then look at the previous attempts by the British government to resolve the conflict. Particularly, we specify the different institutions that the British proposed and implemented. We examine each proposal in detail and then discuss why these institutions failed to promote peace in the region. In the third section we outline the Good Friday Agreement and its institutions. This section pays special attention to the unique cross-border parliamentary institutions and the international aspects of the agreement.

The next section posits the structure of the European Union (EU) as an analogy to the structure of the Good Friday Agreement. This section links chapter 3 to this chapter. We contend that the cross-border parliamentary institutions of the Agreement are similar to those of the EU. Following this, in the last section, we present our argument that the Agreement offers an institutional structure that promotes overlapping identities and pools sovereignty. The diminution of exclusive identities, constructed through cross-national institutions, contributes to a resolution of the Northern Ireland conflict. At the end of this section we propose that the Agreement is a model that could provide a possible solution to other nationalist and ethnic conflicts present in the twenty-first century.

The Internal and External Sources of Conflict in Northern Ireland

Getting at the heart of the intercommunity conflict in Northern Ireland is no easy task. A great wealth of literature has sought to explain the formation of the competing communities and the reasons for the continued division. Two broad trends in the theoretical literature are identified: (1) the emphasis on the "internal" nature of the conflict and (2) the historical process (read: "external") by which the divisions were created. Although one may view these two alternative approaches as being mutually exclusive, they are not necessarily so. We argue that both capture a portion of the process leading up to the current situation in Northern Ireland. The internal model rightly points out the development of exclusive in-group distinctions between the two communities. The external model illustrates the role of external actors, particularly state actors such as Britain, in perpetuating the internally derived group divisions. To reiterate our argument, we posit that any solution to the conflict in Northern Ireland must address both the internal and external causes.

To understand fully the existing conflict, we provide a brief summary of the creation of Northern Ireland.[5] After French consolidation of their control on the European continent in 1540, English expansion turned from Europe toward Wales, Scotland, and Ireland. Settlement of Ireland by English and Scottish settlers was rapid. "By 1641 Protestant settlers owned 41 percent of the land in Ireland and held a majority of seats in both house[s] of the Irish parliament."[6] The victory of Cromwell over the Irish in 1640 led to the confiscation of Irish-owned land. This pattern repeated itself in 1690 with the defeat of the Catholic supporters of James II. The Catholic population receded into that of a peripheral nationality on its own island.

A Catholic revival in the nineteenth century led to calls for Irish independence. Prior to World War I, Irish Republican political struggles created what the English parliamentarians called the "Ulster crisis." In short, a discussion of whether Ireland should have Home Rule was debated on both sides of the Irish Sea. A small group of Republicans felt that the outbreak of the First World War offered an opportunity to strike at British rule while the British were occupied on the European continent. The 1916 Easter Rebellion ended in defeat for the rebels, the British execution of fifteen of the Republican leaders, and the subsequent turn toward terrorism by the new IRA. The British authorities imposed martial law, which only further inflamed the Republican resistance. The Anglo-Irish War (as the British called it; the Irish called it the "Troubles") lasted from 1919 to 1921, with much violence perpetrated by both sides.[7]

Britain eventually went to the negotiating table with the idea of partition as a solution to the violence. The plan was for the nine northeastern counties in the historic area of Ulster to remain a part of Britain while the remaining counties, all predominantly Catholic, would be given Home Rule under British dominion. Eventually only six counties in Ulster would be considered for partition, and of those six, Catholics were the majority in two, Fermanagh and Tyrone, and in the city of Derry. The British Parliament passed the Government of Ireland Act in 1920, effectively dividing the North from the South. Negotiations in the remaining twenty-six counties in the South as to their status eventually led to Home Rule, a civil war, and eventual development of a new Constitution and Republic in 1937.[8]

Returning to our discussion of the factors that led to the development of identity in Northern Ireland, the internal model posits that the source of the sectarian division is endogenous to the Northern counties.[9] The model does not ignore the important role played by external powers, but rather places an emphasis on the particular internal factors leading to intercommunity conflict. In this model, there is no essential conflict between the British and Irish states, or even between the British and Irish people. Rather, the divisions between the two Northern communities give rise to crisis.

As an example, supporters of this theory point to the civil rights movement in the late 1960s and its genesis in the Catholic community. A stronger Catholic middle class was developing as the result of education and business reforms in the 1940s and 1950s that liberalized Catholic entry into the workforce. Catholics organized themselves into political pressure groups. Their goals were to influence the government to make fairer decisions regarding housing, education, employment, basic services, and other local issues.[10] For example, the first of these groups was the Campaign for Social Justice (CSJ). The CSJ sought housing improvements among Catholic renters and equal treatment by the local urban district council. Over time a multitude of pressure groups with almost exclusive Catholic membership organized to fight for social rights.[11]

The culmination of this grassroots effort was the setting up of the Northern Ireland Civil Rights Association (NICRA) in January 1967. By the summer of 1968 the NICRA was leading the Catholic community in public protests demanding civil and social rights. Loyalists gathered for counterdemonstrations and violence was the inevitable result. The Protestant community divided as the Reverend Ian Paisley launched his virulent form of anti-Catholicism and found many adherents. The resulting crisis among the Protestant community and eventual British intervention in 1969 was the product of this demonstration of Catholic voice.[12] In relation to the internal model, actions by the Catholic community in response to internal conditions forced action by external actors, not the other way around.

According to the internal model, the ascriptive differences between the two communities becomes institutionalized in all facets of society. The two communities live divided by religion, socioeconomic status, residence, and many other factors. The distinctiveness of the in-group from the out-group is made more clear and boundaries between the two are maintained.[13]

The second large body of literature concentrates on the historical and external derivation of the conflict. The theoretical link between all accounts that stress the external aspects is that the two communities (Protestant/British vs. Catholic/Irish) are the product of external forces. The communal division is the result of the battle between the invading people, culture, and religion of the British mainland and the Irish people, culture, and religion. Internal disputes in Northern Ireland are all predicated on the divisions shaped by the external forces.

Most authors link the development of communal division into an overall pattern of colonialism and partition of the Island of Ireland. Events such as the seventeenth-century colonization of the northeast of Ireland by Scottish and English settlers produced a system of relationships that insured British control over Ireland. English settlement created a privileged position for Protestant settlers while marginalizing Irish natives. The conflicting ideologies of unionism and nationalism that grew during the British occupation of the nineteenth century are seen not as the result of tensions between two communities, but rather as tension between an occupying group supported by an outside state versus an occupied people fighting to retain their independence. Furthermore, the nature of the struggle between the two states creates a difference in access to power and resources. This long-lasting difference in access produces lasting conflict as the marginalized group seeks access to that which they are denied.[14]

The period of partition in the early twentieth century is another key moment that supports the external school of thought. The territory enclosed within the nation of Northern Ireland is artificial, the result of the balance of power between the British capacity to control Ireland and the strength of the Irish nationalists in 1920. Even later events depict the role of actors external to Northern Ireland, such as during the time of British direct rule of Northern Ireland beginning in 1974. Both communities viewed the British occupation forces as a foreign intervention into the politics of Northern Ireland, although the Protestant community welcomed the intervention but the Catholic community did not.[15]

Both models produce a compartmentalization of the conflict that does not do full justice to its complexity. Yet, both point to key aspects that we seek to address, that is, the building of the internal divisions and the role of external actors in exacerbating those same divisions. Joseph Ruane and Jennifer Todd contend that a more sophisticated model is necessary, one that integrates both bodies of literature. They see the conflict as deriving from a system of interlocking levels in which there are three key relationships: a set of real objective differences between the two communities; a tendency toward communal division, and a structure of dominance, dependence, and inequality.[16]

First, Ruane and Todd argue that understanding the objective differences between the Catholic and Protestant communities is essential to viewing the source of ethnic conflict. They emphasize that five objective differences between the two communities exist: religion, ethnicity, settler-native status, concepts of progress and backwardness, and national identity and allegiance.[17] In short the religious differences revolve around differences in doctrine and religious organization. Ruane and Todd note that a difference in class overlaps this religious difference. Catholics are predominantly from the lower class while Protestants range from the lowest social classes to the most upper social classes.[18]

The ethnic differences are the direct result of colonization. British settlement brought the Scots and English to Ireland. Before British settlement the dominant ethnic people were those of Irish-Gaelic stock. As Ruane and Todd acknowledge, the close relationship between ethnicity and religion makes it difficult to specify the exact importance of ethnicity. Also related to the above two factors is that of settler-native status. The former group would occupy most of Northern Ireland but does not identify with the customs, history, or culture of Ireland. The latter group feels disenfranchised from its customs, history, and culture.[19]

The concepts of progress and backwardness are important in creating the strong in-group versus out-group images. The Protestant settlers saw themselves as a modernizing force in Irish society. They came from a nation that was industrializing and had a liberal, modern, and progressive governmental structure. They viewed the Irish natives as barbaric, icon-worshiping, and backward. The Irish, on the other hand, viewed the invaders as just that, invaders, not as a modernizing and civilizing force.[20]

The last objective difference, that of national identity and allegiance, is based on nineteenth- and twentieth-century ideologies and concepts of the nation and state. Irish nationalism emerged in the nineteenth century alongside similar nationalist movements throughout most of Western Europe. Imported from the French Revolution, nationalism inspired ethnic groups to seek self-determination. The end desire of nationalism is the creation of a nation-state. This Irish political ambition for statehood ran counter to the desire of Protestant settlers to remain in union with Britain. Thus, the dueling ideologies of nationalism and unionism appeared.[21]

The second key relationship is that the perceived and actual differences are crystallized into a difference of "community." An observer must understand the sense of community that is so salient to an inhabitant of Northern Ireland in order to view the conflict in the correct context. Without immersion into the nature of community, it is hard for an outside observer to perceive the reasons and motivations behind the actions of many participants in the conflict.[22]

Communities are "emergent entities, products of structurally conditioned social practices which, however, possess some general properties including a level of self-consciousness, integrating organizational networks and a capacity for boundary maintenance."[23] With this definition, one can identify the main political actors in Northern Ireland as the dual communities of Protestants and Catholics. However, this is not to say that overlapping and multiple identities do not or cannot exist. (Recent survey research demonstrates that a considerable number of Protestants and Catholics in Northern Ireland claim a Northern Irish identity, 27% and 28%, respectively.)[24]

In fact, to the contrary, the development of distinct communities was a slow process and not all communities are bounded perfectly. For example, "[p]rior to partition, Unionists classified themselves as 'Irish'—they were, after all, 'Irish' within the political context of the United Kingdom of Great Britain and Ireland."[25] Likewise, internal divisions within the communities exist. On this last point, the two communities both have sub-divisions. Protestants differ in their constitutional desire for the future of Northern Ireland. Unionists desire to remain a part of the United Kingdom while Loyalists would be happy with an autonomous or independent Ulster. Likewise, the Catholic community divides among Republicans who seek a united Ireland and Nationalists who envision an independent Northern Ireland.

In addition, the political parties in Northern Ireland represent both the community division and the intracommunity segmentation. The two main Catholic parties, the Social Democratic and Labour Party (SDLP) and Sinn Fein, draw greater support from the Nationalist and Republican segments of the Catholic community, respectively. Moreover, the two parties' leaders (John Hume of the SDLP, Gerry Adams of Sinn Fein) have defined Irish identity differently. In an analysis of speeches by Hume and Adams in a two-year period (1984–1986), Andrea K. Grove and Neal A. Carter found that although both leaders use the terms *Catholics, Nation-*

alists, *Irish*, and *this community*, their meanings of these terms differ tremendously.[26] Prior to and following the negotiation of the 1985 Anglo-Irish Agreement (AIA, or Hillsborough Agreement), Hume stressed that the "primary political group is the community of Northern Ireland, including Protestants." When Adams refers to "this community," which is infrequently, he does not include Protestants/Unionists. Thus, Hume's understanding of identity remains inclusive, while Adams's understanding is exclusive. Unlike Adams, Hume's inclusiveness overlaps: when referring to the ingroup he sometimes focuses on the people of Northern Ireland, people on the entire Island of Ireland, people in Britain and Ireland, and people in Europe and in the world.[27]

The literature on Northern Ireland stresses many dimensions of identity difference between the two communities. Most accounts center on differences that result from four different historical processes: ethnic origin, religious indoctrination, colonialism, and ideology.[28] Polar opposition is the usual expression of these differences: Gaelic-Irish versus English/Scottish, Catholic versus Protestant, native versus settler, or nationalism versus unionism. An example of this polarization is how each community defines its national identity. In a poll conducted in 1989, Catholics identified themselves as Irish (60%), Northern Irish (25%), British (8%), and Ulster (2%); Protestants identified themselves as British (68%), Ulster (10%) and Northern Irish (16%), and Irish (3%).[29] A 2001 survey found similar results. Catholics identifies themselves as British (12%), English (1%), European (4%), Irish (65%), Northern Irish (28%), and Ulster (1%). Protestants identified themselves as British (73%), English (2%), European (2%), Irish (4%), Northern Irish (27%), and Ulster (16%).[30] Table 4.1 displays this data.

The two communities have an almost exact opposite ordering of identity. As many authors point out, the tendency toward communal division emerged because of the overlap of these dimensions of differences. For example, English settlers were often supporters of Protestantism and fiercely loyal to Britain and to a British identity. Native Irish were predominantly Catholic and harbored sentiments against Britain. The lack of shared identities polarized the two communities. This relationship stresses the external nature of the genesis of the sharp divisions.

Last, to Ruane and Todd the structure of dominance, dependence, and inequality in Northern Ireland highlights both the internal and external nature of the conflict. The integration of Ireland into the British state from the sixteenth to twentieth centuries

Table 4.1. Identity in Northern Ireland by Religion (percentage)

		British	English	European	Irish	Northern Irish	Ulster
1989	Protestant	68	n.a.	n.a.	3	16	10
	Catholic	8	n.a.	n.a.	60	25	2
2001	Protestant	73	2	2	4	27	16
	Catholic	12	1	4	65	28	1

Source: Edward Moxon-Browne, "National Identity in Northern Ireland," in *Social Attitudes in Northern Ireland*, eds. Peter Stringer and Gillian Robinson (Belfast: Blackstaff, 1991); "Life and Times" Survey, 2001, http://www.ark.ac.uk/nilt/.

secured an alliance between the Protestant settlers and Britain. Both needed each other: the British crown needed the settlers to control Ireland, while the settlers needed the power of Britain to maintain their hegemony on the island. Partition in 1920 did not change this relationship much. The Protestant majority in Northern Ireland enjoys access to resources and power (economic and political) denied to the Catholic minority. The structure of Protestant dominance relies on both their numerical superiority and also the support (tacit or otherwise) of the British government. Protestant dominance has resulted in long-term inequality between the communities. The gradual ascension of the Catholic community, both numerically and substantively, slowly undermines the Protestant position of dominance by reversing the inequality. The erosion of the Protestant position forces the Protestant community to lean heavily on its dependence on British support.[31]

To summarize, the conflict is rooted in both the internal, communal divisions and the role of external actors in perpetuating a set of unequal relationships. These unequal relationships, perceptions of threat, and enemy images reinforce the ethnic security dilemma in Northern Ireland. As Protestants became more dominant in areas such as employment, housing, and governmental administration, Catholics became increasingly insecure, fostering further perceptions of threat and mistrust. Efforts to increase the security of one group only served to reduce the security of the other group. Moreover, this pattern of conflict, be it internally or externally derived, exists under political control by a British parliament across the Irish Sea from Northern Ireland. British sovereignty resides in one place: Westminster. The British government has sole authority over Northern Ireland. It can use policy to dictate events inside Northern Ireland. The British government has used its authority on occasion in an attempt to control the conflict in Northern Ireland.

Previous British Attempts at Resolving the Conflict

The purpose of this section is to show how previous attempts to resolve the conflict have failed to address the issue of promoting overlapping identities. We show that British proposals to end the conflict mirror the changing conceptions of the root of the conflict. Early proposals viewed the conflict as merely an internal one; as an example they cited the British attempt to establish an internal solution (e.g., the Stormont Parliament of 1973). When the British (and Irish) governments perceive the conflict as having not only an internal component but also an external one, the structures that they propose become less "consociational" and more incorporative of overlapping identities.

That the actions of the British government contribute to conflict in Northern Ireland cannot be debated. Exactly how they contribute can be. Britain has conflicting goals in regard to Northern Ireland. On the one hand, Britain has maintained a relationship with Northern Ireland that can be termed *postcolonial*. Northern Ireland has never been fully integrated into Britain. While the Protestant majority may feel a "British" identity, the British on the mainland still refer to the Protestants as "Irish." In the perceptions of the British political elite, Northern Ireland is seen more as an integral part of the Island of Ireland than as a part of Great Britain.[33] Moreover, this view is certainly held by the British populace. Polls of the British population in 1991 and 1992 reveal that nearly half of the British polled believed that Northern Ireland should leave the United Kingdom.(36) Moreover, no poll from 1974 to 1996 has shown that more than a third of the British populace supports maintaining union with Northern Ireland.[34]

Furthermore, British support of the principle of majority rule (as opposed to proportional representation) has exacerbated the conflict in Northern Ireland by reinforcing the in-group (i.e., Protestant) versus out-group (i.e., Catholic) distinction. A hallmark of British territorial management is the belief in the right of the majority to rule. This belief is the cornerstone on which the Protestant community is dependent upon continued British support. The majoritarian principle gives reason for the Protestants to maintain communal solidarity in the face of a growing Catholic minority.

On the other hand, Britain has certainly shown a sincere desire to reach a settlement in Northern Ireland.[35] In the time since partition, the British government has made numerous proposals and initiatives toward ending the conflict. The changing conceptions of identity have paralleled many of the proposals. Chief among these was the short-lived consociational power-sharing Assembly of 1973 (Sunningdale Agreement). It contained all of the provisions spelled out by consociational theorists: power-sharing, minority veto, legislative coalitions, and proportional representation of minority groups. In addition, the Sunningdale Agreement called for the creation of an all-Ireland institution, the Council of Ireland. However, the Agreement faced strong opposition from the Protestants. Five months after the conclusion of the Agreement, the Ulster Workers Council incited strikes that led to the fall of the Assembly and to the establishment of direct British rule of Northern Ireland.[36]

The failure of the consociational arrangement shows the weakness of consociational solutions. The Agreement contained only a single cross-border institution with two important flaws. First, even if it had been established, the Council of Ireland would not have been an effective governing or administrative body as it lacked any real authority. Second, the Council of Ireland gave the Irish in the North a place of representation but did not give the Protestants in the North any similar body. The Protestant community rightfully protested this asymmetry. The talks themselves were not inclusive either. Only three parties were present at the talks: the Ulster Unionists, the Alliance, and the SDLP.[37] Perhaps due to the ease with which the two communities could criticize the agreement and take their case to the British mainland in the way of voice or violence, neither was required to accept the British-led political arrangement. Moreover, the Agreement failed to induce a change in the self-image of the Unionists vis-à-vis their relationship with the Nationalists.[38] The lesson from the Sunningdale Agreement is that the external nature of the struggle in Northern Ireland prohibits any solution that relies solely on regional institutions (i.e., consociational) without a commensurate change in identity.[39]

In light of the failure of the British government's 1973 Sunningdale Agreement and the lack of movement over the next decade to deal with the Northern Irish problem, the Republic of Ireland established the New Ireland Forum in 1983. The purpose of this Forum was to begin taking into account Unionist concerns about Nationalist and Republican attitudes toward unification. The New Ireland Forum sought to push for all-party negotiations to seek solutions to the conflict, instead of the seemingly unchanging demand for unification of all of Ireland. With the Forum, the Irish government recognized the interests and identity of the Unionists and attempted to reconstruct the identity of the Republic of Ireland to include those residents of Northern Ireland who were not ethnically Irish.[40] The secularization process, reduction of the Catholic Church's political authority, and extensive abhorrence of IRA violence all contributed to the Irish government's willingness to reconstruct the Irish identity in order to resolve the conflict. Despite this positive step, the Unionist parties boycotted the talks while the Thatcher government and Unionist parties rejected the three options (unitary united Ireland, federal united Ireland, and joint British-Irish authority over Northern Ireland) presented by the Forum.[41]

The 1985 Anglo-Irish Agreement was based on the policy that only parties acting in a constitutional manner should be privy to peace talks.[42] The notable inclusion of Ireland in a consultative role and the willingness of the Irish government to accept the notion of consensus for the North for constitutional change marked a significant turning point in the process of resolving the conflict.[43] Thus the agreement stressed the *"Irish* ethnic dimension"—rather than an internal Northern Ireland settlement—to the future political structure for Northern Ireland.[44]

The British government's enticement to the Unionists for acceptance of the AIA rested on the diminished role of the Irish government in the North—if the Unionists agreed to an internal solution with the Nationalists.[45] Yet, the 1985 Agreement failed because the Unionist parties refused to participate in the negotiations. Their refusal can be explained in their understanding of their interests and identity. The historical and religious identity of the Protestants is opposed to the interests of the British and Irish governments in the peace process. Protestants perceive the Catholics as the Other—out-group—and are thus unwilling to reach agreement with the Republic of Ireland.[46] Moreover, the failure of the 1985 Agreement emphasized that the Republican wing of the Catholic community could not be excluded from a viable political solution. Without Republican consent, the communal violence, and indeed interstate terrorism, continued.

A change in the British position vis-à-vis Northern Ireland occurred in 1993 when Britain began to acknowledge the link between the internal and external causes for the conflict. The government of Conservative Prime Minister John Major realized the island-wide nature of the conflict and made overtures to the Irish government in Dublin and to Sinn Fein. The goal of both governments became the inclusion of *all* communities (British, Irish, Catholic, and Protestant) with a stake in the conflict, which marked a significant change from previous attempts at resolution.

The Downing Street Declaration (DSD) of 1993 was the result of this new interstate approach. Britain declared that "it is for the people of the island of Ireland alone, by agreement between the two parts respectively, to exercise their right of self-determination on the basis of consent." The Irish government accepted that "the democratic right of self-determination by the people of Ireland as a whole must be exercised with, and subject to the agreement and consent of a majority of the people of Northern Ireland."[47] In other words, Britain protected the Protestant majority by including the majority principle.

Yet, Britain also accepted a new, important role of both the Irish government and the Irish community, and particularly Sinn Fein. Eight months prior to the Declaration, Sinn Fein and the SDLP met in secret talks. These talks paved the way for the IRA's willingness to compromise on its demand for unification in return for the British government's offer to allow Sinn Fein a seat at the negotiating table. In response, the Republic of Ireland began to move toward a softening of the overt threat contained in Articles 2 and 3 of its own Constitution, the articles calling for the eventual unification of the Island of Ireland. The Irish government also issued a statement commending the commitment of the IRA to accept the democratic process for constitutional change.[48]

Two years later, in February 1995, the British and Irish governments published a document entitled "Frameworks for the Future." The Frameworks document contained two new proposals: devolution of British authority to a government in Northern Ireland and a new framework for agreement detailing the exact relations between Northern Ireland, the Republic, and Britain. The Frameworks document specified "the creation of new cross-border institutions and the guarantee of a referendum" for any future constitutional change for the North.[49] Importantly, the Frameworks document attempted to construct a new identity for the North. The document concentrated on revising the interests and identity of the Unionists away from an in-group-out-group division of Protestants versus Catholics toward an identity and interest that complemented and overlapped with those of the Irish Catholics and the Republic of Ireland. It did this in two ways. First, by proposing "devolved institutions with legislative and executive responsibilities over a wide range of areas, including security—and an elaborate system of checks and balances to protect minority interests."[50] Second, it elaborated both North-South intergovernmental bodies, as well as an "East-West" intergovernmental conference supported by a permanent staff from both the British and Irish governments. While these cross-border institutions did not become a reality immediately, the focus on the necessity for such institutions is illustrative of the new focus on seeing the common identities. Correspondingly, the Frameworks document had broad support of most Unionist parties (with the exception of the Democratic Unionist Party), the Catholic Social Democratic and Labour Party, and the ambiguous support of Sinn Fein.[51]

Despite a resumption of IRA terrorism in February 1996 and Unionist retaliatory intimidation, an election was held and all-party talks commenced, with former senator George Mitchell as chair of the talks.[52] However, the peace talks initially failed to achieve much. Distrust of the new Irish influence led Unionists to use their position in the House of Commons to push for concessions (e.g., exclusion of Sinn Fein from the talks) from Major's government.[53] Major's slim parliamentary majority left him dependent on Unionist votes. Thus, the peace talks appeared on the brink of collapse until the 1997 British general election and the victory of Tony Blair and the Labour Party. Labour's landslide victory left Blair with a large majority, one large enough to discount any Unionist blackmail.

The British-Irish (Good Friday) Peace Agreement of April 1998 signaled the new direction taken by Blair's Labour government.[54] The Blair government moved quickly to a settlement of the problem in a manner consistent with its handling of other regional disputes on the British periphery, including the devolution of power to Scotland and Wales. The goal was to allow the people of Northern Ireland to run their own government *and* to determine the eventual fate of the six Northern counties. However, Britain would maintain a role in the final solution through participation in various international parliamentary institutions.[55] Furthermore, significant Nationalist and Unionist leaders changed their views of the Other as illegitimate to legitimate, signaling a willingness to find common ground for settlement of the conflict. Unionists recognized the implications of the changing demographics of the north: in three Northern Ireland elections in 1996–1997, Unionist parties garnered 50.3% of the vote, Nationalists, 38.2% on average (a middle and moderate bloc including members of the Alliance Party and Women's Coalition received the remainder of the vote). Unionists and Nationalists became more flexible in their negotiating stance. The Unionists agreed to power-sharing institutions; the Nationalists agreed to keep Northern Ireland as part of the United Kingdom if supported by the majority.[56]

The Agreement needed to be ratified by referendum in Northern Ireland and by a separate referendum to amend the Constitution in the Republic of Ireland. The Agreement called for the Republic to drop Articles 2 and 3 of its Constitution, the articles that contained its territorial claim of Northern Ireland and its goal of eventual unification of North and South. While turnout was low (56.3%) for the referendum on May 22, 1998, the vote was overwhelmingly positive toward the constitutional amendment (94.4% in favor of dropping Articles 2 and 3).[57] The referendum in Northern Ireland was a bit more contentious. Of the main political parties, only the Democratic Unionist Party (DUP) opposed a yes vote. Turnout was very high (81.1%) with 71.12% voting in favor of the Agreement, with a pro-Agreement majority in 17 of the 18 Westminster constituencies (i.e., all but Ian Paisely's district of North Antrim).[58]

Institutions of the British-Irish Peace Agreement

The British-Irish Peace Agreement creates four new democratic institutions for Northern Ireland: the Northern Irish Assembly, the North/South Ministerial Council, the British-Irish Council, and the British-Irish Intergovernmental Conference. Additionally, the text of the Agreement links to the European Union (EU), the fifth institution in which sovereignty is pooled and promotes overlapping identities (cross-categories). Unlike the prescription of internal institutions for consociational governments, this Agreement specifically has an international institutional component.[59] Furthermore, Articles 2 and 3 of the Irish Constitution have been amended to delete reference to the goal of complete unification of the Island of Ireland. The British government also agreed to respect any free decision of the majority of the people of both Northern Ireland and the Republic of Ireland as to the relationship between Northern Ireland and Britain.

Northern Ireland Assembly

The new Northern Ireland Assembly "will exercise full legislative and executive authority in respect of those matters currently within the responsibility of the six Northern Ireland Government Departments, with the possibility of taking on responsibility for other matters."[60] Thus, while London will financially support the new assembly in Belfast, it allows the Assembly to exercise devolved decision-making capability for Northern Ireland affairs.

The Assembly contains much of the same consociational devices as the earlier 1973 power-sharing Assembly, plus the new mechanism of "parallel consent." The new 108-member assembly will use the Single Transferable Vote (STV) to elect its members. To do so, it combines existing districts used for elections to the House of Commons into larger, multimember districts. This proportional system allows for equal representation of the Northern Ireland communities.[61] Legislation requires a simple majority except in decisions where a cross-community basis is required. In these instances "parallel consent" is necessary, that is, a majority of support from representatives of both communities or "a weighted majority (60%) of members present and voting, including at least 40% of each of the nationalist and unionist designations present and voting."[62] This supermajority requirement results in a de facto minority veto. Decisions requiring cross-community support can be designated in advance by the petition of 30 of the 108 Assembly members. A grand coalition is almost assured as the posts of first minister and deputy first minister must also be decided upon by cross-community consent.

Elections to the Northern Ireland Assembly occurred in June 25, 1998. Six seats were available in each of the 18 Westminster constituencies, for a total of 108 seats. For the first time in the history of Northern Ireland, a Catholic party won the largest share of the vote, though not the seats. The SDLP won 22.0% of the vote and 24 seats. The Ulster Unionist Party (UUP) gained 28 seats, the most, from 21.3% of the vote, its lowest national vote percentage yet. Over 73% of the population voted for pro-Agreement parties with the anti-Agreement parties (DUP; the UK Unionists,UKUP; and three independent Unionist parties) netting only 28 seats.[63] The Assembly met for the first time on July 1, 1998, and elected David Trimble (Ulster Unionist Party, UUP) first minister, and Seamus Mallon (SDLP) deputy minister, creating a cross-community government. On December 1, 1999, the British government in Westminster granted devolved authority to the Northern Irish Assembly, allowing Trimble and Mallon to begin work.

This Assembly has undergone a difficult existence. The issue of the decommissioning of the paramilitary forces (detailed in the next section) has elicited the British government to suspend the Assembly on occasion. Specifically, Secretary of State Peter Mendelson suspended the Northern Ireland Assembly from February 11, 2000 to May 29, 2000 because of disagreement over the reluctance of the IRA to decommission its arsenal. The secretary for Northern Ireland, John Reid, also suspended the Assembly for one day (August 11, 2001) over the same issue. The lack of continuity in governance hinders the ability of the Northern Ireland government to pass significant legislation. The result is that the Northern Ireland Assembly has yet to use effectively its devolved authority.

As a case in point, at the time of writing, the political parties returned to the Stormont Assembly after its operation had been suspended for more than a year. Despite a recent election to fill the Assembly, no new speaker was selected, no ministers appointed, and no real power devolved. The British secretary of state, Paul Murphy, has asked all parties to begin a "party review" process by which the differences can be bridged and the Assembly put back into action. However it is not clear that the largest party following the recent elections, the DUP headed by Reverend Ian Paisley, will attend the review or not.

North-South Ministerial Council

The North-South Ministerial Council deals with the "totality of relationships" between the governments of Northern Ireland and the Republic of Ireland. The purpose of the North-South Council is to "develop consultation, co-operation and action within the island of Ireland—including through implementation on an all-island and cross-border basis—on matters of mutual interest."[63] This new Council has the ability to make decisions on matters of implementation for common policy in the two political regions, as well as separate implementation in each jurisdiction. Participation in the North-South Council is limited to ministers of the two governments, with plenary sessions held at least twice a year.

British-Irish Council

The British-Irish Council (BIC) comprises membership from all national and devolved assemblies on the British Isles. Representatives of the British and Irish national governments will be joined by representatives from the new assemblies in Northern Ireland, Scotland, and Wales (with a provision for representatives from the Isle of Man and Channel Islands). The BIC will "exchange information, discuss, consult and use best endeavours to reach agreement on cooperation on matters of mutual interest within the competence of the relevant administrations."[65] The operating procedure will be consensus, with full agreement of all members participating in any common policy. Dissenting members "may opt not to participate in such common policies."[66]

British-Irish Intergovernmental Conference

The last new institution is the British-Irish Intergovernmental Conference. The British prime minister and Irish Taoiseach will meet at a summit to "promote bilateral co-operation at all levels on all matters of mutual interest within the competence of both Governments."[67] Of special note is the provision for the Conference "of the extent to which issues of mutual concern arise in relation to Northern Ireland" to have "regular and frequent meetings."[68] Such meetings are to address security matters and in particular "rights, justice, prisons and policing."[69] The Intergovernmental Conference is also charged with the duty of reviewing the workings of the institutions created by the British-Irish Peace Agreement.

Confidence-Building Areas of the Agreement: Police Reform, Early Release of Prisoners, and Decommissioning

A number of provisions of the Good Friday Peace Agreement deal with confidence-building measures. These measures support the Agreement by providing the pre-conditions for the smooth working of the institutions. The provisions calling for police reform, the early release of prisoners and the de-commissioning of arms by the IRA build trust between the two communities. The participation of each community in these provisions reduces the perceived security dilemma and establishes a pattern of mutual cooperation that is necessary in order for leaders to seek consensus and compromise. Because these measures are preconditions to the institutions we do not dwell on them long here. However, we will now provide a brief sketch of these measures so that the reader may see the pattern of confidence-building that these measures can promote.

Reform of the police, known as the Royal Ulster Constabulary (RUC), is a major demand of the Catholic community. Ronald Weitzer contends that

> policing in communally divided societies is organised around the defence of a sectarian regime and the preservation of a social order based on institutionalised inequality between dominant and subordinate ethnic, racial, or religious groups. To a greater extent than in more integrated societies, the police in divided societies are politicised, tend to be biased against the subordinate group, are unencumbered by effective mechanisms of accountability, wield extensive powers over civilians, and are responsible for both ordinary crime and security problems.[70]

The maintenance of law and order is not separate from the sectarian divide. The Catholic community demanded reform of the RUC during the civil rights movement of the late 1960s. Specifically, they called for repeal of the Special Powers Act of 1922, which gave the police exceptional security powers and militarized force, recruitment of Catholics as the RUC was overwhelmingly Protestant, an expansion of community relations programs, and an investigation into citizen complaints, among other things.[71] The demands of the Catholic community for police reform in the late 1990s were hardly different.

The Agreement calls for an independent commission on policing to form. Its goal is to plan a way to get to a set of principles that the Agreement proscribes: a police system characterized by "professionalism, effectiveness, efficiency, fairness, impartiality, freedom from partisan control and accountability both under the law and to the wider community."[72] At the time of writing the Commission has proposed a number of reforms along the lines proposed by the Catholic community for decades. The implementation of these reforms has barely begun, but progress is being made.

The planned early release of paramilitary prisoners from both communities is another measure aimed at building trust. Both the Irish and the British governments passed legislation in June 1998 establishing a date of June 2000 to release prisoners associated with paramilitary groups maintaining the cease-fire. Indeed, in June and July 2000 approximately 428 prisoners walked away from prisons in Northern Ireland. Most of these left the Maze, the notorious prison that housed political, paramilitary, and terrorist prisoners at the site of a disused airfield near Lisburn.[73]

The decommissioning of weapons, especially weapons in the hands of the IRA, is the most controversial of the trust-building measures. The Agreement creates an Independent International Commission on De-Commissioning (IICD) to oversee the turnover of weapons.[74] The British and Irish governments created a timetable to turn over the weapons that was similar to that of the release of prisoners. However, events since 1998 show how difficult decommissioning is to achieve. The IRA refused to contact the IICD until the Northern Ireland Assembly was functioning. Therefore, the IRA did not appoint a member to the IICD until December 2, 1999. This action and reaction pattern would repeat itself many times over (see the next section). Between the ratifying of the Agreement and December 1999, a series of terrorist acts occurred, of which splinter groups from the IRA claimed most of the responsibility. Included among these is the devastating explosion in Omagh on August 15, 1998 that killed 29 and left over 200 wounded.[75]

After Mendelson's suspension of the Assembly in February 2000, the IRA withdrew its member from the IICD. Mendelson promptly issued a statement saying that it was unlikely that decommissioning would occur by the May 22 deadline in the Agreement. However, by May 2000, the IRA released a statement that it was ready to begin a process by which it would "completely and verifiably" put its arms beyond use, but only if Mendelson restored the Assembly. Inspection of IRA arms dumps occurred throughout 2000. However, on October 26 the IICD chair, General John de Chastelain of Canada, reported that that no progress had been made on actual paramilitary disarmament. Two days later Trimble banned Sinn Fein from ministerial meetings of the North-South Council. In typical tit-for-tat reciprocity, the IRA refused to continue putting aside its weapons. The Belfast High Court overturned the ban in December but it was not until March 2001 that the IRA was ready to work with the IICD again. The game between the IRA and the Unionists continues currently, with the IRA's political wing, Sinn Fein, demanding political inclusion before decommissioning while the Unionists demand decommissioning before inclusion of Sinn Fein.[76]

The parties to the Agreement did not fully resolve these measures (i.e., police reform, release of prisoners, and decommissioning) in the Agreement. Rather, they are intended to be future developments that will bolster the Agreement. To this end, the second has been accomplished successfully, the first is underway, albeit under an atmosphere of contention, and the third is a stuttering miasma of gamesmanship, brinksmanship, and accusation. We do not wish to make any predictions here, but we make a qualified assessment that if these trust-building measures progress so will confidence in the governing institutions. If these trust-building measures regress (e.g., if the IRA refuses to decommission) then support for the institutions will falter.

The European Union and the Agreement

As members of the EU, both Britain and Ireland have a vested interest in resolving the conflict, particularly as political and economic integration in the EU has deepened. For the Republic, funding from the EU has significantly contributed to the positive economic situation of Ireland. Concern over unification with the economically depressed North may prove to be more of a hindrance, and thus the willingness to revise Ireland's demand for unification. In addition, the EU has provided funding for Northern Ireland, through the International Fund for Ireland and the Special Support Programme for Peace and Reconciliation in Northern Ireland and the border counties of Ireland, as significant incentives for cooperation and settlement of the conflict.[77] Thus, the link to the EU was not lost on the 1998 Agreement.[78]

This link was built upon "the *modus operandi* of EU institutions [which] have encouraged cooperation and agreement between the British and Irish governments."[79] The EU Commission and Council created formal equality in Anglo-Irish relations within a European context. This helped break older, conflictual patterns of contact between the two nation-states. The bilateral nature of the current peace process and the notion of "pooled sovereignty" (which we discuss later) in Northern Ireland have their origins in British and Irish participation in the decision-making institutions of the EU.

Furthermore, the EU, while not explicitly referred to as a separate institution, per se, within the Agreement's structure, provides a final layer of representation for the various parties to the Agreement. The Agreement stipulates that the Northern Ireland Assembly's "[t]erms will be agreed between appropriate Assembly representatives and the Government of the United Kingdom to ensure effective co-ordination and input by Ministers to national policy-making including on EU issues."[80] With regards to the North-South Ministerial Council, "[a]rrangements [are] to be made to ensure that the views of the Council are taken into account and represented appropriately at relevant EU meetings."[81]

Additionally, the EU itself provides the opportunity for the representation and expression of overlapping identities as a supranational institution, as well as through cross-border institutions. In terms of the level of the EU, Northern Ireland is a single constituency with three Members of the European Parliament (MEPs) in the European Parliament (EP), the legislative body of the EU. These MEPs are also members of the various political parties in Northern Ireland and yet "speak with one voice" in the various committees on which they serve.[82] In essence, the fact that they "speak with one voice" indicates a possible common group identity as "Northern Irish" MEPs. As Cathal McCall argues, these MEPs "act as a conduit between the EU center and the Northern Ireland periphery, leading delegations from Northern Ireland to Brussels on fact-finding and lobbying missions, as well as hosting visits of European Commissioners to Northern Ireland."[83] She further asserts that the EU may serve "as a potential catalyst that will effect change in communal identities in Northern Ireland.[84] Additionally, cross-border identities may overlap when Irish and Northern Irish MEPs, through the EP, act in concert in areas of national/regional interests.[85]

In terms of cross-border institutions, and their link to the possibility of an overlapping identity, the EU has recognized the border region between the Republic of Ireland and Northern Ireland as sharing common economic problems. As Etian Tannam argues, "these groups may feel they share more in common with each other than they do with groups in Dublin, Belfast or Westminster. Thus, a sense of regional identity and of regional interests in straddling the border may be encouraged by EU efforts to achieve a Europe of the Regions."[86]

The EU provides an interesting analogy to that of the Good Friday Agreement. As discussed in chapter 3, the governing institutions of the EU represent our model: cross-border parliamentary institutions that pool sovereignty. The institutions of the Agreement also contain some of these same elements. The next section outlines how the Agreement institutions provide multiple forums for representation and pool sovereignty across the communities and across the whole of the British Isles.

Overlapping Identities Through Layers of Representation and Pooling of Sovereignty

One cannot but help to notice the similar flavor of the institutions of the British-Irish Peace Agreement and the institutions of the EU. The British Irish Council (BIC) is an inclusive assembly of more regional assemblies, much like the European Parliament. While the latter has legislative ability and the former does not, the former can act without ratification of other institutions. The North-South Ministerial Council is reminiscent of the European Council of Ministers, albeit once again without the legislative ability (but perhaps with the executive ability of implementation). The British-Irish Intergovernmental Conference has a format of summitry much like that of the European Council. We do not wish to push this analogy too far. Yet we hope that it is clear to the observer that the general "framework" is the same: a set of international institutions at different levels of government (e.g., ministerial and assembly) with broadly parliamentary features (e.g., representative and voting) derived from national and sub-national governments.

Importantly, in both the EU and in the new British-Irish Peace Agreement, these international institutions play three vital roles: (1) the promotion of overlapping identities through differing layers of representation (European identity, Northern Irish identity, and party identification); (2) a framework for credible commitments (British and Irish governments); and (3) a pooling of sovereignty (Irish-British communities and Protestant-Catholic communities). It should be abundantly clear from this discussion that the new institutions in the British Isles allow all actors multiple forums to which to bring their concerns. The end result is that *both* Northern Ireland communities should feel more secure (thereby reducing the ethnic security dilemma) because policy does not rest in a single political arena (e.g., the British House of Commons or the Northern Ireland Assembly). Likewise, the two national governments have created institutions in which they can consult and cooperate in the creation and implementation of policy—fostering a credible commitment by all parties to the Agreement.[87]

Three new relationships are of particular importance. First, the Catholic community can now interact in a structured manner with the Irish government in Dublin. In this way, the minority community in Northern Ireland can turn to other political bodies for redress if the new Northern Ireland Assembly does not meet its needs. The Agreement also satisfies the Republican movement's goal of bringing the conflict into the context of an "Irish" question and not a question of British internal policy. Of course, the Irish government has not always, and may not now, support the Republican movement. The Irish in the South harbor no strong idealistic notions about Irish unification. For example, a 1995 *Guardian/ Irish Times* poll found, for the first time, that a majority of those in the South opposed unification with the North.[88] Instead, the matter is often seen with an eye toward the pragmatic and tangible benefits and costs that would result.[89]

Including the "Irish" question into the peace calculus could heighten competition within the Catholic community. For the Social Democratic and Labour Party (SDLP) and the Nationalists it represents, the different layers of representation allow their voice to be heard. Previously they were often ignored beneath the constant din of Sinn Fein's Republican cries for unification. This intracommunity division exists at the level of identity and behavior. Nationalists disagree with Republicans on many issues. A 1996 poll found that supporters of Sinn Fein (Republicans) were more likely than SDLP supporters (Nationalists) to say that peace talks would fail, support unification with the Republic, seek reform of the Royal Ulster Constabulary, and approve of American interest in Irish affairs.[90] In addition, in previous elections (1986 by-election, 1987 UK parliamentary elections, and 1989 local and European elections) votes for the SDLP increased relative to Sinn Fein, further demonstrating differences in support of their respective positions.[91] Finally, regarding voting behavior, vote transfers between Sinn Fein and SDLP are relatively modest compared to the solidarity of Unionist transfers.[92]

The second new relationship is the increased representation of the Protestant majority. Unionist parties have often been influential in the British House of Commons. For example, from 1992 to 1997 John Major's government relied on the Unionists to preserve the Conservative's slim majority in the House of Commons. Now, the Unionist parties can participate in their own regional parliament (where they surely will be the majority), in the BIC, and also in the North-South Council. Unionists who would rather reject or undermine the Agreement's institutions face a problem: no input into the policies that will be implemented without them.[93] In addition, one should not discount the possible impact of a Protestant first minister having regular meetings with the Irish Taoiseach. Given the aforementioned attitude of past Irish governments, the Protestant leader may be able to persuade the Irish government as to the usefulness of continued partition. Perhaps a crafty Protestant leader could even secure Irish aid in building a strong Northern Ireland, one in which the Catholic Nationalists may eventually distance themselves from the Republicans.

It is important to note that the new institutions provide incentives for the two communities to recognize the objective nature of the other. It is clear that the two communities are not homogenous blocs, but rather each contains sharp divisions and distinguishable sub-divisions.[94] Recognition that the "other" is not a Cyclopean, monolithic group allows for intersectarian negotiation. Polling evidence suggests that knowledge of the differing views of both "self" and "other" is fairly widespread in both communities.[95] Moreover, more lucid views of the "other" engender trust and compromise, both of which are necessary for the success of the peace process and democratic consolidation. For example, a new generation of leaders (Gerry Adams and Martin McGuinness of Sinn Fein, the political arm of the IRA; and David Ervine of the Progressive Unionist Party, the political arm of the Ulster Volunteer Force) has moved to end the sectarian violence through pressuring their respective paramilitary organizations to establish and maintain cease-fires. Andrew Reynolds notes that "these forty-something former combatants appear to have much in common with each other and genuine respect for their opponents' histories and motivations."[96] From this, these more muted views of the other paved the way for compromise and enhanced the prospects for peace.

The institutions allow each community to see the set of overlapping identities. This occurs because political division within each community becomes transparent. For instance, after the 1998 Assembly elections, the split between Nationalists and Unionists was clear from self-declaration. However, the split between "Yes" Unionists and "No" Unionists was also clear, with the former tacitly on the same side of the agreement as the Nationalists.[97]

The link between the British and Irish governments marks the third relationship. The new international institutions pool the sovereignty of both governments regarding Northern Ireland. In the new set of institutions, while the British government retains some power over the six northern counties, the Dublin government has perhaps more influence. This devolution works both ways of course. Financial outlays will still flow from London to Belfast, but the new devolution will allow the House of Commons to further its policy of marginalizing Northern Irish politics.

The Irish government, on the other hand, gains a measure of control over events and politics north of its border and even more control over its own sovereign territory. For example, if an island-wide policy of policing and antiterrorism is established, the Irish police force could now move more freely against clandestine (and armed) Republican hideouts in the Republic. The past hesitation to respond, due to a fear of weakening the position of the Catholic community in the North, would vanish.

These examples make it clear that the multiple layers of representation create greater security for the British and Irish states, but also for the Catholic and Protestant communities in Northern Island by recognizing and institutionalizing the "bistatal" nature of the situation. The links of the two groups with two different states gives it the "bistatal dimension": Protestants see themselves as British, and thus connected to the United Kingdom; whereas the Catholic minority sees itself as Irish, and hence linked to Ireland.[98] The Agreement's provisions for majority support in the Assembly and proportionality of both Nationalists and Unionists affords an opportunity for building much-needed trust in order to surmount historic animosities.[99] The pooling of sovereignty between the Irish and British governments allows Britain to change the scope of the regional conflict from one of an internal problem to that of an Irish, or island-wide, problem. Importantly, the involvement of both governments provides a credible commitment to the Agreement and to the future of the region.

Conclusion

The Good Friday British-Irish Peace Agreement has led to much euphoria and a counterimpulse of pessimism. Some view the recent settlement as one that places a new set of institutions onto a centuries-old conflict without addressing the deep societal divisions that separate the Protestant and Catholic communities. We disagree with this view. Unlike previous attempts at solving the conflict, for the first time all the parties to the conflict are active participants in the Agreement. Importantly, an opportunity for resolution to the long-standing conflict has presented itself through the establishment of institutions that promote overlapping identities, provide for multiple layers of representation, and pool sovereignty. The key to the success of the new Agreement will be the degree to which trust is established, security dilemmas are ameliorated, and the security of all parties is ensured. As John Lloyd notes, "[t]he success of the agreement may lie in its very looseness and ambiguity. Neither side has what it wants . . . each side can agree to differ while also agreeing to govern."[100] In the end, any resolution to intractable conflicts must come from the people themselves. They must be willing to promote a common, overlapping identity that transcends in-group/out-group differences and mistrust, and promotes peace instead.

5

Conclusion

Institutions and the
Construction of Identity

How can conflicts within and between states among various nationalist/ethnic groups be ameliorated, or reduced, so that inequality in wealth and power can be overcome? This is the research question, or puzzle, that this book has attempted to answer. Through an incorporation of the social psychology literature on identity with the political science literature on institutions, we demonstrate how democratic international institutional structures that promote multiple and overlapping identities and pool sovereignty provide a mechanism for resolving issues of identity and perceptions of inequality that lead to group conflict. We argue that, unlike internal (consociational or federal) institutions, international institutions afford the opportunity for conflicting groups to reduce the enemy image, ethnic security dilemma, and mistrust—three aspects that are linked directly to perceived inequality among groups and lead to conflict. Cross-border institutions have an effect on the expression of multiple group identities that can then lead to a reduction in tension by creating an atmosphere where different ethnic groups lose their strict definitions of the Self and Other (i.e., enemy images). Moreover, pooling sovereignty across a number of international (and national) representative bodies leads to increased access to governmental policy making for all parties involved, with each party having a stake in government.

This chapter briefly revisits the theoretical argument and summarizes the findings of the three cases used to illustrate our argument. We conclude by offering areas for future research.

Promoting Overlapping Identities and International Institutions

We assert that cross-border institutions can promote (and perhaps construct) overlapping social identities if they possess the following attributes: allow multiple forums for group representation, promote cross-community trust, and encourage groups to see a common identity in pooled sovereignty. The cases examined, Spain, the European Union (EU), and Northern Ireland, serve to illustrate our argument. In the Northern Ireland case cross-border institutions were established in order to address the various grievances between the two ethnic groups. The EU is an international institution that addresses the interests and concerns of its member states. In one case (Spain), the government promoted an internal (federal) institution. In each case there is evidence of an overlapping identity (Spanish, European, and Northern Irish). There is also variance in terms of the dependent variable (reduction of ethnic/nationalist conflict). The EU provides a means for member states to resolve their differences without resort to violent conflict. In Spain, the *Euskadi Ta Askatasuna* (ETA, Basque Homeland and Liberty) continues to engage in violent acts as a means to advance Basque demands for independence. The level of violence between Catholics and Protestants has diminished significantly since the signing of the Good Friday Agreement, particularly as the Ulster Unionist Party (UUP) has continued to support Sinn Fein's existence in the Northern Ireland Assembly.

We tested several hypotheses using our cases. First, the establishment of cross-border institutions should promote the growth of overlapping identities among the groups in conflict. If our theory is correct, as communities gain representation in new forums, they should begin to express multiple, and overlapping, identities. This should be evident in cross-community cooperation and alliances in these new forums. If groups refuse to work together and maintain strict, unitary identities, such evidence would disprove our hypothesis. The evidence from the *Eurobarometer* (EB) surveys demonstrate that indeed an overlapping European identity has emerged. In the case of Northern Ireland, a Northern Irish identity exists that transcends Protestant and Catholic identities, enhanced as members of the European Parliament (MEPs) as well as through representation in the cross-border institutions of the Good Friday Agreement.

Second, the intensity with which an individual holds her primary identity should decline with the continuation of functioning cross-border institutions. *Eurobarometer* data continues to show an increase in identification with Europe, and slight lessening, on average, of national identities.

Third, group identification of the Self and Other should become more complex and less antagonistic over time. Such a reduction in antagonism would reduce the ethnic security dilemma. Evidence that the intensity of primary identity increases with involvement in cross-border institutions or that each group's definition of Self and Other becomes more monolithic would disprove our theory. Thus, if over time the new Northern Ireland Assembly reinforced strong Protestant and Catholic identities rather than constructing a new Northern Irish identity, our hypothesis would be disproven.

Last, the final indicator of the success or failure of the theory is the eventual reduction of the conflict. One could argue that the historical antagonism between Germany and France has declined significantly with their membership in the European Union. In Northern Ireland, violent conflict between the two groups has decreased significantly with the Good Friday Agreement's institutions. The inclusion of Sinn Fein, the political arm of the Irish Republican Army (IRA), has had a profound impact on lessening of violence.

The Model Revisited

In chapter 1 we outlined our argument about the link between institutions, identity, and ethnic conflict. We also argued that consociational models of solving ethnic conflict were inadequate if the source of identity crossed national borders. Consociational models take identity as static and immutable. Moreover, consociational institutions promote elite cooperation but do not address identity as a source of ethnic conflict. We argued that consociational models can exacerbate conflict at worst, and at best only conceal the ethnic conflict behind a screen of strained, elite governance.

Figure 5.1 presents the Consociational Model of ethnic conflict and our "Constructive Model" of ethnic conflict. The Consociational

Figure 5.1. Two Models of Ethnic Conflict

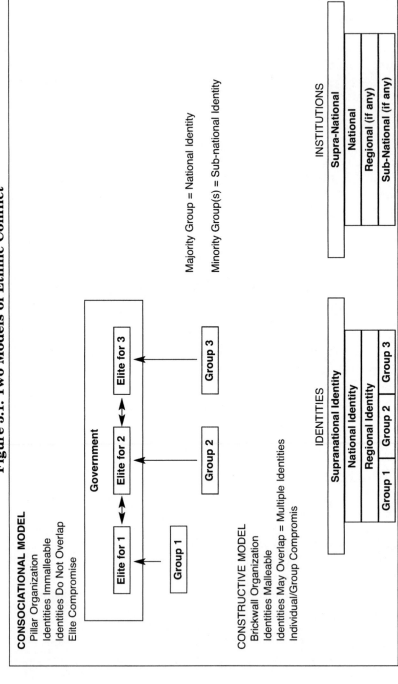

CONSOCIATIONAL MODEL
Pillar Organization
Identities Immalleable
Identities Do Not Overlap
Elite Compromise

Government

Elite for 1 ⟷ Elite for 2 ⟷ Elite for 3

Group 1   Group 2   Group 3

CONSTRUCTIVE MODEL
Brickwall Organization
Identities Malleable
Identities May Overlap = Multiple Identities
Individual/Group Compromis

Majority Group = National Identity

Minority Group(s) = Sub-national Identity

IDENTITIES

Supranational Identity
National Identity
Regional Identity
Group 1 | Group 2 | Group 3

INSTITUTIONS

Supra-National
National
Regional (if any)
Sub-National (if any)

Model views conflict organized into "pillars."[1] Each pillar represents a different ethnic group. Each ethnic group is separate from the other groups, and identity does not overlap. Elites represent each group and only one group each. The majority group, in other words the group that controls most of the socioeconomic resources, creates the national identity. The minority group(s) retains a subnational identity and does not identify strongly with the nation. The elites from each group negotiate with each other in government. Consociational institutions (e.g., proportional representation and grand coalition) promote elite negotiation, cooperation, and compromise.

If we view the Consociational Model in this manner, we can see how federalism would exacerbate ethnic tension instead of ameliorating it. The principle of consociationalism is to keep ethnic groups apart from each other while bringing their leaders into negotiation. If the model is to work, the elites must have a need for national government to succeed. Federalism creates a source of power, authority, and security for elite at the level of their supporting group. Thus, federalism erodes the "pillar" organization by providing incentives for elites to concentrate their efforts at the sub-national level and refusing to negotiate at the national level.

Our Constructive Model portrays ethnic conflict as being organized into a "Brickwall." Identities exist at different layers and multiple layers overlap. From figure 5.1, identities exist at four different levels, with each level being an aggregation of the levels beneath it: sub-national, regional, national, and supranational. Thus, an individual might possess a group identity, as well as a separate and overlapping regional identity, national identity, and/or supranational identity. Unlike the Consociational Pillar Model, the Brickwall Model displays the reality that individuals with different group identity might have a similar identity at a different level.

Our Constructive Model portrays institutions in a similar Brickwall organization. Parliamentary and/or representational institutions exist in a hierarchical structure with supranational institutions (if any) layered on top of national institutions, regional institutions, and/or sub-national institutions. The congruence between the layers of identity and the layers of institution highlight the relationship between the two. When institutions exist, they promote an overlapping identity at that level. In chapter 2 we argued that the federal system in Spain has constructed sub-national identities among the non-historical minorities while also reinforcing the sub-national identity of the historical minorities. In chapter 3 we explored how the creation of EU institutions has promoted a European identity, which did not exist in any measurable way before the creation of the EU. When institutions do not exist, identities remain "unconstructed." In other words, identities continue to exist if they already do, and if they do not exist, they do not come into existence. In chapter 4 we investigated the persistence of the salience of Protestant and Catholic identity in Northern Ireland. Without any cross-border institutions, these identities continued to dominate Northern Irish politics, while an overlapping identity remained noticeably absent.

Figure 5.2 provides an example derived from chapter 4. It illustrates how both the Consociational and the Constructive models view the ethnic conflict in Northern Ireland. The Consociational Model views the conflict as stemming from two communities that are separate and exclusive. Different political parties represent each community. The UUP and Democratic Unionist Party (DUP), for example, represent the majority Protestant community and the Social Democratic and Labour Party (SDLP) and Sinn Fein represent the minority Catholic community. Elites meet in the Northern Ireland Assembly and attempt to compromise on differences in order to govern effectively. The underlying social division remains and is not addressed directly.

The Constructive Model highlights three different aspects: the multiple and overlapping identities, the external (cross-border) factors, and the multiple and overlapping institutions. The Brickwall Model displays how a member of the Protestant community in Northern Ireland could potentially possess up to four identities: Protestant, Northern Ireland/Ulster, British, and European. We presented information and data in chapters 3 and 4 showing that some members of the Protestant community do indeed recognize other identities and even hold multiple identities. The Brickwall Model allows us to see the complexity of multiple identities and also allows us to see how individuals from one group may share a common identity with individuals from another group.

The cross-border nature of identity shows up in our Constructive Model. From figure 5.2 (and chapter 4), one can see, for instance, that the Protestant community also exists outside of Northern Ireland. In fact, most British citizens are members of this wider community. To be fair, most non-Northern Irish Protestants do not identity as strongly with the Protestant community as those in Northern Ireland. However, this highlights the ties between the

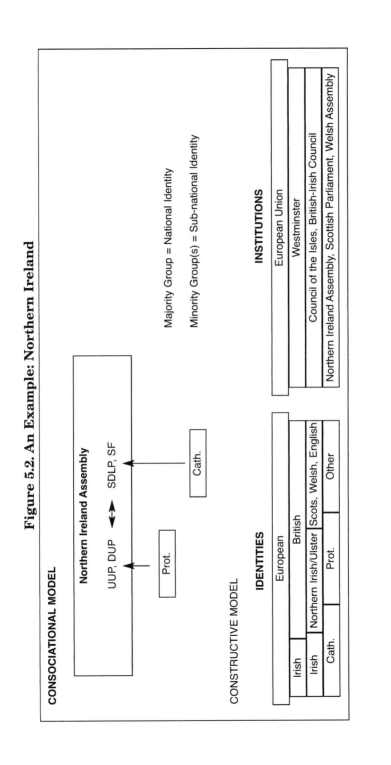

Figure 5.2. An Example: Northern Ireland

CONSOCIATIONAL MODEL

Northern Ireland Assembly

UUP, DUP ⟷ SDLP, SF

Prot.

Cath.

Majority Group = National Identity

Minority Group(s) = Sub-national Identity

CONSTRUCTIVE MODEL

IDENTITIES

European

British

Irish

Irish | Northern Irish/Ulster | Scots, Welsh, English | Other

Cath. | Prot.

INSTITUTIONS

European Union

Westminster

Council of the Isles, British-Irish Council

Northern Ireland Assembly, Scottish Parliament, Welsh Assembly

Ulster Protestants and the British on the mainland. Figure 5.2 also highlights the existence of other regional identities (e.g., Scottish nd Welsh) that exist in Britain. It also displays the cross-border nature of the Catholic identity and its links to an Irish identity more sympathetic with the Republic of Ireland. The supranational European identity also exists "on top" of the other identities.

The Constructive Model also illustrates the multiple forums of representation and participation resulting from overlapping institutions. This is evident in the case of Northern Ireland from the regional assembly established by the 1998 Good Friday Agreement and under the umbrella of Prime Minister Tony Blair and his program of devolution all the way to the governing institutions of the EU. There are also a number of institutions promoting cooperation between Great Britain and the Republic of Ireland, the Republic and Northern Ireland, and even between the different nations of Britain (i.e. Scotland, Wales, and Northern Ireland). These different cross-border forums, some of which are the product of the Agreement, allow for the construction of overlapping identities (as we explained in chapter 4).

The Constructive Model highlights the concept of pooled sovereignty. It is clear from figure 5.2 that the British Parliament is in reality a shared parliament of four different nations: England, Scotland, Wales, and Northern Ireland. Thus, what appears to be a "national" parliament, and is often thought of that way, can be understood (using this model) as an assembly of pooled governance. Indeed, one of the most common complaints from Scottish and Welsh nationalist Members of Parliament is that Westminster runs more like an English Parliament even though it is supposed to represent all of Britain.

In sum, these two models provide very different outcomes for the reduction of conflict in divided societies. One, the Consociational Model, reinforces existing identity and group differences, while the other, the Brickwall Model, provides an avenue for the reduction of conflict through pooled sovereignty and for promotion of overlapping and multiple identities.

Cases Revisited

In chapter 2, we demonstrated that internal institutional solutions do not alleviate nationalist concerns that arise because of perceived inequality. The nature of the autonomous communities and the federal system in Spain promotes nation-building at the expense of state-building. Rather than leading to a centralized state, the decentralization of politics and issues of identity has led to calls for sub-national government and even independence. The division of Spain into autonomous communities promoted the building of an exclusive identity in each community. While federalism was introduced as a solution to the nationalist demands of two regional and cultural minority groups, the Basques and Catalans, such a structure exacerbated these sub-national demands by segmenting the society into exclusive political communities. The failure of federalism is that it institutionalized ethnic/national differences in Spain, rather than promoting recognition of an overarching state identity. Specifically, the exclusive self-identification of the Basques precludes the development of overlapping identities. The Catalan identity is more inclusive of a Spanish identity, while the Basque identity is primarily an exclusive identity, a result of three elements: a difference in the main forms of acceptable political participation, a difference in the salience of language, and the impact of modernization. Catalan nationalism defines itself as a civic/political identity, while Basque nationalism is defined in terms of a cultural/ethnic identity. As the survey data show, the federal structure has not led to a strong Spanish identity. In both Catalan and the Basque Country, the percent of natives who self-identified themselves as being at least "as Spanish as Catalan/Basque" has steadily declined since 1979.[2] Thus, Spain's federalist experiment, in allowing for greater regional autonomy and the emergence of regional parliaments to administer autonomous competencies, has led to nationalist-regional parties seeking elections (and hence representation) through the promotion of national/regional identities. It appears that federalism in Spain has heightened the ethnic security dilemma rather than ameliorating it.

Moreover, the federal structure has created new national identities where they did not exist before. For example, in the regions of Andalucia and Galicia strong regional parties have emerged. Interestingly, Spanish inclusion in the EU provides the regions another forum in which to present their concerns. The process of Europeanization appears to be leading toward an acceptance of Europe and a European identity among the regions. Thus supranationalism and regionalism pull the construction of identities in Spain two directions: toward the larger community of Europe and toward the small national community.

Identity building in the EU constitutes our second case. While nationalist conflicts do not directly affect the relationships between the member states, the EU is a useful example of how international institutions promote an overlapping identity—a European identity—through representation at the local, regional, national, and supranational levels. EU citizens maintain their national identity, but also have taken on a European identity. As we have discussed, recent *Eurobarometer* surveys indicate that of those polled, on average more than half feel both a European and national identity (with an additional 4% "feeling European only").

The member states recognize that they have shared attitudes that are then able to form the basis of a European identity and citizenship. These shared attitudes have found their way in various declarations from the EU over the past several decades. Importantly, the Tindemans' "Report on European Union" in 1975 introduced the term, *Citizen's Europe*. The EU went further in 1985 with the Adonnino Committee's reports that recommended several symbols to promote a European identity such as a flag, anthem, and passport. In doing so, the EU deliberately sought to promote, if not construct, a European identity for its citizens. The 1992 Maastricht Treaty further solidified the promotion and institutionalization of European citizenship. As just noted, more than half of the respondents to the *Eurobarometer* surveys claim both a European and national identity.

The various institutions, such as the European Parliament (EP), provide the mechanism by which to express that identity, as well as to foster further cooperation between the national governments. These different layers of representative institutions pool sovereignty. The EP is the only institution in which EU citizens directly elect their representatives. While voter turnout has been low relative to national elections, those that voted express high levels of trust for EU institutions, with the EP ranked first.

Moreover, transnational party groups provide the arena for direct representation of EU citizens and promotion of an overlapping European identity. As discussed in the chapter, the Maastricht Treaty explicitly notes "parties at the European level," thus recognizing the pooled sovereignty across national lines at the supranational level. The existence of transnational parties at the EP level permits the promotion of overlapping and multiple memberships of their national governments as well as at the European level. These multiple memberships also permit the promotion of a European identity as these MEPs advocate at the supranational level while also consulting with representatives from their national governments.

The challenge for the EU is to overcome the perceived democratic deficit in order to enhance democratic participation and hence increased representation. Currently, EU citizens are more satisfied with their national democracy than with the way democracy works in the EU.

Finally, the unequal relationship between Protestants and Catholics in Northern Ireland in the areas of employment, housing, and governmental administration plays a significant role in the continuing ethnic/nationalist conflict and perception of an ethnic security dilemma. Various institutional attempts at resolving the conflict were internal solutions—that is, until the 1998 Good Friday Agreement. For example, the 1973 Sunningdale Agreement contained all the provisions of a consociational power-sharing arrangement, yet failed in the end when one of the parties, the Protestants, opposed. Although there was a proposed cross-border institution, the Council of Ireland, it lacked real authority and only gave the Irish in the North a place of representation but not the Protestants, a glaring asymmetry in representation.

The 1983 New Ireland Forum moved the two parties closer, and even promoted the reconstruction of the identity of the Republic of Ireland to include those residents of Northern Ireland who were not ethnically Irish. Due to Unionist boycott of the talks and rejection of the options presented by the Forum (i.e., unitary united Ireland, federal united Ireland, and joint British-Irish authority over Northern Ireland), this also failed.

With the 1995 "Frameworks for the Future," a document published by the British and Irish governments, the beginnings of a new identity for the North emerged that corresponded with new proposed intergovernmental bodies that would focus on common interests and identities between Catholics and Protestants. This Frameworks document paved the way for the 1998 Good Friday Agreement.

Importantly, the Good Friday Agreement adds the element of cross-border institutions that allow both sides to express their grievances and to obtain representation at different levels. Identity is strong, and yet the existence of a Northern Irish identity that overlaps with Protestant (Unionist) and Catholic (Nationalist) provides an avenue for cooperation and common links. In fact, the political divisions within each community provide for the emergence of overlapping identities. For example, in the referendum on the Agreement, divisions emerged between Unionists voting "yes" and those voting "no." Thus, those Unionists voting "yes" could be linked to a common interest, and perhaps identity, with those Nationalists who also supported the Agreement.

The four new democratic institutions for Northern Ireland (and the link to the EU, in essence the fifth institution in which sovereignty is pooled) move beyond an internal (consociational) institutional solution to an international one. For example, the North-South Ministerial Council deals with common policy issues between the governments of Northern Ireland and the Republic of Ireland, while the British-Irish Council comprises members from all national and devolved assemblies on the British Isles. Representatives from the assemblies in Northern Ireland, Scotland, and Wales will join with representatives from the British and Irish national governments. In addition, Northern Ireland's three MEPs tend to unify in their efforts at the various committees on which they serve in the EP (thus the possibility of expression of a common Northern Irish identity at this international institutional body). Thus, both ethnic groups in Northern Ireland have several institutions in which to obtain representation and to seek redress for their grievances.

Overall, these cases demonstrate both theoretical links as well as policy implications. In terms of theoretical links, we argue that bringing together the literature on social identity theory and institutions can provide a more thorough understanding of ethnic/ nationalist conflicts, and the means to resolve them. Looking only at identity issues or only at institutions leaves part of the theoretical puzzle of resolving ethnic/nationalist conflicts unanswered, given the existence of ethnic security dilemmas and perceptions of inequality and mistrust between groups. As we discussed in chapter 1, social identity theory helps to explain why people develop ethnic/nationalist group identities (as well as other identities) resulting from the social psychological need to belong and to be distinct from other groups. Moreover, perceptions of threat to identity can lead to enemy images about other groups, contributing to conflict. Importantly, the literature on cross-categorization shows that people can have multiple, and thus possibly overlapping, social identities that can provide the basis for common ground between conflicting groups. Overlapping memberships in different groups can lead to decreased intergroup bias and decreased conflict between in-groups and out-groups.

Additionally, international institutions can have an effect on the expression of multiple (and overlapping) group identities that can, in turn, reduce tension by creating an atmosphere where different ethnic/nationalist groups lose their strict definition of the Self and Other—that is, enemy images. It is the interaction between these two concepts, overlapping identities and international institutions, which can account for the reduction in ethnic/nationalist conflict.

In terms of policy implications, international institutions can play an important role in promoting overlapping identities as a means to overcome conflict between ethnic/nationalist (and other) groups. By finding a common identity, and thus common ground, groups become vested in the positive and beneficial outcomes. Consequently, in order to resolve many such contemporary conflicts around the world, the international community and individual states themselves should focus on promoting (and possibly creating) overlapping identities through representative cross-border institutions, rather than focusing solely on internal solutions.

Future Research

While we believe that we have gone a long way toward building a new theory in this book, and shown its contribution to the larger discussion of conflict resolution, we still see the need for further research. In particular, the hypotheses that we derive from our theory require confirmation through rigorous empirical analysis. Further comparative studies would be helpful such as cases of cross-border institutions in other nationalist/ethnic conflicts. Perhaps the role of the EU in the dispute between the two main groups in Belgium, the Walloons, and Flemish, might provide useful and important insights. An examination of the nationalist aspirations of Quebec inside a federal Canadian state could be valuable as well. The African nation of Nigeria has experimented with both consociational and federal arrangements; thus looking at identity construction in Nigeria would prove useful in testing our theory. Also of possible interest would be an examination of whether cross-border institutions promote identity change of leaders, citizens, or both.

In sum, this book links identity and institutions as a means to resolve nationalist/ethnic conflicts that emerge as a result of inequality. It shows how institutions can promote overlapping identities, which may lead to a reduction of tension. Overlapping identities also reduce the security dilemma between ethnic groups and lessen strict "us versus them" group relations. Multiple forums of representation allow all interested parties to a conflict to have their voices heard and contribute. Multiple forums also diffuse conflict into many different arenas, reducing the possibility that any one group will constantly feel threatened by the power and/or authority of other groups.

However, in the end, any resolution to such conflicts must come from the people themselves. They must be willing to promote a common, overlapping identity that transcends in-group/out-group differences and mistrust, and promotes peace instead. The proper institutions can help people develop and promote these identities, but the final resolution of the conflict lies on the shoulders of the people involved.

Notes

Chapter 1

1. Arend Lijphart, *Democracy in Plural Societies* (New Haven: Yale University Press, 1977).

2. Ibid.

3. To some degree our argument is about access points. In most parliamentary systems, let's think of the British model as an example, there is only one forum for representation, that is, the national parliament. Minority groups often have little access. A good example would be the Scottish Nationalist Party (or any of the other nationalist parties for that matter). It wins a handful of seats but it does not participate in government. Therefore it does not legislate and has almost no voice. If it had access through multiple forums (e.g., another parliament or perhaps a regional council) it could find expression for its voice. It also might display a more complex policy agenda that represents the multiple identities of the Scottish people (e.g., British and Scottish).

4. David A. Lake and Donald Rothchild, "Spreading Fear: The Genesis of Transnational Ethnic Conflict," in *The International Spread of Ethnic Conflict: Fear, Diffusion, and Escalation*, eds. Lake and Rothchild (Princeton: Princeton University Press, 1998), 9.

5. Michael A. Hogg, Deborah J. Terry, and Katherine M. White, "A Tale of Two Theories: A Critical Comparison of Identity Theory with Social Identity Theory," *Social Psychology Quarterly* 58 (1995): 255–269.

6. Henri Tajfel, *Human Groups and Social Categories: Studies in Social Psychology* (Cambridge: Cambridge University Press, 1981); see also Marilynn B. Brewer and Wendi Gardner, "Who Is This 'We'? Levels of

Collective Identity and Self-Representations," *Journal of Personality and Social Psychology* 71 (1996): 83–93.

7. Hogg, Terry, and White, "A Tale of Two Theories."

8. Ted Hopf, "The Promise of Constructivism in International Relations Theory," *International Security* 23 (1998): 171–200.

9. Brewer, "The Social Psychology of Intergroup Relations: Can Research Inform Practice?" *Journal of Social Issues* 53 (1997): 203–204; Brewer, "Ingroup Identification and Intergroup Conflict: When Does Ingroup Love Become Outgroup Hate?" in *Social Identity, Intergroup Conflict, and Conflict Reduction*, eds. Richard D. Ashmore, Lee Jussim, and David Wilder (Oxford: Oxford University Press, 2001), 21–22.

10. D. Katz, "Nationalism and Strategies of International Conflict Resolution," in *International Behavior: A Social-Psychological Analysis*, ed. Herbert C. Kelman (New York: Holt, 1965), 356–390.

11. John McGarry, "Political Settlements in Northern Ireland and South Africa," *Political Studies* 46 (1998): 853–870.

12. Ronald J. Fisher, *The Social Psychology of Intergroup and International Conflict Resolution* (New York: Springer Verlag, 1990), 29; Dean G. Pruitt, "Definition of the Situation as a Determinant of International Action," in *International Behavior*; 393–432.

13. Fisher, *The Social Psychology of Intergroup and International Conflict Resolution*, 149; Pruitt, "Definition of the Situation as a Determinant of International Action," 393–432; Myron Rothbart, "Intergroup Perception and Social Conflict," in *Conflict between People and Groups: Causes, Processes, and Resolutions*, eds. Stephen Worchel and Jeffry A. Simpson (Chicago: Nelson-Hall, 1993), 93–109. See also the following for a discussion of image theory and the role of images on decision making: Richard K. Herrmann and Michael P. Fischerkeller, "Beyond the Enemy Image and Spiral Model: Cognitive-Strategic Research after the Cold War," *International Organization* 49, 3 (Summer 1995): 415–450; Shoon Kathleen Murray and Jonathan A. Cowden, "The Role of 'Enemy Images' and Ideology in Elite Belief Systems," *International Studies Quarterly* 43 (1999): 455–481; Mark Schafer, "Images and Policy Preferences," *Political Psychology* 18, 4 (1997): 813–829; Philip E. Tetlock, "Policy-Makers' Images of International Conflict," *Journal of Social Issues* 39, 1 (1983): 67–86; Michael D. Young and Schafer, "Is There Method in Our Madness? Ways of Assessing Cognition in International Relations," *Mershon International Studies Review* 42 (1998): 63–96.

14. Shannon Lindsey Blanton further notes that "If an actor maintains an image that incorrectly portrays an enemy or dependent as threatening and uncompromising, then it is unlikely that peaceful resolution of the conflict will follow." Blanton, "Images in Conflict: The Case of Ronald

Reagan and El Salvador," *International Studies Quarterly* 40, 1 (March 1996): 41.

15. Fisher, *The Social Psychology of Intergroup and International Conflict Resolution*, 159.

16. Robert Jervis, *Perception and Misperception in International Politics* (Princeton: Princeton University Press, 1976).

17. Barry R. Posen, "The Security Dilemma and Ethnic Conflict," *Survival* 35 (1993): 28.

18. Ibid; Barbara F. Walter and Jack Snyder, eds. *Civil Wars, Insecurity, and Intervention* (New York: Columbia University Press, 1999).

19. Fisher, *The Social Psychology of Intergroup and International Conflict Resolution*.

20. Posen, "The Security Dilemma and Ethnic Conflict," 38.

21. Rothbart, "Intergroup Perception and Social Conflict."

22. Pruitt, "Definition of the Situation as a Determinant of International Action."

23. Deborah W. Larson, "Trust and Missed Opportunities in International Relations," *Political Psychology* 18 (1997): 721.

24. Agreement between the Government of the United Kingdom of Great Britain and Northern Ireland and the Government of Ireland (10 April 1998).

25. Daniele Conversi, *The Basques, the Catalans and Spain: Alternate Routes to Nationalist Mobilisation* (Reno: University of Nevada Press, 1997), 142–143.

26. Larson, "Trust and Missed Opportunities in International Relations."

27. Ibid.

28. The constructivist approach challenges realism, which claims that state interests and identities are exogenously given (i.e., "self-help is given by anarchic structure exogenously to process") (Alexander Wendt, "Anarchy Is what States Make of It: the Social Construction of Power Politics," *International Organization* 46, 2 [Spring 1992]: 394). In understanding structure, "neorealists think it is made only of a distribution of material capabilities, whereas constructivists think it is also made of social relationships" (Wendt, "Constructing International Politics," *International Security* 20, 1 [Summer 1995]: 73). Social relationships affect how states relate to one another; "states act differently toward enemies than they do toward friends because enemies are threatening and friends are not . . . It

is collective meanings that constitute the structures which organize our actions" (Wendt, "Anarchy Is what States Make of It," 397). See also the following on social constructivism and international relations: Jeffrey T. Checkel, "The Constructivist Turn in International Relations Theory," *World Politics* 50, 2 (January 1998): 324–348; Hopf, "The Promise of Constructivism in International Relations Theory," 171–200; Rey Koslowski and Friedrich V. Kratochwil, "Understanding Change in International Politics: the Soviet Empire's Demise and the International System," *International Organization* 48, 2 (Spring 1994): 215–247; Wendt, "Collective Identity Formation and the International State," *American Political Science Review* 88, 2 (June 1994): 384–396.

29. See James M. Goldgeier, "Psychology and Security," *Security Studies* 6 (1997): 137–166.

30. Wendt, "Collective Identity Formation and the International State," 385.

31. Paul C. Stern, "Why Do People Sacrifice for Their Nations?" *Political Psychology* 16 (1995): 217–235.

32. It can be argued that this was a main part of the solution instituted by Josip Tito in the face of ethnic hostility in post-Second World War Yugoslavia. In this case, the ruling Communist Party attempted to foster a dual identity: a Yugoslav identity and an ethnic identity (Serb, Croat, Slovene, etc.).

33. Brewer, "The Social Psychology of Intergroup Relations"; John Coakley, "Introduction: The Territorial Management of Ethnic Conflict, in *The Territorial Management of Ethnic Conflict*, ed. Coakley (London: Frank Cass, 1993).

34. Karen Trew and Denny E. Benson, "Dimensions of Social Identity in Northern Ireland," in *Changing European Identities: Social Psychological Analyses of Social Change*, eds. Glynis M. Breakwell and Evanthia Lyons Speri (Oxford: Butterworth-Heinemann, 1996), 123–143; Trew, "The Northern Irish Identity," in *A Question of Identity*, ed. Anne J. Kershen (Aldershot, England: Ashgate, 1998), 60–76.

35. Nurcan Ensari and Norman Miller, "Effect of Affective Reactions by an Out-Group on Preferences for Crossed Categorization Discussion Partners," *Journal of Personality and Social Psychology* 75 (1998): 1503–1527; Samuel L. Gaertner, John F. Dovidio, Phyllis A. Anastasio, Betty A. Bachman, and Mary C. Rust, "The Common Ingroup Identity Model: Recategorization and the Reduction of Intergroup Bias," *European Review of Social Psychology* 4 (1993): 1–26; Miles Hewstone, Mir Rabiul Islam, and Charles M. Judd, "Models of Crossed Categorization and Intergroup Relations," *Journal of Personality and Social Psychology* 64 (1993): 779–793; Lynn M. Urban and Miller, "A Theoretical Analysis of Crossed

Categorization Effects: A Meta-Analysis," *Journal of Personality and Social Psychology* 74 (1998): 894–908.

36. Urban and Miller, "A Theoretical Analysis of Crossed Categorization Effects."

37. George J. Mitchell, *Making Peace* (New York: Knopf, 1999), 110.

38. In examining the causes of nationalist/ethnic conflict, scholars have looked at several mechanisms, or solutions, for addressing such conflict, including partition (physically separate the warring parties) and third-party intervention (economic sanctions, coercive intervention, etc.). We, however, focus on cross-border institutions as a means of promoting overlapping identities that will lead to cross-categorization and thus to the reduction of conflict. See *Nationalism and Ethnic Conflict*, eds. Michael E. Brown, Owen R. Cote Jr., Sean M. Lynn-Jones, and Steven E. Miller (Cambridge: MIT Press, 2001).

39. J. G. March and J. P. Olsen, "The Institutional Dynamics of International Political Orders," *International Organization* 52 (1998): 943–969.

40. Robert O. Keohane and Lisa L. Martin, "The Promise of Institutionalist Theory," *International Security* 20 (1995): 39–51. In examining institutions as "settled or routinized practices established and regulated by norms," Koslowski and Kratochwil note, "the constructivist research program identifies institutions as both elements of stability and as strategic variables for the analysis of [system-transforming] change" (Koslowski and Kratochwil, "Understanding Change in International Politics: the Soviet Empire's Demise and the International System," 222, 227).

41. Alicia Levine, "Political Accommodation and the Prevention of Secessionist Violence," in *The International Dimensions of Internal Conflict*, ed. Michael E. Brown (Cambridge: MIT Press, 1996), 311–340; Lijphart, *Democracy in Plural Societies*.

42. Ibid.

43. Ibid. 331.

44. Donald L. Horowitz, *Ethnic Groups in Conflict* (Berkeley: University of California Press, 1995), 626.

45. For a thorough discussion of the many different forms of federalism, as well as associated governmental forms such as confederations, see Ronald L. Watts, *Comparing Federal Systems*, 2d ed. (Kingston, Ontario: Queen's University Press, 1999); Daniel J. Elazar, *Exploring Federalism* (Tuscaloosa: University of Alabama, 1987).

46. Graham Smith, "Mapping the Federal Condition: Ideology, Political Practice and Social Justice," in *Federalism: The Multiethnic Challenge*, ed. Smith (London: Longman, 1995), 1–28.

47. David C. Nice, *Federalism: The Politics of Intergovernmental Relations* (New York: St. Martin's, 1987).

48. Smith, "Mapping the Federal Condition."

49. Alexander Murphy, "Belgium's Regional Divergence: Along the Road to Federation," in *Federalism*, 73–100.

50. Sharda Rath, *Federalism Today: Approaches, Issues and Trends* (New Dehli: Sterling Publishers Private, 1984).

51. K. C. Wheare, *Federal Government*, 4th ed. (London: Oxford University Press, 1963).

52. Jonathan Lemco, *Political Stability in Federal Governments* (New York: Praeger, 1991).

53. Brendan O'Leary and John McGarry, "Regulating Nations and Ethnic Communities," in *Nationalism and Rationality*, eds. Albert Breton, Gianluigi Galeotti, Pierre Salmon, and Ronald Wintrobe (Cambridge: Cambridge University Press, 1995), 245–289.

54. George Schopflin, "The Rise and Fall of Yugoslavia," in *The Politics of Ethnic Conflict Regulation*, eds. McGarry and O'Leary (London: Routledge, 1993), 172–203.

55. Levine, "Political Accommodation and the Prevention of Secessionist Violence."

56. Ibid.

57. Lijphart, *Democracy in Plural Societies*.

58. I. William Zartman, "Putting Humpty-Dumpty Together Again," in *The International Spread of Ethnic Conflict*, 317–336.

59. Lijphart, *Democracy in Plural Societies*; Lijphart, *Conflict and Coexistence in Belgium: The Dynamics of a Culturally Divided Society* (Berkeley: University of California Press, 1981).

60. Horowitz, *Ethnic Groups in Conflict*.

61. Cameron Ross, "Federalism and Democratization in Russia," *Communist and Post–Communist Studies* 33 (2000): 403–420.

62. Eric A. Nordlinger, *Conflict Regulation in Divided Societies* (Cambridge: Center for International Affairs, Harvard University, 1972).

63. Levine, "Political Accommodation and the Prevention of Secessionist Violence."

64. Ibid.

65. Lijphart, *Democracy in Plural Societies*.

66. Ian S. Lustick, "Lijphart, Lakatos, and Consociationalism," *World Politics* 50 (1997): 90.

67. Ibid. 99–100.

68. Ibid. 108.

69. M. P. C. M. Van Schendenlen, "The Views of Arend Lijphart and Collected Criticisms," *Acta Politica* 19 (1984): 26.

70. Lustick, "Lijphart, Lakatos, and Consociationalism," 110.

71. Ibid. 112; see also David D. Laitin, "South Africa: Violence, Myths, and Democratic Reform," *World Politics* 39 (1987): 258–279; McGarry and S. J. R. Noel, "The Prospects for Consociational Democracy in South Africa," *Journal of Commonwealth and Comparative Politics* 27 (1989): 3–22.

72. Lijphart, "The Puzzle of Indian Democracy: A Consociational Interpretation," *American Political Science Review* 90 (1996): 258–268.

73. Maureen Covell, "Ethnic Conflict and Elite Bargaining: The Case of Belgium," *West European Politics* 4 (1981): 216. See also Brian Barry, "The Consociational Model and Its Dangers," *European Journal of Political Research* 3 (1975): 393–412.

74. Peride Kaleagasi, "Belgium and Switzerland: A Comparative Study of Federalism in Multiethnic Democracies," *Annual Meeting of the Midwest Political Science Association* (Chicago: April 27–30, 2000): 16.

75. Michael O'Neill, "Belgium: Language, Ethnicity and Nationality," *Parliamentary Affairs* 53 (2000): 124.

76. Clive H. Church, "Switzerland: A Paradigm in Evolution," *Parliamentary Affairs* 53 (2000): 98.

77. Ibid.

78. Robert Senelle, "The Reform of the Belgian State," in *Federalizing Europe?* eds. J. Hesse and V. Wright (Oxford: Oxford University Press, 1996), 266–324.

79. It is interesting to compare Belgium and Switzerland in this regard. Belgium's political and electoral structures are constructed on ethnicity. See Kaleagasi, "Belgium and Switzerland."

80. Rotimi T. Suberu, *Federalism and Ethnic Conflict in Nigeria* (Washington DC: United States Institute of Peace, 2001), 1.

81. Ibid.

82. Robert Ladrech, "Partisanship and Party Formation in European Union Politics," *Comparative Politics* 29 (1997): 167–185; Brigid Laffan,

"The Politics of Identity and Political Order in Europe," *Journal of Common Market Studies* 34 (1996): 81–102.

83. Commission of the European Union, *Eurobarometer Report Number 58* (Brussels: European Commission, 2002).

84. Paul Bew and Elizabeth Meehan, "Regions and Borders: Controversies in Northern Ireland about the European Union," *Journal of European Public Policy* 1 (1994): 102.

85. Ferran Requejo, "Cultural Pluralism, Nationalism and Federalism: A Revision of Democratic Citizenship in Plurinational States," *European Journal of Political Research* 35 (1999): 272.

86. Lake and Rothchild, "Spreading Fear," 13.

87. Ibid.

88. James D. Fearon, "Commitment Problems and the Spread of Ethnic Conflict," in *The International Spread of Ethnic Conflict: Fear, Diffusion, and Escalation*, eds. Lake and Donald Rothchild (Princeton: Princeton University Press, 1998), 123.

89. Ibid.

90. Alexander L. George, "Case Studies and Theory Development: The Method of Structured, Focused Comparison," in *Diplomacy: New Approaches in History, Theory, and Policy*, ed. Paul Gordon Lauren (New York: Free Press, 1979), 43–68; Gary King, Robert O. Keohane, and Sidney Verba, *Designing Social Inquiry: Scientific Inference in Qualitative Research* (Princeton: Princeton University Press, 1994), 93, 115, 206.

91. Comparison of cases with different outcomes refers to John Stuart Mill's "Method of Difference," cited in Stephen M. Walt's *Revolution and War* (Ithaca: Cornell University Press, 1996), 14.

92. Amitai Etzioni, *Political Unification Revisited: On Building Supranational Communities* (Lanham, MD: Lexington Books, 2001), 304.

93. Ibid. 303.

94. Ibid. 139, 149, 178.

Chapter 2

1. Good examinations of multinational and multicultural Spain are available readily. Some examples are Miquel Siguan, *Multilingual Spain* (Amsterdam: Swets and Zeitlinger, 1993); Helen Graham and Jo Labanyi, "Culture and Modernity: The Case of Spain," in *Spanish Cultural Studies,*

An Introduction: The Struggle for Modernity, eds. Helen Graham and Labanyi (New York: Oxford University Press, 1995), 1–20; David Corkill, "Race, Immigration and Multiculturalism in Spain," in *Contemporary Spanish Cultural Studies*, eds. Barry Jordan and Rikki Morgan-Tamosunas (New York: Oxford University Press, 2000), 48–57. Readings on one or more ethnic minority groups are also available: Marianne Heiberg, *The Making of the Basque Nation* (Cambridge: Cambridge University Press, 1989); Carner-Ribalta, *The Catalan Nation and Its People*; Albert Balcells, *Catalan Nationalism* (London: Macmillan, 1996).

2. Paul Heywood, *The Government and Politics of Spain* (New York: St. Martin's, 1995), 11.

3. The figures are for those who identify "Having own language as a first language" when Spanish is not their "own language." If one compares those who "speak own language" or who "understand own language" than the numbers would be slightly different. Siguan, *Multilingual Spain*, provides figures for each autonomous community.

4. Ibid., 70–72.

5. This concentration does not preclude the existence of linguistic groups in other regions. For instance, a number of Catalan speakers reside in Aragon. Moreover, Aragonese is also spoken in Aragon, much like Asturian is still spoken in rural areas of Asturias and Aranese in Val d'Aran. Ibid.

6. Ibid., 70–71.

7. Heywood, *The Government and Politics of Spain*, 34.

8. Juan Díez Medrano, *Divided Nations: Class, Politics, and Nationalism in the Basque Country and Catalonia* (Ithaca: Cornell University Press, 1995), 175.

9. Heywood, *The Government and Politics of Spain*, 143.

10. Ibid., 145–146.

11. Antoni Monreal, "The New Spanish State Structure," in *Federalism and Federation in Western Europe*, ed. Michael Burgess (London: Croom Helm, 1986), 59–75.

12. Heywood, *The Government and Politics of Spain*, 143.

13. Seymour M. Lipset and Stein Rokkan, *Party Systems and Voter Alignments: Cross-National Perspectives* (New York: Free Press, 1967) present a clear theory about the tension between nation and state, and the development of center-periphery cleavages. Spain is a typical West European example of how state-building changes a latent center-periphery cleavage into a manifest cleavage.

14. Heywood, *The Government and Politics of Spain*, chapter 1.

15. Stanley Payne, *Spanish Catholicism: An Historical Overview* (Madison: University of Wisconsin Press, 1984) portrays both sides of this interpretation. Layne asserts that the traditional view is that of the Spanish Church as the "champion of the Counter-Reformation and the sword of international Catholicism" (46). He claims that this interpretation is too simplistic and does not do justice to the complexity of relations between the Spanish church and the Papacy. He provides examples, such as the anti-Spanish bent of Pope Paul IV (1555–1559), to back up his assertion.

16. Juan Linz, "Early State-Building and Late Peripheral Nationalisms against the State: The Case of Spain," in *Building States and Nations*, eds. S. N. Eisenstadt and S. Rokkan (London: Sage, 1973), 38–49; Heywood, *The Government and Politics of Spain*, 2.

17. Clare Mar-Molinero and Angel Smith, "The Myths and Realities of Nation-Building in the Iberian Peninsula," in *Nationalism and the Nation in the Iberian Peninsula:*, 2.

18. Ken Medhurst, "Basques and Basque Nationalism," in *National Separatism*, ed. C. H. Williams (Vancouver: University of British Columbia, 1982), 236–237.

19. Heywood, *The Government and Politics of Spain*, 2.

20. Jose Alvarez Junco, "The Nation-Building Process in Nineteenth-Century Spain," in *Nationalism and the Nation in the Iberian Peninsula*, 89–90.

21. Ibid., 90.

22. Ibid.

23. Ibid., 91.

24. See, for example, Payne, *Basque Nationalism* (Reno: University of Nevada Press, 1975); Balcells, *El nacionalismo catalán* (Madrid: Universidad de Valencia, 1991); Balcells, *Catalan Nationalism*; Carner-Ribalta, *The Catalan Nation and Its People*.

25. Medrano, *Divided Nations*; Montserrat Guibernau, "Catalan Nationalism and the Democratisation Process in Spain," in *Democratisation in the New Europe*, ed. K. Cordell (New York: Routledge, 1999), 77–90.

26. Alvarez Junco, "The Nation-Building Process in Nineteenth-Century Spain," 93.

27. Medhurst, "Basques and Basque Nationalism," 237.

28. Ibid., 238.

29. Ibid., 238–239.

30. Ibid., 239.

31. See the following for historical accounts of this period: Alvarez Junco, *La ideología política del anarquismo español (1868–1910)* (Madrid: Siglo XXI, 1976); J. Nadal, "The Failure of the Industrial Revolution in Spain, 1830–1914," in *The Fontana Economic History of Europe, Vol. 6, part 2; The Emergence of Industrial Nations*, ed. C. M. Cipolla (Hassocks: Harvester Press, 1976), 533–626; Jose Varela-Ortega, *Los amigos políticos: Partidos, elecciones y caciquismo en la Restauración, 1875–1900* (Madrid: Alianza Editorial, 1977); Raymond Carr, *Spain 1808–1875*, 2d ed. (Oxford: Clarendon Press, 1982); Adrian Shubert, *A Social History of Modern Spain* (London: Unwin Hyman, 1990).

32. Alvarez Junco, "The Nation-Building Process in Nineteenth-Century Spain," 99.

33. Heywood, *The Government and Politics of Spain*, 3; Sebastian Balfour, "'The Lion and the Pig': Nationalism and National Identity in *Fin-de-Siècle* Spain," in *Nationalism and the Nation in the Iberian Peninsula*, 108.

34. Histories of the Spanish-American War can be found in Varela-Ortega, "Aftermath of Splendid Disaster: Spanish Politics before and after the Spanish-American War of 1898," *Journal of Contemporary History* 15 (1980): 317–344; Joseph Smith, *The Spanish-American War: Conflict in the Caribbean and the Pacific, 1895–1902* (London: Longman, 1994); Michael Golay, *The Spanish-American War* (New York: Facts on File, 1995).

35. Balfour, "'The Lion and the Pig,'" 109–112.

36. Ibid., 110–112.

37. Ibid., 114.

38. Medhurst, "Basques and Basque Nationalism," 240–241.

39. Francisco Romero Salvadó, "The Failure of the Liberal Project of the Spanish Nation-State, 1909–1938," in *Nationalism and the Nation in the Iberian Peninsula*, 122.

40. Romero Salvadó, "The Failure of the Liberal Project of the Spanish Nation-State, 1909 -1938," 124–127.

41. Ibid., 126–127.

42. Ibid., chapter 3.

43. Reliable and good accounts of the Second Republic can be found in Manuel Tuñon de Lara, *La II República* (Madrid: Siglo XXI, 1976); Tuñón de Lara, *Poder y sociedad en España, 1900–1931* (Madrid: Colección

Austral, 1992); Shlomo Ben-Ami, *The Origins of the Second Republic of Spain* (Oxford: University Press, 1978); Ben-Ami, *Fascism from Above: The Dictatorship of Primo de Rivera in Spain, 1923–1930* (Oxford: University Press, 1983); Jose Luis García Delgado ed, *La crisis de la Restauración: España entre la primera guerra mundial y la segunda Republica* (Madrid: Siglo XXI, 1986); María Teresa González Calbet, "La destrucción del sistema político de la Restauración: El golpe de septiembre de 1923," in *La Crisis de la Restauración*, 101–120; Nicolas Sánchez-Albornoz (ed.) *The economic Modernization of Spain, 1830–1930* (New York: New York University Press, 1987); T. Carnero, "Política sin democracia en España, 1874–1923," *Revista de Occidente* 83 (1988): 43–58; Benjamin Martin, *The Agony of Modernization: Labour and Industrialization in Spain* (Ithaca: ILR Press, 1990); Payne, *Spain's First Democracy: The Second Republic, 1931–1936* (London: University of Wisconsin Press, 1993); Payne, *Fascism in Spain, 1923–1977* (Madison: University of Wisconsin Press, 1999).

44. Graham, "Community, Nation and State in Republican Spain, 1931–1938," in *Nationalism and the Nation in the Iberian Peninsula*, 133–134.

45. Ibid., 133.

46. Reliable and good accounts of the Spanish Civil War can be found in Gabriel Jackson, *The Spanish Republic and the Civil War, 1931–1939*, 5th ed. (Princeton, NJ: Princeton University Press, 1972); Hugh Thomas, *The Spanish Civil War*, 3rd ed. (Harmondsworth: Penguin, 1986); Michael Alpert, *A New International History of the Spanish Civil War* (London: Macmillan, 1994); Paul Preston, *The Coming of the Spanish Civil War: Reform, Reaction and Revolution in the Second Republic, 1931–1936* (London: Macmillan, 1978); Preston, *The Coming of the Spanish Civil War: Reform, Reaction and Revolution in the Second Republic* (London: Routledge, 1994); Preston, *A Concise History of the Spanish Civil War* (London: HarperCollins, 1996).

47. Daniele Conversi, *The Basques, the Catalans and Spain: Alternate Routes to Nationalist Mobilisation* (Reno: University of Nevada Press, 1997), 74.

48. Palomar Aguilar, "The Memory of the Civil War in the Transition to Democracy: The Peculiarity of the Basque Case," *West European Politics* 21 (1998): 9.

49. Ibid., 9–11.

50. Ibid., 10–11.

51. Ironically, the opposing Basque forces were both fighting for the same thing: autonomy from a centralized state. The opposition of the

Basques to each other shows how confusing the political situation was in Spain in the 1930s. Ibid. 16–17.

52. Excellent texts on Franco's rule and the Fascist regime are available. Arguably the most complete are Payne, *The Franco Regime: 1936–1975* (Madison: University of Wisconsin Press, 1987); Payne, *Fascism in Spain, 1923–1977*. Other texts include Preston, *The Coming of the Spanish Civil War*; Preston, *Franco: A Biography* (London: HarperCollins, 1993); Juan Pablo Fusi, *Franco: Autoritarismo y poder personal* (Madrid: El País, 1985).

53. Michael Richards, "Constructing the Nationalist State: Self-Sufficiency and Regeneration in the Early Franco Years," in *Nationalism and the Nation in the Iberian Peninsula*, 149–167; Richards, "Collective Memory, the Nation-State and Post-Franco Society," in *Contemporary Spanish Cultural Studies*, 38–47; Conversi, *The Basques, the Catalans and Spain*.

54. Payne explains that by 1936 the Spanish Catholic Church was "much more conservative and even reactionary, producing a spirit of religious restoration highly susceptible to the political movement of the military rebels" (Payne, *Spanish Catholicism*, 171). Franco used the willingness of the Church to reestablish a close relationship between the Church and state. The result was "National Catholicism." Payne points out that the support of the Catholic Church preserved Franco's rule at the close of World War II. It did so by confirming a Catholic, and thus non-fascist, identity for Franco's rule. The church then became an institutionalized part of the Franco government, holding important cabinet seats including the foreign ministry (Ibid. 179–191). Audrey Brassoloff argues that division always existed in the Spanish Catholic Church and that compliance with Franco's government was never complete nor constant. In particular, reemergence of support among clergy in the nationalist regions for local autonomy undermined the façade of National Catholicism. Brassoloff, *Religion and Politics in Spain: The Spanish Church in Transition 1962–1996* (New York: St. Martin's, 1998). William J. Callahan, *The Catholic Church in Spain, 1987–1998* (Washington, DC: Catholic University of America Press, 2000) provides a similar commentary.

55. Conversi, *The Basques, the Catalans and Spain*, 11.

56. Ibid., chapters 5 and 6.

57. Ibid., 87.

58. The struggle of ETA and the history of terrorism in the Spanish state is also not a central theme of this book. Excellent accounts of these topics are available, for example, J. L. Hollyman, "Separatismo Vasco Rev-

olucionario: ETA," in *España en crisis: La evolución y decadencia del régimen de Franco*, ed. Paul Preston (Madrid: Fondo de cultura económica, 1977), 212–233; Clark, *The Basques: The Franco Years and Beyond* (Reno: University of Nevada Press, 1979); John Sullivan, *ETA and Basque Nationalism: The Fight for Euskadi* (London: Routledge, 1988); Joseba Zulaika, *Basque Violence: Metaphor and Sacrament* (Reno: University of Nevada Press, 1988); L. Núñez Astrain, *The Basques: Their Struggle for Independence* (Wales: Welsh Academic Press, 1997).

59. Conversi, *The Basques, the Catalans and Spain*, 109; Payne, "Catalan and Basque Nationalism: Contrasting Patterns," in *Ethnic Challenges to the Modern Nation State*, eds. S. Ben-Ami and Y. Peled (London: Macmillan, 2000), 101.

60. Goldie Shabad, "After Autonomy: The Dynamics of Regionalism in Spain," in *The Politics of Democratic Spain*, ed. S. G. Payne (Chicago: Chicago Council of Foreign Relations, 1986), 111–180.

61. Heywood, *The Government and Politics of Spain*, 37–40.

62. Excellent accounts of the transition from the Franco regime to democracy occur in David Gilmour, *The Transformation of Spain: From Franco to the Constitutional Monarchy* (London: Quartet, 1985); Preston, *The Triumph of Democracy in Spain* (London: Methuen, 1986); Victor M. Pérez-Díaz, *The Return of Civil Society: The Emergence of Democratic Spain* (Cambridge: Harvard University Press, 1993).

63. Graham, *Spain: Change of a Nation* (London: Michael Joseph, 1984); Gilmore, *The Transformation of Spain*; Preston, *The Triumph of Democracy in Spain*.

64. Of those voting in the December 1978 referendum, 87.9% favored the new constitution. Among the Basques, 51.1% abstained from voting while 23.5 percent of those who did vote, voted against the Constitution. Clark, *The Basques*, 361–363.

65. Heywood, *The Government and Politics of Spain*, 45.

66. Ibid., 45–46.

67. Guibernau, "Spain: Catalonia and the Basque Country, *Parliamentary Affairs* 53 (2000)."

68. Ibid.

69. Conversi, *The Basques, the Catalans and Spain*, 142.

70. Aguilar, "The Memory of the Civil War in the Transition to Democracy."

71. Medrano, *Divided Nations*.

72. Josep M. Colomer, "The Spanish 'State of Autonomies': Non-Institutional Federalism," *West European Politics* 21 (1998): 40–52.

73. Heywood, *The Government and Politics of Spain*, 51–53; Colomer, "The Spanish 'State of Autonomies,'" 42–43.

74. Shabad, "After Autonomy," 114–115; Heywood, *The Government and Politics of Spain*, 51–53; Colomer, "The Spanish 'State of Autonomies,'" 41–42.

75. Heywood, *The Government and Politics of Spain*, 52.

76. L. López Guerra, *Sobre la Personalidad Jurídica del Estado*, Revista del Departamento de Derecho Político (Madrid: UNED, 1980).

77. The region of Navarre, a region comprised of the Basque minority, declared itself as a separate region from the Basque Country. It did this so that it could maintain its separate system of fueros and maintain its own independent autonomy. John Gibbons, *Spanish Politics Today* (New York: Manchester University Press, 1999), 19.

78. Ibid., 19–21.

79. J. Solé-Villanova, "Spain: Developments in Regional and Local Government," in *Territory and Administration in Europe*, ed. R. Bennett (London: Pinter, 1989), 209–215.

80. Shabad, "After Autonomy," 116.

81. Ibid.

82. Heywood, *The Government and Politics of Spain*, 144–145.

83. Shabad, "After Autonomy," 117–118.

84. As quoted in Ibid. 118.

85. Gibbons, *Spanish Politics Today*.

86. Ferran Requejo points out that most analyses of federalism have concentrated on the historical example of the United States. He argues that the American example is not linked to cultural pluralism, but is rather a federalism based on territorial decentralization. As such, the symmetrical federalism of the American model does not address the inherent questions about democratic citizenship, identity and regional distinction that must be answered in the Spanish case. Requejo argues that Spain must create a new model of federalism without any firm historical precedent as guidance. Requejo, "Cultural Pluralism, Nationalism and Federalism: A Revision of Democratic Citizenship in Plurinational States," *European Journal of Political Research* 35 (1999): 255–286.

87. Payne, "Catalan and Basque Nationalism," 95.

88. Guibernau, "Spain: Catalonia and the Basque Country."

89. R. Richard Ford, *Las Cosas de España* (Madrid: Cara Raggio, 1974); Jeremy MacClancy, "Bilingualism and Multinationalism in the Basque Country," in *Nationalism and the Nation in the Iberian Peninsula,* 207–220.

90. Medrano, *Divided Nations.*

91. Clark, *The Basque Insurgents: ETA 1952–1980* (Madison: University of Wisconsin Press, 1984); Clark, *Negotiating with ETA: Obstacles to Peace in the Basque Country, 1975–1988* (Reno: University of Nevada Press, 1990); G. Jáuregui Bereciartu, *Ideología y Estragia Politica de ETA: Análisis de su Evolución entre 1959 y 1968,* 2d ed. (Madrid: Siglo XXI, 1985), 475–496.

92. Medrano, *Divided Nations.*

93. Ibid.

94. Payne, "Catalan and Basque Nationalism," 105.

95. Ibid., 105.

96. For example, Joseba Zulaika, *Basque Violence: Metaphor and Sacrament* (Reno: University of Nevada, 1988).

97. Conversi, *The Basques, the Catalans and Spain.*

98. Kathryn A. Woolard, *Double Talk: Bilingualism and the Politics of Ethnicity in Catalonia* (Stanford: Stanford University Press, 1989), 38.

99. As quoted in Conversi, *The Basques, the Catalans and Spain,* 195–196.

100. Conversi notes that Catalan is a rarity among "minority" languages in Europe. The number of speakers is rapidly expanding, while most minority languages are rapidly losing speakers. Ibid. chapters 7 and 8. Along a similar line of thinking, Hutchinson suggests that the typical pattern of decline occurs when language is not the primary symbol of nationality, but only secondary or tertiary. He argues that a "plausible reason for the decline of the [Irish] language is that, as a symbol of nationality, most Irish men and women regard it as definitely secondary to religion." Hutchinson, *The Dynamics of Cultural Nationalism: The Gaelic Revival and the Creation of the Irish Nation State* (London: Allen and Unwin, 1987), 308.

101. Medrano, *Divided Nations.*

102. In both regions the number of natives self-identified as "Only Spanish" accounted for a large portion of the drop. In the Basque Country

such respondents went from 9.7% to 3.8%, and in Catalonia from 16.9% to 4.1%. Ibid.

103. Gary Marks computes the average of four surveys taken from 1991 to 1994. We use the end date in the text for sake of simplicity. Marks, "Territorial Identities in the European Union," in *Regional Integration and Democracy: Expanding on the European Experience*, ed. J. J. Anderson (Lanham, MD: Rowman and Littlefield, 1999), 69–91.

104. The survey results differ, sometimes dramatically, from year to year and thus should be considered only tentative evidence. Heywood reports polls from the mid-1980s that show that self-identification of multiple identities decreased in both Catalonia and the Basque Country. Heywood, *The Government and Politics of Spain*, 34.

105. Medrano, *Divided Nations*. S. McDonough, H. Barnes, A. López Pina with D. C. Shin and J. Á. Moisés, examine feelings of "closeness to Spain" in citizens in each autonomous community. They find that migrants in every region feel closer to Spain than natives of that region. There is also a positive association between the feelings of the migrants and the natives in each region. Regarding our work, natives in the Basque Country and Catalonia feel the least close to Spain. Likewise, migrants in the Basque Country and Catalonia register two of the three lowest feelings of closeness to Spain among all migrant groups. S. McDonough, et. al., *The Cultural Dynamics of Democratization in Spain* (Ithaca: Cornell University Press, 1998).

106. Ministerio de Cultura, *Encuesta de Equipamiento*, Prácticas y Consumos Culturales (Madrid, 1990).

107. Gershon Shafir, *Immigrants and Nationalists: Ethnic Conflict and Accommodation in Catalonia, the Basque Country, Latvia, and Estonia* (Albany: State University of New York Press, 1995), 118–119.

108. Ibid., 119–120.

109. Benjamin Tejerina Montaña, "Language and Basque Nationalism: Collective Identity, Social Conflict and Institutionalisation," in *Nationalism and the Nation in the Iberian Peninsula*, 231–234.

110. Ibid., 234.

111. As quoted in Conversi, *The Basques, the Catalans and Spain*, 173.

112. Ibid., 174.

113. MacClancy, "Bilingualism and Multinationalism in the Basque Country."

114. Davydd J. Greenwood, "Continuity in Change: Spanish Basque Ethnicity as a Historical Process," in *Ethnic Conflict in the Western World*, ed. Milton J. Esman (Ithaca: Cornell University Press, 1977), 81–102.

115. There are of course other national symbols of both communities; we have focused on language as illustration. For further elaboration of nationalism in Spain see Jordi Solé-Tura,. *Nacionalidades y Nacionalismos en España: Autonomias Federalismo Autodeterminacion* (Madrid: Alianza Editorial, 1985); Medrano, *Divided Nations*; Conversi, *The Basques, the Catalans and Spain*; Kenneth Bollen and Juan Diez Medrano, "Who are the Spaniards? Nationalism and Identification in Spain" *Social Forces* 77 (1998): 587–622; Cynthia L. Irvin, *Militant Nationalism: Between Movement and Party in Ireland and the Basque Country* (Minneapolis: University of Minnesota Press, 1999); Paulina Raento, "The Geography of Spanish Basque Nationalism," in *Nested Identities: Nationalism, Territory and State*, eds. Guntram H. Herb and David H. Kaplan (Lanham, MD: Rowman and Littlefield, 1999), 219–235; John Hargraves, *Freedom for Catalonia: Catalan Nationalism, Spanish Identity and the Barcelona Olympic Games* (New York: Cambridge University Press, 2000); Guibernau, "Catalan Nationalism and the Democratisation Process in Spain"; Guibernau, "Spain: Catalonia and the Basque Country."

116. Ole Waever, "Identity, Integration and Security: Solving the Sovereignty Puzzle in E.U. Studies," *Journal of International Affairs* 48 (1995): 389–431.

117. Gibbons, *Spanish Politics Today*, 23.

118. Conversi, *The Basques, the Catalans and Spain*.

119. Payne, "Catalan and Basque Nationalism," 97.

120. Ibid., 98.

121. Medrano, *Divided Nations*, 119–121; Shafir, *Immigrants and Nationalists*, 42.

122. Payne, "Catalan and Basque Nationalism," 102.

123. Ibid., 102.

124. Spain has also experienced a significant increase in immigration, primarily from North Africa. An estimate of the immigrant population is around 200,000 or more in 1994. Martin Baldwin-Edwards and Joaquin Arango, eds, *Immigrants and the Informal Economy in Southern Europe* (London: Frank Cass, 1999), 24.

125. Medrano, *Divided Nations*, 175.

126. Bollen and Medrano, "Who Are the Spaniards?"

127. Heywood, *The Government and Politics of Spain*, 144.

128. Ibid., 145–154. The 1978 Constitution allows Andalucía, the Canary Islands, Catalonia, Galicia, Navarra, the Basque Country, and Ceuta and Melilla a high level of powers (Article 151). Article 142 grants low powers to Aragón, Astruias, the Balearic Islands, Cantabria, Castile y León, Castile-La Mancha, Extremadura, Madrid, Murcia, Rioja and Valencia.

129. Shabad, "After Autonomy," 114–115; Heywood, *The Government and Politics of Spain*, 125.

130. Heywood, *The Government and Politics of Spain*, 124.

131. Ibid.

132. Ibid.

133. Gibbons, *Spanish Politics Today*, 25–27.

134. Colomer, "The Spanish 'State of Autonomies': Non-Institutional Federalism,'" *West European* Politics 21 (1998): 40–52.

135. F. Morata, "Spanish Regions in the EC," in *The European Union and the Regions*, eds. B. Jones and M. Keating (Oxford: Clarendon Press, 1995), 115–133.

136. Ibid.

137. Heywood, *The Government and Politics of Spain*.

138. Many texts on the European Union provide details about the European Regional and Development Fund (ERDF) and structural funds. Perhaps the most comprehensive is David Allen, "Cohesion and the Structural Funds: Transfers and Trade-Offs," in *Policy-Making in the European Union*, 4th ed., eds. Helen Wallace and William Wallace (New York: Oxford University Press, 2000), 243–265.

139. Ibid., 254.

140. M. Keating, "Europeanism and Regionalism," in *The European Union and the Regions*, 1–22; Keating and L. Hooghe, "By-passing the Nation State? Regions and the EU Policy Process," in *European Union: Power and Policy-Making*, ed. J. Richardson (London: Routledge, 1996), 216–229.

141. Morata, "Spanish Regions in the EC."

142. Commission of the European Union, *Eurobarometer Report Number 52* (Brussels, European Commmission, 2000), 26.

143. Ibid., *Number 52*, 33.

144. Ibid., *Number 58*, 28.

145. Maria Ros, Carmen Huic and Angel Gomez, "Comparative Identity, Category Salience and Intergroup Relations," in *Social Identity Processes: Trends in Theory and Research*, eds. D. Capozza and R. Brown (London: Sage, 2000), 94.

146. Jose Luis Garcia Sangrador, *Identidades, actitudes y estereotipos en la España de las autonomies* (Madrid: Centro de Investigaciones Sociologias, 1996).

147. López Guerra, "Sobre la Personalidad Jurídica del Estado," *Revista del Departamento de Derecho Político* (Madrid: UNED, 1980); Colomer, "The Spanish 'State of Autonomies'"; Heywood, *The Government and Politics of Spain*.

148. Requejo, "Cultural Pluralism, Nationalism and Federalism," 272.

Chapter 3

1. Daniela Obradovic, "Policy Legitimacy and the European Union," *Journal of Common Market Studies* 34 (1996): 191–221; Anthony D. Smith, "National Identity and the Idea of European Unity," *International Affairs* 68 (1992): 55–76.

2. Commission of the European Union. *Eurobarometer Report Number 59* (Brussels: European Commission, 2003), 36.

3. Ibid., *Number 54* (Brussels: European Commission, 2001), 11.

4. Robert Ladrech, "Partisanship and Party Formation in European Union Politics," *Comparative Politics* 29, 2 (January 1997): 167–185.

5. Wayne Sandholtz, "Membership Matters: Limits of the Functional Approach to European Institutions," *Journal of Common Market Studies* 34 (September 1996): 426.

6. Ole Waever, "Identity, Integration and Security: Solving the Sovereignty Puzzle in E.U. Studies," *Journal of International Affairs* 48 (Winter 1995): 389–431.

7. Commission on the European Union, *Number 42* (Brussels: European Commission, 1995), 66.

8. Derek W. Urwin, *A Dictionary of European History and Politics 1945–1995* (London: Longman, 1996), 124.

9. Ibid., 124.

10. Carolyn Rhodes, *Pivotal Decisions: Selected Cases in Twentieth Century International Politics* (Fort Worth: Harcourt College Publishers, 2000), 64, 67.

11. Ibid., 67.

12. Monnet's vision corresponds with the functionalist idea of international cooperation: cooperation in functional areas (e.g., economic resources) would lead to cooperation in other areas, thereby diminishing the potential for conflict and war. Rhodes, *Pivotal Decisions*, 70.

13. As quoted in Desmond Dinan, *Ever Closer Union: An Introduction to European Integration*, 2d ed. (Boulder, CO: Lynne Rienner Publishers, 1999), 11.

14. Interestingly, while visiting Paris, Secretary of State Dean Acheson received the proposal from Monnet and Schuman. While Acheson supported the plan, he did so with caution as he worried that the "Plan was a clever cover for 'a gigantic European cartel.'" He was concerned that in the future such a European organization's push for economic competition would challenge the US. Ibid., 22.

15. Rhodes, *Pivotal Decisions*, 68–69.

16. Ibid., 70.

17. Ibid., 71, 78.

18. Ibid., 71.

19. Dinan, *Ever Closer Union*, 43.

20. Amitai Etzioni, *Political Unification Revisited: On Building Supranational Communities* (Lanham, MD: Lexington Books, 2001), 267.

21. With the failure of the EDC, the Western European Union (WEU) was formed in 1955. The WEU, an outgrowth of the 1948 Treaty of Brussels, resulted from the continuing fears of a revived German military, "but this organization by itself had little practical value." Ibid., 241–242, 267.

22. Rhodes, *Pivotal Decisions*, 71–72.

23. Dinan, *Ever Closer Union*, 45, 54.

24. Ibid., 67–68.

25. As quoted in Brian T. Hanson, "What Happened to Fortress Europe?: External Trade Policy Liberalization in the European Union," *International Organization* 52, 1 (Winter 1998): 68.

26. Rhodes, *Pivotal Decisions*, 77.

27. Ibid.

28. Dinan, *Ever Closer Union*, 103–104.

29. Ibid., 120.

30. Ibid., 131–132.

31. Richard C. Eichenberg and Russell J. Dalton, "Europeans and the European Community: The Dynamics of Public Support for European Integration," *International Organization* 47, 4 (Autumn 1993): 57; Derek W. Urwin, *A Dictionary of European History and Politics 1945–1995*, 392.

32. Urwin, *A Dictionary of European History and Politics 1945–1995* (London: Longman, 1996), 393.

33. As quoted in Ibid., 168.

34. Dinan, *Ever Closer Union*, 182.

35. Christine Lemke, "Citizenship and European Integration," *World Affairs* 160, 4 (Spring 1998): 215.

36. As quoted in Antje Wiener, "Promises and Resources-the Developing Practice of 'European' Citizenship," in *European Citizenship: An Institutional Challenge*, ed. Massimo La Torre (The Hague: Kluwer Law, 1998), 401.

37. Daniela Obradovic, "Policy Legitimacy and the European Union," *Journal of Common Market Studies* 24 (1996).

38. As quoted in Chris Shore, "Inventing the 'People's Europe': Critical Approaches to European Community 'Cultural Policy,'" *Manchester Journal of the Royal Anthropological Institute* 28 (1993): 787–788.

39. Wiener, "Promises and Resources," 401.

40. Shore, "Transcending the Nation-State?: The European Commission and the (Re-)Discovery of Europe," *Journal of Historical Sociology* 9 (1996).

41. Urwin, *A Dictionary of European History and Politics 1945–1995*.

42. Shore, "Transcending the Nation-State?"

43. Ulrich K. Preuss, "Citizenship in the European Union: A Paradigm for Transnational Democracy?" in *Re-imagining Political Community: Studies in Cosmopolitan Democracy*, eds. Daniele Archibugi, David Held, and Martin Kohler (Stanford: Stanford University Press, 1998), 142.

44. Shore, "Transcending the Nation-State?"

45. Obradovic, "Policy Legitimacy and the European Union"; Shore, "Transcending the Nation—State?"

46. As quoted in Shore, "Transcending the Nation-State?" 479.

47. Ibid.

48. Ibid., 480. The flag's design is twelve yellow stars on a blue background. "Twelve was the symbol of perfection and plenitude, associated equally with the apostles, the sons of Jacob, the tables of the Roman legislator, the labours of Hercules, the hours of the day, the months of the year, or the signs of the Zodiac. Lastly, the circular layout denoted union" (as quoted in Ibid.).

49. Wiener and Vincent Della Salla, "Constitution-making and Citizenship Practice-Bridging the Democracy Gap in the EU?" *Journal of Common Market Studies* 35 (1997): 595–614.

50. Brigid Laffan, "The Politics of Identity and Political Order in Europe," *Journal of Common Market Studies* 34 (1996): 96.

51. Ibid.

52. Ibid., 97.

53. Ingmarr Karlsson, "European Identity," *The New Presence* (1998), 2, http://www.new−presence.cz/98/12/karlsson.html.

54. Shore, "Transcending the Nation-State?"

55. Lemke, "Citizenship and European Integration," 215.

56. Ibid.

57. As a point of information, the ratification of Maastricht did not go smoothly in some member states, namely Denmark and France. Some in France worried about the loss of sovereignty that would invariably result from ratification, and narrowly passed. The first Danish referendum actually opposed ratification, but the second approved. Concerns over joint citizenship and loss of sovereignty were reflected in a post-referendum poll: 73% of those Danes polled opposed joint citizenship. The contentiousness of the ratification process raised questions about the extent of feeling of a European community. Laffan, "The Politics of Identity and Political Order in Europe."

58. Sandholtz, "Membership Matters," 425.

59. As quoted in Shore, "Transcending the Nation-State?" 482.

60. Laffan, "The Politics of Identity and Political Order in Europe," 97.

61. As quoted in Preuss, "Citizenship in the European Union," 139.

62. Wiener, "Promises and Resources," 409.

63. Lemke, "Citizenship and European Integration."

64. As quoted in Rey Koslowski, "A Constructivist Approach to Understanding the European Union as a Federal Polity," *Journal of European Public Policy* 6, 4 (Special Issue 1999): 572.

65. Jeffrey T. Checkel, "The Europeanization of Citizenship," in *Transforming Europe: Europeanization and Domestic Change*, eds. Maria Green Cowles, James Caporaso, and Thomas Risse (Ithaca: Cornell University Press, 2001), 187.

66. Preuss, "Citizenship in the European Union," 139.

67. Commission of the European Union, "Programme 'Culture 2000'" (Brussels: European Commission, 2000), http://www.europa.eu.int/scadplus/leg/en/lvb/l29006.htm.

68. Ibid., "Culture: Current state and prospects" (Brussels: European Commission), http://www.europa.eu.int/scadplus/leg/en/lvb/l29001.htm.

69. Dinan, *Ever Closer Union*, 430.

70. Wiener, "Promises and Resources," 407.

71. From 1982 to June 1992, the *Eurobarometer* question varied: "In addition to feeling your nationality, what frequency do you feel European? Often, sometimes, or never"; "Do you ever think of yourself as not only (Nationality), but also European? Does this happen often, sometimes, or never?"; "Does the thought ever occur to you that you are not only (nationality) but also European?" From December 1993 to 2003, the question read: "In the near future do you see yourself as: nationality only, nationality and European, European and nationality, or European only?"

72. Commission of the European Union, *Eurobarometer Report Number 59*, 36.

73. Ibid., *Number 38* (Brussels: European Commission, 1992), A34.

74. Ibid., *Number 38*, 45.

75. Ibid., *Number 38*, A35.

76. Ibid., *Number 54*, 15.

77. Ibid., *Number 59*, 33.

78. Another body in the EU is the European Council (not to be confused with the Council of Ministers), which is the "collective organ of the heads of the member states." The heads of government meet informally and the European Council's initiatives "have been framed as broad principles and then passed to the Commission and Council of Ministers for further consideration and discussion." The Treaty on European Union made the European Council the "only body with the authority across the pillars

of the European Union" (Urwin, *A Dictionary of European History and Politics 1945–1995*, 151–152). It is the meeting of the European Council, the summits, that "stand out as turning points in the EU's history"-Milan led to the Single European Act; Maastricht led to the TEU; Amsterdam led to the Amsterdam Treaty (Dinan, *Ever Closer Union*, 237).

79. Urwin, *A Dictionary of European History and Politics 1945–1995*.

80. Waever, "Identity, Integration, and Security," 420.

81. Laffan, "The Politics of Identity and Political Order in Europe"; Urwin, *A Dictionary of European History and Politics 1945–1995*, 110.

82. Dinan, *Ever Closer Union*, 239–240.

83. Ibid., 240.

84. Ibid., 241.

85. Laffan, "The Politics of Identity and Political Order in Europe"; Urwin, *A Dictionary of European History and Politics 1945–1995*.

86. Dinan, *Ever Closer Union*, 255.

87. Ibid., 257.

88. Commission of the European Union, *Eurobarometer Report Number 59*, 70.

89. Ibid., *Number 59*, 71.

90. Laffan, "The Politics of Identity and Political Order in Europe."

91. Urwin, *A Dictionary of European History and Politics 1945–1995*.

92. Dinan, *Ever Closer Union*, 215.

93. Ibid.

94. Ibid., 207.

95. Ibid., 215.

96. Ibid., 225.

97. Amie Kreppel, *The European Parliament and Supranational Party System: A Study in Institutional Development* (New York: Cambridge University Press, 2002); Urwin, *A Dictionary of European History and Politics 1945–1995*.

98. Ladrech, "Partisanship and Party Formation in European Union Politics"; George Tsebelis, "The Power of the European Parliament as a Conditional Agenda Setter," *American Political Science Review* 88 (1994): 128–142.

99. Dinan, *Ever Closer Union*, 267.

100. Ibid., 273.

101. Ladrech, "Partisanship and Party Formation in European Union Politics," 174.

102. Ibid., 179.

103. Dinan, *Ever Closer Union*, 275.

104. Ladrech, "Partisanship and Party Formation in European Union Politics," 180.

105. Ibid.

106. Dinan, *Ever Closer Union*, 277.

107. Ladrech, "Partisanship and Party Formation in European Union Politics."

108. As quoted in Dinan, *Ever Closer Union*, 274–275.

109. Dinan, *Ever Closer Union*, 297–298.

110. Commission of the European Union, *Eurobarometer Report Number 52*, 81–82.

111. Obradovic, "Policy Legitimacy and the European Union."

112. Laffan, "The Politics of Identity and Political Order in Europe," 93.

113. Commission of the European Union, *Eurobarometer Report Number 54*, 94–96.

114. Ibid., *Number 59*, 74.

115. Ibid., *Number 59*, 75.

116. Ibid., *Number 52*, 85.

117. Ibid., *Number 52*, 82–83.

118. Ibid., *Number 52 (Highlights)*, 1.

119. Ibid., *Number 52*, 89.

120. Laffan, "The Politics of Identity and Political Order in Europe."

121. Koslowski, "A Constructivist Approach to Understanding the European Union as a Federal Polity"; Laffan, "The Politics of Identity and Political Order in Europe."

122. Ladrech, "Partisanship and Party Formation in European Union Politics"; Laffan, "The Politics of Identity and Political Order in Europe";

Committee of the Regions (Brussels: Committee of the Regions, 2000), http://www.cor.eu.int.

123. Committee of the Regions.

124. EPP Group, "EPP Mission: The Reasons for Our Commitment," *Committee of the Regions* (2001), http://www.cor.eu.int/presentation/down/ EPP/mission.html.

125. PES Group, "Policy Papers: Political Priorities for the Second Term of Office (1998–2002)," *Committee of the Regions*, http://www.cor.eu. int/presentation/down/Pes/PolicyPapers.html.

126. Alexander B. Murphy, "Rethinking the Concept of European Identity," in *Nested Identities: Nationalism, Territory, and Scale*, eds. Guntram H. Herb and David H. Kaplan (Lanham, MD: Rowman and Littlefield, 1999), 63.

127. Ibid.

128. As quoted in Ibid.

129. Importantly, the variation in individual countries in their attachment to the EU is quite large: a high of 75% of those respondents from Luxembourg felt attached to the EU, and a low of 24% for those from Finland. Commission of the European Union, *Eurobarometer Report Number 58*, 26–27.

130. Ibid., *Number 59*, 69.

131. Ladrach, "Partisanship and Party Formation in European Union Politics," 169.

132. Lemke, "Citizenship and European Integration," 213.

133. Commission of the European Union, *Eurobarometer Report Number 59*, 67–68.

134. Ibid., *Number 59*, 94–95.

135. Marco Cinnirella, "A Social Identity Perspective on European Integration," in *Changing European Identities: Social Psychological Analyses of Social Change*, eds. Glynis M. Breakwell and Evanthia Lyons Speri (Oxford: Butterworth-Heinemann, 1996), 267–268.

136. Lemke, "Citizenship and European Integration."

137. Shore, "Transcending the Nation-State?"; Smith, "National Identity and the Idea of European Unity."

138. Smith, "National Identity and the Idea of European Unity," 70.

139. Waever, "Identity, Integration and Security," 412.

140. Ibid., 430.

141. Laffan, "The Politics of Identity and Political Order in Europe"; Elizabeth Meehan, "Citizenship and the European Community," *Political Quarterly* 64, 2 (April-June 1993): 172—186.

142. Martin Marcussen, Thomas Risse, Daniela Englemann-Martin, Hans Joachim Knopf, and Klaus Roscher, "Constructing Europe? The Evolution of French, British and German Nation State Identities," *Journal of European Public Policy* 6, 4 (Special Issue 1999): 631.

Chapter 4

1. Adrian Guelke reports these figures. Guelke, "Political Violence and the Paramilitaries," in *Politics in Northern Ireland*, eds. Paul Mitchell and Rick Wilford (Boulder, CO: Westview, 1999), 220–241.

2. Brendan O'Leary and John McGarry, *The Politics of Antagonism: Understanding Northern Ireland* (London: Athlone, 1993), 36.

3. Malcolm Sutton, *Bear in Mind These Dead . . .: An Index of Deaths from the Conflict in Ireland, 1969–1993* (Belfast: Beyond the Pale Publications, 1994).

4. For example, our interpretation of the events of the year 2000 when the British Northern Ireland secretary Peter Mendelson suspended the Northern Ireland Assembly supports this claim. Since 1997, Labour has a huge majority, as opposed to the slim Conservative majority for Major's government. Major had to rely on Unionist support to pass legislation and to prop up his government, for example, during the 1992 Maastricht Treaty vote and vote of confidence. The current Labour government no longer needs the support of Unionist parties. That David Trimble had to threaten resignation to gain some voice in Westminister shows the depth of desperation in which the Unionist parties find themselves.

5. There are good sources on the history of Northern Ireland readily available. See, particularly, Thomas Hennessey, *A History of Northern Ireland* (New York: St. Martin's, 1997).

6. Joseph Ruane and Jennifer Todd, *The Dynamics of Conflict in Northern Ireland: Power, Conflict and Emancipation* (Cambridge: Cambridge University Press, 1996), 20.

7. T. W. Moody and F. X. Martin, *The Course of Irish History* (Cork, Ireland: Mercier, 1967), 309–311.

8. Ibid.; Ruane and Todd, *The Dynamics of Conflict in Northern Ireland.-*

9. John H. Whyte, *Interpreting Northern Ireland* (Oxford: Clarendon, 1991).

10. Hennessey, *A History of Northern Ireland*, 126–138.

11. Ibid.

12. Ibid., 151, 156, 162, 166–167.

13. Richard Breen and Paula Devine, "Segmentation and Social Structure," in *Politics in Northern Ireland*, eds. Paul Mitchell and Rick Wilford (Boulder, CO: Westview, 1999), 52–65; Ruane and Todd, *The Dynamics of Conflict in Northern Ireland*.

14. D. George Boyce, *Ireland 1828–1923: From Ascendancy to Democracy* (Oxford: Blackwell, 1992); Louis Cullen, *The Emergence of Modern Ireland 1600–1900* (London: Batsford, 1981); K. Theodore Hoppen, *Ireland since 1800: Conflict and Conformity* (London: Longman, 1989).

15. Ruane and Todd, *The Dynamics of Conflict in Northern Ireland*, chapter 3.

16. Ibid., chapter 2.

17. Ibid., 22.

18. Ibid., 23.

19. Ibid.

20. Ibid., 26–28.

21. Ibid., 28–29.

22. Ibid., 43–46.

23. Ibid., 9.

24. "Life and Times" Survey, 2001, http://www.ark.ac.uk/nilt/; Karen Trew, "The Northern Irish Identity," in *A Question of Identity*, ed. Anne J. Kershen (Aldershot, England: Ashgate, 1998), 60–76; Trew and Denny E. Benson, "Dimensions of Social Identity in Northern Ireland," in *Changing European Identities: Social Psychological Analyses of Social Change*, eds. Glynis M. Breakwell and Evanthia Lyons Speri (Oxford: Butterworth-Heinemann, 1996), 123–143.

25. Cathal McCall, *Identity in Northern Ireland* (New York: St. Martin's, 1999), 147.

26. Andrea K. Grove and Neal A. Carter, "Not All Blarney Is Cast in Stone: International Cultural Conflict in Northern Ireland," *Political Psychology* 20 (1999): 725–765.

27. Ibid., 733, 737.

28. Good sources, for example, are Benedict Anderson, *Imagined Communities: Reflections on the Origin and Spread of Nationalism* (London: Verso, 1991); Desmond Bowen, *The Protestant Crusade in Ireland, 1800–70: A Study of Protestant-Catholic Relations between the Act of Union and Disestablishment* (Dublin: Gill and Macmillan, 1978); R. H. Buchanan, "The Planter and the Gael: Cultural Dimensions of the Northern Ireland Problem," in *Integration and Division: Geographical Perspectives on the Northern Ireland Problem*, eds. F. W. Boal and J. N. Douglas (London: Academic Press, 1982), 49–73; Conor Cruise O'Brien, *Ancestral Voices: Religion and Nationalism in Ireland* (Dublin: Poolbeg, 1994); Henry Patterson, *Class Conflict and Sectarianism: The Protestant Working Class and the Belfast Labour Movement 1868–1920* (Belfast: Blackstaff, 1980).

29. Ruane and Todd, *The Dynamics of Conflict in Northern Ireland*; Edward Moxon-Browne, "National Identity in Northern Ireland," in *Social Attitudes in Northern Ireland*, eds. Peter Stringer and Jillian Robinson (Belfast: Blackstaff, 1991), 25.

30. "Life and Times" Survey.

31. The increasing size of the Catholic minority and its eventual ascension to majority status in Northern Ireland can be found in Paul Doherty, "The Numbers Game: The Demographic Context of Politics," in *Northern Ireland Politics*, eds. A. Aughey and D. Morrow (London: Longman, 1996), 199–209. This demographic change is also clear in the increasing size of the vote for Catholic parties as opposed to Protestant parties. From the 1970s to the 1990s, the average size of electoral support for the "Unionist Bloc" fell from 59.4% to 50.5%. Over this same time period, the "Nationalist Bloc" share increased from 25.8% to 37.0%. Paul Mitchell, "The Party System and Party Competition," in *Politics in Northern Ireland*, eds. Mitchell and Rick Wilford (Boulder, CO: Westview, 1999), 91–116. In elections to the Northern Ireland Assembly on June 25, 1998, the Unionist Bloc won 47.3% to the Nationalist Bloc's 39.7% (Northern Ireland Assembly, http://www.ni-assembly.gov.uk/).

32. O'Leary and McGarry, *The Politics of Antagonism*; Merlyn Rees, *Northern Ireland: A Personal Perspective* (London: Methuen, 1985).

33. O'Leary, "Public Opinion and Northern Irish Futures," *Political Quarterly* 63 (1992): 143–170.

34. Peter F. Trumbore points out that while the British public favors disengagement, they do not agree on how to substantiate that desire. Polls taken in the 1990s show that while making Northern Ireland an "Independent state" is often the leading response (roughly 1/3), the other three options of "Remain part of the UK," "Union with Ireland," and "Don't Know" are close behind with just under 1/4 of the response. Trumbore,

"Public Opinion as a Domestic Constraint in International Negotiations: Two-Level Games in the Anglo-Irish Peace Process," *International Studies Quarterly* 42 (1998): 545–565.

35. Paul Bew, *Northern Ireland 1921–1994: Political Forces and Social Classes* (London: Serif, 1995); O'Leary, "Public Opinion and Northern Irish Futures"; Charles Townshend, *Political Violence in Ireland: Government and Resistance since 1848* (Oxford: Clarendon Press, 1983).

36. Arend Lijphart, *Democracy in Plural Societies* (New Haven: Yale University Press, 1997).

37. Rick Wilford, "Regional Assemblies and Parliament," in *Politics in Northern Ireland*, eds. Paul Mitchell and Rick Wilford (Boulder, CO: Westview, 1999), 117–141.

38. Bill McSweeney, "Security, Identity and the Peace Process in Northern Ireland," *Security Dialogue* 27 (1996): 167–178.

39. As we posit, a major weakness of consociational solutions is that they can and do only see the problem between two or more communities as *internal* to the particular state. The rapidity of the fall of the Stormont government is perhaps an indicator of the external factors contributing to conflict in Northern Ireland. Moreover, Lijphart argues that Northern Ireland demonstrates the limits of consociationalism because "it cannot be imposed against the will of one of the segments, especially if it is a majority segment. Most of the Protestant leaders as well as the rank and file remain opposed to sharing power with the Catholics." With one group able to dominate over the other, no equilibrium between the two parties and no overarching national identity, a consociational solution will not work. Lijphart, *Democracy in Plural Societies*, 137–-138.

40. McSweeney, "Security, Identity and the Peace Process in Northern Ireland."

41. Ibid.

42. Arthur Aughey, "Northern Ireland," in *Developments in British Politics*, 5th ed., ed. P. Dunleavy, A. Gamble, I. Holliday, and G. Peele (New York: St. Martin's, 1997), 241–252.

43. McSweeney, "Security, Identity and the Peace Process in Northern Ireland."

44. J. Vincent, "Ethnicity and the State in Northern Ireland," in *Ethnicity and the State*, ed. J. D. Toland (New Brunswick: Transaction Publishers, 1993), 123–146.

45. John McGarry, "Political Settlements in Northern Ireland and South Africa," *Political Studies* 46 (1998): 853–870.

46. McSweeney, "Security, Identity and the Peace Process in Northern Ireland."

47. Aughey, "Northern Ireland."

48. McSweeney, "Security, Identity and the Peace Process in Northern Ireland."

49. Ibid., 169.

50. Ruane and Todd, *The Dynamics of Conflict in Northern Ireland*, 298.

51. Opinion in the Republic of Ireland also favored the intent of the documents. Public opinion polls show that majorities in both the North and the South agreed on the "consent principle," that is, that constitutional change in Northern Ireland should not be imposed by any outside body against the wishes of the residents. Moreover, support moved against the position of Sinn Fein and toward that of the nationalists. Brian Girvin, "Northern Ireland and the Republic," in *Politics in Northern Ireland*, eds. Paul Mitchell and Rick Wilford (Boulder, CO.: Westview, 1999), 220–241.

52. Colm McKeogh, "Northern Ireland: The Good Friday Solution," *New Zealand International Review* 23 (1998): 2–6.

53. The Protestants were also distrustful of American involvement. A poll from September 1996 reports that 64% of the non-Catholics polled believed that American interests in the affairs of Northern Ireland would be likely to "hinder" attempts at securing a settlement (with 26% saying that it would "help" and 11% with no opinion). The Catholic response was 14%, 75%, and 11% with respect to "hinder," "help," and "no opinion" (MRBI on behalf of the *Sunday Times*, September 1996).

54. McKeogh, "Northern Ireland."

55. Polls in both 1996 and 1997 show that the proposed solution (a local parliament for Northern Ireland within the UK with power-sharing between the local parties but with cross-border institutions) is more highly favored by the Catholic community than by the Protestant community. In general, this solution is second-favored by Catholics (behind Union with Ireland) and fourth- or fifth-favored by Protestants (who favor continued Union with the UK). In 1997, the poll asked respondents if any of the proposed solutions were "unacceptable." The difference between the two communities is striking: only 2.7% of Catholics would find such a solution unacceptable versus 15.5% of Protestants. The source for the 1996 poll is MRBI on behalf of the *Sunday Times*, September 1996. The source for the 1997 poll is Coopers & Lybrand for BBC, September 1997.

56. McGarry, "Political Settlements in Northern Ireland and South Africa," 858–859, 865.

57. Rick Wilford, "Epilogue," in *Politics in Northern Ireland*, eds. Paul Mitchell and Wilford (Boulder, CO: Westview, 1999), 298–300.

58. Ibid.

59. For an argument about how the Good Friday Agreement, in whole or in part, differs from a consociational agreement see Rupert Taylor, "Northern Ireland: Consociation or Social Transformation?" in *Northern Ireland and the Divided World: The Northern Ireland Conflict and the Good Friday Agreement in Comparative Perspective*, ed. McGarry (Oxford: Oxford University Press, 2001), 36–52. For a counterargument stating that the agreement is indeed consociational, see Donald L. Horowitz, "The Northern Ireland Agreement: Clear, Consociational and Risky," in ibid., 89–108. For an argument about how the participants managed to agree on such a convoluted agreement, see Horowitz, "Explaining the Northern Ireland Agreement: The Sources of an Unlikely Constitutional Consensus," *British Journal of Political Science* 32 (2002): 193–220.

60. Strand 1: Paragraph 2. Agreement between the Governments of the United Kingdom of Great Britain and Northern Ireland and the Government of Ireland (10 April 1998).

61. Each member of the Assembly must upon being first seated register a designation of identity: Nationalist, Unionist, or other (Strand 1: Paragraph 6). Agreement between the Governments of the United Kingdom of Great Britain and Northern Ireland and the Government of Ireland (10 April 1998).

62. Strand 1: Paragraph 5:cii. (10 April 1998).

63. Wilford, "Epilogue," 302.

64. Strand 2: Paragraph 1. (10 April 1998).

65. Strand 2: Paragraph 5. (10 April 1998).

66. Strand 2: Paragraph 7. (10 April 1998).

67. Strand 3: Part 2: Paragraph 2. (10 April 1998).

68. Strand 3: Part 2: Paragraph 5. (10 April 1998).

69. Strand 3: Part 2: Paragraph 6. (10 April 1998).

70. Ronald Weitzer, "Policing and Security," in *Politics in Northern Ireland*, eds. Paul Mitchell and Rick Wilford (Boulder, CO: Westview, 1999), 170.

71. Ibid., 171–172.

72. Wilford, "Epilogue," 297.

73. BBC Online, *Timelines of Events in Northern Ireland since the Signing of the Good Friday Agreement* (British Broadcasting Corporation).

74. Wilford, "Epilogue," 296.

75. BBC Online, *Timelines of Events in Northern Ireland since the Signing of the Good Friday Agreement.*

76. Ibid.

79. McSweeney, "Interests and Identity in the Construction of the Belfast Agreement," *Security Dialogue* 29 (1998): 303–314; Etian Tannam, *Cross-Border Cooperation in the Republic of Ireland and Northern Ireland* (New York: St. Martin's, 1999).

78. Elizabeth Meehan, "'Britain's Irish Question: Britain's European Question?' British-Irish Relations in the Context of European Union and the Belfast Agreement," *Review of International Studies* 26 (2000): 83–97.

79. Ruane and Todd, *The Dynamics of Conflict in Northern Ireland*, 281.

80. Strand 1: Paragraph 31. (10 April 1998).

81. Strand 2: Paragraph 17. (10 April 1998).

82. Paul Bew and Elizabeth Meehan, "Regions and Borders: Controversies in Northern Ireland about the European Union," *Journal of European Public Policy* 1 (1994): 104.

83. McCall, *Identity in Northern Ireland*, 86.

84. Ibid.

85. Tannam, *Cross-Border Cooperation in the Republic of Ireland and Northern Ireland*, 119.

86. Ibid., 109.

87. O'Leary uses a consociational framework to view the institutions of the Good Friday Agreement and comes to the conclusion that it has "co-sovereignty built in; and it promises a novel model of 'double protection.'" O'Leary, "The 1998 British-Irish Agreement: Power-Sharing Plus," *Scottish Affairs* 26 (1999): 15. In this way, O'Leary sees the same multiple forums and pooled sovereignty that we see, but his focus on consociationalist theory limits his analysis of the connection between the institutions and promoting overlapping identities.

88. McKeogh, "Northern Ireland."

89. Ruane and Todd, *The Dynamics of Conflict in Northern Ireland.*

90. The source for the poll is MRBI on behalf of the *Sunday Times*, September 1996.

91. Grove and Carter, "Not All Blarney Is Cast in Stone."

92. Whyte, *Interpreting Northern Ireland*.

93. McGarry, "Political Settlements in Northern Ireland and South Africa."

94. Breen and Devine, "Segmentation and Social Structure."

95. A question in 1996 asked, "There has been some discussion as to whether the Orange Order represents the views of the Protestant community as a whole. To what extent would you say the views of Protestants in general are reflected in the statements and actions of the Orange Order?" Thirty-eight percent of Catholic respondents said that this statement was only sometimes or never true, while 51 percent of the non-Catholics responded the same way. The source for the poll is MRBI on behalf of the *Sunday Times*, September 1996.

96. Andrew Reynolds, "A Constitutional Pied Piper: The Northern Irish Good Friday Agreement," *Political Science Quarterly* 114 (1999–2000): 624.

97. Out of 108 seats, the Nationalists claimed 42, 'Yes Unionists' 30, 'No Unionists' 28 and others 8.

98. McGarry, "Political Settlements in Northern Ireland and South Africa."

99. Ibid.

100. John Lloyd, "Ireland's Uncertain Peace," *Foreign Affairs* 77 (1998): 109–122.

Chapter 5

1. George Tsebelis, *Nested Games: Rational Choice in Comparative Politics* (Berkeley and Los Angeles: University of California Press, 1990), 173–181.

2. Juan Díez Medrano, *Divided Nations: Class, Politics, and Nationalism in the Basque Country and Catalonia* (Ithaca: Cornell University Press, 1995), 175.

Bibliography

Agreement between the Governments of the United Kingdom of Great Britain and Northern Ireland and the Government of Ireland (10 April 1998).

Aguilar, Palomar. "The Memory of the Civil War in the Transition to Democracy: The Peculiarity of the Basque Case." *West European Politics* 21 (1998): 5–25.

Allen, David. "Cohesion and the Structural Funds: Transfers and Trade-Offs." In *Policy-Making in the European Union*, 4th ed., edited by Helen Wallace and William Wallace, 243–265. New York: Oxford University Press, 2000.

Alpert, Michael. *A New International History of the Spanish Civil War.* London: Macmillan, 1994.

Alvarez Junco, Jose. *La ideología política del anarquismo español (1868–1910).* Madrid: Siglo XXI, 1976.

———. "The Nation-Building Process in Nineteenth-Century Spain." In *Nationalism and the Nation in the Iberian Peninsula: Competing and Conflicting Identities*, edited by Clare Mar-Molinero and Angel Smith, 89–106. Oxford: Berg, 1996.

Anderson, Benedict. *Imagined Communities: Reflections on the Origin and Spread of Nationalism.* London: Verso, 1991.

Aughey, Arthur. "Northern Ireland." In *Developments in British Politics*, 5th ed., edited by P. Dunleavy, A. Gamble, I. Holliday, and G. Peele, 241–252. New York: St. Martin's, 1997.

163

Balcells, Albert. *El nacionalismo catalán*. Madrid, Universidad de Valencia, 1991.

———. *Catalan Nationalism*. London: Macmillan, 1996.

Baldwin-Edwards, Martin, and Joaquin Arango, eds. *Immigrants and the Informal Economy in Southern Europe*. London: Frank Cass, 1999.

Balfour, Sebastian. "'The Lion and the Pig': Nationalism and National Identity in *Fin-de-Siècle* Spain." In *Nationalism and the Nation in the Iberian Peninsula: Competing and Conflicting Identities*, edited by Clare Mar-Molinero and Angel Smith, 107–118. Oxford: Berg, 1996.

Barry, Brian. "The Consociational Model and Its Dangers." *European Journal of Political Research* 3 (1975): 393–412.

Barton, Robert. *Notes for a Lecture*. MS 1093/14. Public Records Office (PRO): Dublin.

BBC Online. *Timelines of Events in Northern Ireland since the Signing of the Good Friday Agreement*. British Broadcasting Corporation.

Ben-Ami, Shlomo. *The Origins of the Second Republic of Spain*. Oxford: University Press, 1978.

———. *Fascism from Above: The Dictatorship of Primo de Rivera in Spain, 1923–1930*. Oxford: University Press, 1983.

Bew, Paul. *Northern Ireland 1921–1994: Political Forces and Social Classes*. London: Serif, 1995.

Bew, Paul, and Elizabeth Meehan. "Regions and Borders: Controversies in Northern Ireland about the European Union." *Journal of European Public Policy* 1 (1994): 95–113.

Blanton, Shannon Lindsey. "Images in Conflict: The Case of Ronald Reagan and El Salvador." *International Studies Quarterly* 40, 1 (March 1996): 23–44.

Bollen, Kenneth, and Juan Diez Medrano. "Who Are the Spaniards? Nationalism and Identification in Spain." *Social Forces* 77 (1998): 587–622.

Bowen, Desmond. *The Protestant Crusade in Ireland, 1800–70: A Study of Protestant-Catholic Relations between the Act of Union and Disestablishment*. Dublin: Gill and Macmillan, 1978.

Boyce, D. George. *Ireland 1828–1923: From Ascendancy to Democracy*. Oxford: Blackwell, 1992.

Brassaloff, Audrey. *Religion and Politics in Spain: The Spanish Church in Transition 1962–1996*. New York: St. Martin's, 1998.

Breen, Richard, and Pauline Devine. "Segmentation and Social Structure." In *Politics in Northern Ireland*, edited by Paul Mitchell and Rick Wilford, 52–65. Boulder, CO: Westview, 1999.

Brewer, Marilynn B. "The Social Psychology of Intergroup Relations: Can Research Inform Practice?" *Journal of Social Issues* 53 (1997): 197–211.

———. "Ingroup Identification and Intergroup Conflict: When Does Ingroup Love

Become Outgroup Hate?" In *Social Identity, Intergroup Conflict, and Conflict Reduction*, edited by Richard D. Ashmore, Lee Jussim, and David Wilder, 17–41. Oxford: Oxford University Press, 2001.

Brewer, Marilynn B., and Wendi. Gardner. "Who Is This 'We'? Levels of Collective Identity and Self Representations." *Journal of Personality and Social Psychology* 71 (1996): 83–93.

Brown, Michael E., Owen R. Cote Jr., Sean M. Lynn-Jones, and Steven E. Miller, eds. *Nationalism and Ethnic Conflict*. Cambridge: MIT Press, 2001.

Buchanan, R. H. "The Planter and the Gael: Cultural Dimensions of the Northern Ireland Problem." In *Integration and Division: Geographical Perspectives on the Northern Ireland Problem*, edited by F. W. Boal and J. N. Douglas, 49–73. London: Academic Press, 1982.

Callahan, William J. *The Catholic Church in Spain, 1987–1998*. Washington, DC, Catholic University of America Press, 2000.

Carner-Ribalta, Josep. *The Catalan Nation and Its People*. Houston: American Institute for Catalan Studies, 1995.

Carnero, T. "Política sin democracia en España, 1874–1923." *Revista de Occidente* 83 (1988): 43–58.

Carr, Raymond. *Spain 1808–1875*, 2d ed. Oxford: Clarendon Press, 1982.

Checkel, Jeffrey T. "The Constructivist Turn in International Relations Theory." *World Politics* 50, 2 (January 1998): 324–348.

———. "The Europeanization of Citizenship?" In *Transforming Europe: Europeanization and Domestic Change,* edited by Maria Green Cowles, James Caparosa, and Thomas Risse, 180–97. Ithaca: Cornell University Press, 2001.

Church, Clive H. "Switzerland: A Paradigm in Evolution." *Parliamentary Affairs* 53 (2000): 96–113.

Cinnirella, Marco. "A Social Identity Perspective on European Integration." In *Changing European Identities: Social Psychological*

N

Analyses of Social Change, edited by Glynis M. Breakwell and Evanthia Lyons Speri, 253–274. Oxford: Butterworth-Heinemann, 1996.

Clark, Robert P. *The Basques: The Franco Years and Beyond*. Reno: University of Nevada Press, 1979.

———. *The Basque Insurgents: ETA 1952–1980*. Madison: University of Wisconsin Press, 1984.

———. *Negotiating with ETA: Obstacles to Peace in the Basque Country, 1975–1988*. Reno: University of Nevada, 1990.

Coakley, John. "Introduction: The Territorial Management of Ethnic Conflict." In *The Territorial Management of Ethnic Conflict*, edited by John Coakley, 1–22. London: Frank Cass, 1993.

Colomer, Josep M. "The Spanish 'State of Autonomies': Non-Institutional Federalism." *West European Politics* 21 (1998): 40–52.

———. "The 2000 General Election in Spain." *Electoral Studies* 20 (2001): 463–501.

Commission of the European Union. "Programme 'Culture 2000.'" Brussels: European Commission, 2000. http://www.europa.eu.int/scadplus/leg/en/lvb/l29006.htm.

———. "Culture: Current State and Prospects." Brussels: European Commission. http://www.europa.eu.int/scadplus/leg/en/lvb/l29001.htm.

———. *Eurobarometer Report Number 42*. Brussels: European Commission, 1995.

———. *Eurobarometer Report Number 50*. Brussels: European Commission, 1999.

———. *Eurobarometer Report Number 53*. Brussels: European Commission, 2000.

———. *Eurobarometer Report Number 52*. Brussels: European Commission, 2000.

———. *Eurobarometer Report Number 54*. Brussels: European Commission, 2001.

———. *Eurobarometer Report Number 58*. Brussels: European Commission, 2002.

———. *Eurobarometer Report Number 59*. Brussels: European Commission, 2003.

———. *Special Report No 7/2000 concerning the International Fund for Ireland and the Special Support Programme for Peace and Recon-*

ciliation in Northern Ireland and the Border Counties of Ireland (1995 to 1999), together with the Commission's Replies. Brussels: European Commission, 2000. http://europa.eu.int/eur-lex/en/lif/dat/2000/en_300Y0525_01.html.

Committee of the Regions. Brussels: Committee of the Regions, 2000. http://www.cor.eu.int.

Conversi, Daniele. *The Basques, the Catalans and Spain: Alternate Routes to Nationalist Mobilisation.* Reno: University of Nevada Press, 1997.

Coogan, Tim Pat, and George Morrison. *The Irish Civil War.* Boulder, CO.: Roberts Rinehart, 1998.

Corkill, David. "Race, Immigration and Multiculturalism in Spain." In *Contemporary Spanish Cultural Studies*, edited by Barry Jordan and Rikki Morgan-Tamosunas, 48–57. New York: Oxford University Press, 2000.

Covell, Maureen. "Ethnic Conflict and Elite Bargaining: The Case of Belgium." *West European Politics* 4 (1981): 197–218.

Cullen, Louis. *The Emergence of Modern Ireland 1600–1900.* London: Batsford, 1981.

De la Rouchefoucauld, Francois. *Maxims.* Translated by Leonard Tancock. New York: Viking, 1982.

Deflem, M., and F. C. Pampel. "The Myth of Postnational Identity: Popular Support for European Unification." *Social Forces* 75 (1996): 119–143.

Dinan, Desmond. *Ever Closer Union: An Introduction to European Integration*, 2nd edition. Boulder: Lynne Rienner, 1999.

Doherty, Paul. "The Numbers Game: The Demographic Context of Politics." In *Northern Ireland Politics*, edited by A. Aughey and D. Morrow, 199–209. London: Longman, 1996.

Eichenberg, Richard C., and Russell J. Dalton. "Europeans and the European Community: The Dynamics of Public Support for European Integration." *International Organization* 47, 4 (Autumn, 1993): 48–57.

Elazar, Daniel J. *Exploring Federalism.* Tuscaloosa: University of Alabama, 1987.

Ensari, Nurcan, and Norman Miller. "Effect of Affective Reactions by an Out-Group on Preferences for Crossed Categorization Discussion Partners." *Journal of Personality and Social Psychology* 75 (1998): 1503–1527.

EPP Group. "EPP Mission: The Reasons for our Commitment." *Committee of the Regions* (2001). http://www.cor.eu.int/presentation/down/EPP/mission.html.

Etzioni, Amitai. *Political Unification Revisited: On Building Supranational Communities*. Lanham, MD: Lexington Books, 2001.

European Parliament Elections: Voter Turnout across the EU (1979–1999) (%). *European Parliament UK Office*. http://www.europarl.org.uk/guide.Gelectionfacts.htm.

Fearon, James D. "Commitment Problems and the Spread of Ethnic Conflict." In *The International Spread of Ethnic Conflict: Fear, Diffusion, and Escalation*, edited by David A. Lake and Donald Rothchild, 107–126. Princeton: Princeton University Press, 1998.

Fisher, Ronald J. *The Social Psychology of Intergroup and International Conflict Resolution*. New York: Springer Verlag, 1990.

Ford, R. Richard. *Las Cosas de España*. Madrid: Cara Raggio, 1974.

Fusi, Juan Pablo. *Franco: Autoritarismo y poder personal*. Madrid: El País, 1985.

Gaertner, Samuel L., John F. Dovidio, Phyllis A. Anastasio, Betty A. Bachman, and Mary C. Rust. "The Common Ingroup Identity Model: Recategorization and the Reduction of Integroup Bias." *European Review of Social Psychology* 4 (1993): 1–26.

García Delgado, Jose Luis, ed. *La crisis de la Restauración: España entre la primera guerra mundial y la segunda Republica*. Madrid: Siglo XXI, 1986.

Garcia Sangrador, Jose Luis. *Identidades, actitudes y estereotipos en la España de las autonomies*. Madrid: Centro de Investigaciones Sociologias, 1996.

George, Alexander L. "Case Studies and Theory Development: The Method of Structured, Focused Comparison." In *Diplomacy: New Approaches in History, Theory, and Policy*, edited by Paul Gordon Lauren, 43–68. New York: Free Press, 1979.

Gibbons, John. *Spanish Politics Today*. New York: Manchester University, 1999.

Gilmour, David. *The Transformation of Spain: From Franco to the Constitutional Monarchy*. London: Quartet, 1985.

Gilner, S. 1984. *The Social Structure of Catalonia*. Anglo-Catalan Society Occasional Publications, no. 1, 1984.

Girvin, Brian. "Northern Ireland and the Republic." In *Politics in Northern Ireland*, edited by Paul Mitchell and Rick Wilford, 220–241. Boulder, CO: Westview, 1999.

Golay, Michael. *The Spanish-American War*. New York: Facts on File, 1995.

Goldgeier, James M. "Psychology and Security." *Security Studies* 6 (1997): 137–166.

González Calbet, Maria Teresa. "La destrucción del sistema político de la Restauración: El golpe de septiembre de 1923." In *La Crisis de la Restauración*, edited by Jose Luis Garcia Delgado, 101–120. Madrid: Siglo XXI, 1986.

Graham, Helen. *Spain: Change of a Nation*. London: Michael Joseph, 1984.

———. "Community, Nation and State in Republican Spain, 1931–1938." In *Nationalism and the Nation in the Iberian Peninsula: Competing and Conflicting Identities*, edited by Clare Mar-Molinero and Angel Smith, 133–148. Oxford: Berg, 1996.

———, and Jo Labanyi. "Culture and Modernity: The Case of Spain." In *Spanish Cultural Studies, An Introduction: The Struggle for Modernity*, edited by Helen Graham and Jo Labanyi, 1–20. New York: Oxford University, 1995.

Greenwood, Davydd J. "Continuity in Change: Spanish Basque Ethnicity as a Historical Process." In *Ethnic Conflict in the Western World*, edited by Milton J. Esman, 81–102. Ithaca: Cornell University Press, 1977.

Grove, Andrea K., and Neal A. Carter. "Not All Blarney Is Cast in Stone: International Cultural Conflict in Northern Ireland." *Political Psychology* 20 (1999): 725–765.

Guibernau, Montserrat. "Catalan Nationalism and the Democratisation Process in Spain." In *Democratisation in the New Europe,* edited by K. Cordell, 77–90. New York: Routledge, 1999.

———. "Spain: Catalonia and the Basque Country." *Parliamentary Affairs* 53 (2000): 55–68.

Guelke, Adrian. "Political Violence and the Paramilitaries." In *Politics in Northern Ireland*, edited by Paul Mitchell and Rick Wilford, 220–241. Boulder, CO: Westview, 1999.

Hanson, Brian T. "External Trade Policy Liberalization in the European Union." *International Organization* 52, 1 (Winter, 1998): 55–86.

Hargraves, John. *Freedom for Catalonia: Catalan Nationalism, Spanish Identity and the Barcelona Olympic Games.* New York: Cambridge University Press, 2000.

Heiberg, Marianne. *The Making of the Basque Nation.* Cambridge: Cambridge University Press, 1989.

Hennessey, Thomas. *A History of Northern Ireland.* New York: St. Martin's, 1997.

Herb, Guntram H., and David H. Kaplan, eds. *Nested Identities: Nationalism, Territory and Scale.* Lanham, MD: Rowman and Littlefield, 1999.

Herrmann, Richard K., et al. "Images in International Relations: An Experimental Test of Cognitive Schemata." *International Studies Quarterly* 41 (1997): 403–433.

Herrmann, Richard K., and Michael P. Fischerkeller. "Beyond the Enemy Image and Spiral Model: Cognitive-Strategic Research after the Cold War." *International Organization* 49, 3 (Summer 1995): 415–450.

Hewstone, Miles, Mir Rabiul Islam, and Charles M. Judd. "Models of Crossed Categorization and Intergroup Relations." *Journal of Personality and Social Psychology* 64 (1993): 779–793.

Heywood, Paul. *The Government and Politics of Spain.* New York: St. Martin's, 1995.

Hogg, Michael A., Deborah J. Terry, and Katherine M. White. "A Tale of Two Theories: A Critical Comparison of Identity Theory with Social Identity Theory." *Social Psychology Quarterly* 58 (1995): 255–269.

Hollyman, J. L. "Separatismo Vasco Revolucionario: ETA." In *España en crisis: La evolución y decadencia del régimen de Franco*, edited by Paul Preston, 212–233. Madrid: Fondo de cultura económica, 1977.

Hopf, Ted. "The Promise of Constructivism in International Relations Theory." *International Security* 23, 1 (1998): 171–200.

Hoppen, K. Theodore. *Ireland since 1800: Conflict and Conformity.* London: Longman, 1989.

Horowitz, Donald L. *Ethnic Groups in Conflict.* Berkeley: University of California Press, 1985.

———. "The Northern Ireland Agreement: Clear, Consociational and Risky." In *Northern Ireland and the Divided World: The Northern Ireland Conflict and the Good Friday Agreement in Comparative Perspective*, edited by John McGarry, 89–108. Oxford: Oxford University Press, 2001.

————. "Explaining the Northern Ireland Agreement: The Sources of an Unlikely Constitutional Consensus." *British Journal of Political Science* 32 (2002): 193–220.

Hutchinson, John. *The Dynamics of Cultural Nationalism: The Gaelic Revival and the Creation of the Irish Nation State.* London: Allen and Unwin, 1987.

Irvin, Cynthia L. *Militant Nationalism: Between Movement and Party in Ireland and the Basque Country.* Minneapolis: University of Minnesota Press, 1999.

Jackson, Gabriel. *The Spanish Republic and the Civil War, 1931–1939*, 5th ed. Princeton: Princeton University Press, 1972.

Jáuregui Bereciartu, G. *Ideología y Estragia Politica de ETA: Análisis de su Evolución entre 1959 y 1968*, 2d ed. Madrid: Siglo XXI, 1985.

Jervis, Robert. *Perception and Misperception in International Politics.* Princeton: Princeton University Press, 1976.

Kaleagasi, Peride. "Belgium and Switzerland: A Comparative Study of Federalism in Multiethnic Democracies." *Annual Meeting of the Midwest Political Science Association.* Chicago: April 27–30, 2000.

Karlsson, Ingmarr. "European Identity." *The New Presence* (1998): 1–4. http://www.new-presence.cz/98/12/karlsson.html.

Katz, D. "Nationalism and Strategies of International Conflict Resolution." In *International Behavior: A Social-Psychological Analysis*, edited by Herbert C. Kelman, 356– 90. New York: Holt, 1965.

Keating, M. "Europeanism and Regionalism." In *The European Union and the Regions*, edited by B. Jones and M. Keating, 1–22. Oxford: Clarendon Press, 1995.

————, and L. Hooghe. "By-passing the Nation State? Regions and the EU Policy Process." In *European Union: Power and Policy-Making*, edited by J. Richardson, 216–229. London: Routledge, 1996.

Keohane, Robert O., and Lisa L. Martin. "The Promise of Institutionalist Theory." *International Security* 20 (1995): 39–51.

King, Gary, Robert O. Keohane, and Sidney Verba. *Designing Social Inquiry: Scientific Inquiry in Qualitative Research.* Princeton: Princeton University Press, 1994.

Koslowski, Rey. "A Constructivist Approach to Understanding the European Union as a Federal Polity." *Journal of European Public Policy* 6, 4 (Special Issue 1999): 561–578.

————, and Friedrich V. Kratochwil. "Understanding Change in International Politics: the Soviet Empire's Demise and the International System." *International Organization* 48, 2 (Spring 1994): 215–247.

Krepel, Amie. *The European Parliament and Supranational Party System: A Study in Institutional Development*. New York: Cambridge University Press, 2002.

Ladrech, Robert. "Partisanship and Party Formation in European Union Politics." *Comparative Politics* 29, 2 (January 1997): 167–185.

Laffan, Brigid. "The Politics of Identity and Political Order in Europe." *Journal of Common Market Studies* 34 (1996): 81–102.

Laitin, David D. "South Africa: Violence, Myths, and Democratic Reform." *World Politics* 39 (1987): 258–279.

Lake, David A., and Donald Rothchild. "Spreading Fear: The Genesis of Transnational Ethnic Conflict." In *The International Spread of Ethnic Conflict: Fear Diffusion, and Escalation*, edited by David A. Lake and Donald Rothchild, 3–32. Princeton: Princeton University Press, 1998.

Larson, Deborah W. "Trust and Missed Opportunities in International Relations." *Political Psychology* 18 (1997): 701–734.

Lemco, Jonathan. *Political Stability in Federal Governments*. New York: Praeger, 1991.

Lemke, Christine. "Citizenship and European Integration." *World Affairs* 160, 4 (Spring 1998): 212–217.

Levine, Alicia. "Political Accommodation and the Prevention of Secessionist Violence." In *The International Dimensions of Internal Conflict*, edited by Michael E. Brown, 311–340. Cambridge: MIT Press, 1996.

Lijphart, Arend. *Democracy in Plural Societies*. New Haven: Yale University Press, 1977.

————. *Conflict and Coexistence in Belgium: The Dynamics of a Culturally Divided Society*. Berkeley: University of California Press, 1981.

————. "The Puzzle of Indian Democracy: A Consociational Interpretation." *American Political Science Review* 90 (1996): 258–268.

Linz, Juan. "Early State-Building and Late Peripheral Nationalisms Against the State: The Case of Spain." In *Building States and Nations*, edited by S. N. Eisenstadt and S. Rokkan, 32–112. London: Sage, 1973.

Lipset, Seymour M., and Stein Rokkan. *Party Systems and Voter Alignments: Cross-National Perspectives*. New York: Free Press, 1967.

Lloyd, John. "Ireland's Uncertain Peace." *Foreign Affairs* 77 (1998): 109–122.

López Guerra, L. "Sobre la Personalidad Jurídica del Estado." *Revista del Departamento de Derecho Político*. Madrid: UNED, 1980.

Lustick, Ian S. "Lijphart, Lakatos, and Consociationalism." *World Politics* 50 (1997): 88–117.

MacClancy, Jeremy. "Bilingualism and Multinationalism in the Basque Country." In *Nationalism and the Nation in the Iberian Peninsula: Competing and Conflicting Identities*, edited by Clare Mar-Molinero and Angel Smith, 207–220. Oxford: Berg, 1996.

March, J. G. and J. P. Olsen. "The Institutional Dynamics of International Political Orders." *International Organization* 52 (1998): 943–969.

Marcussen, Martin, Thomas Risse, Daniela Englemann-Martin, Hans Joachim Knopf, and Klaus Roscher. "Constructing Europe? The Evolution of French, British, and German Nation State Identities." *Journal of European Public Policy* 6, 4 (Special Issue 1999): 614–633.

Marks, Gary. "Territorial Identities in the European Union." In *Regional Integration and Democracy: Expanding on the European Experience*, edited by J. J. Anderson, 69–91. Lanham, MD: Rowman and Littlefield, 1999.

Mar-Molinero, Clare, and Angel Smith, eds. *Nationalism and the Nation in the Iberian Peninsula: Competing and Conflicting Identities*. Oxford: Berg, 1996.

Martin, Benjamin. *The Agony of Modernization: Labour and Industrialization in Spain*. Ithaca: ILR Press, 1990.

McCall, Cathal. *Identity in Northern Ireland*. New York: St. Martin's, 1999.

McDonough, S., H., Barnes, A. López Pina with D. C. Shin and J. Á. Moisés. *The Cultural Dynamics of Democratization in Spain*. Ithaca, NY: Cornell University Press, 1998.

McGarry, John. "Political Settlements in Northern Ireland and South Africa." *Political Studies* 46 (1998): 853–870.

———, and S. J. R. Noel. "The Prospects for Consociational Democracy in South Africa." *Journal of Commonwealth and Comparative Politics* 27 (1989): 3–22.

McKeogh, Colm. "Northern Ireland: The Good Friday Solution." *New Zealand International Review* 23 (1998): 2–6.

McSweeney, Bill. "Security, Identity and the Peace Process in Northern Ireland." *Security Dialogue* 27 (1996): 167–178.

———. "Interests and Identity in the Construction of the Belfast Agreement." *Security Dialogue* 29 (1998): 303–314.

Medhurst, Ken. "Basques and Basque Nationalism." In *National Separatism*, edited by C. H. Williams, 235–261. Vancouver: University of British Columbia, 1982.

Medrano, Juan Díez. *Divided Nations: Class, Politics, and Nationalism in the Basque Country and Catalonia.* Ithaca: Cornell University Press, 1995.

Meehan, Elizabeth. "Citizenship and the European Community." *Political Quarterly* 64, 2 (April-June 1993): 172–186.

———. "'Britain's Irish Question: Britain's European Question?' British-Irish Relations in the Context of European Union and the Belfast Agreement." *Review of International Studies* 26 (2000): 83–97.

Ministerio de Cultura. *Encuesta de Equipamiento, Prácticas y Consumos Culturales.* Madrid, 1990.

Mitchell, George. J. *Making Peace.* New York: Knopf, 1999.

Mitchell, Paul. "The Party System and Party Competition." In *Politics in Northern Ireland*, edited by Paul Mitchell and Rick Wilford, 91–116. Boulder, CO: Westview, 1999.

Monreal, Antoni. "The New Spanish State Structure." In *Federalism and Federation in Western Europe*, edited by Michael Burgess, 59–75. London: Croom Helm, 1986.

Moody, T.W., and F. X. Martin. *The Course of Irish History.* Cork, Ireland: Mercier, 1967.

Morata, F. "Spanish Regions in the EC." In *The European Union and the Regions*, edited by B. Jones and M. Keating, 115–133. Oxford: Clarendon Press, 1995.

Moxon-Browne, Edward. "National Identity in Northern Ireland." In *Social Attitudes in Northern Ireland*, edited by Peter Stringer and Jillian Robinson, 23–30. Belfast: Blackstaff, 1991.

Murphy, Alexander B. "Belgium's Regional Divergence: Along the Road to Federation." In *Federalism: The Multiethnic Challenge*, edited by Graham Smith, 73–100. London: Longman, 1995.

———. "Rethinking the Concept of European Identity." In *Nested Identities: Nationalism, Territory, and Scale*, edited by Guntram H. Herb and David H. Kaplan, 53–73. Lanham, MD: Rowman and Little-field, 1999.

Murray, Shoon Kathleen, and Jonathan A. Cowden. "The Role of 'Enemy Images' and Ideology in Elite Belief Systems." *International Studies Quarterly* 43 (1999): 455–481.

Nadal, J. "The Failure of the Industrial Revolution in Spain, 1830–1914." In *The Fontana Economic History of Europe,* Vol. 6, part 2; *The Emergence of Industrial Nations*, edited by C. M. Cipolla, 533–626. Hassocks: Harvester Press, 1976.

Nice, David C. *Federalism: The Politics of Intergovernmental Relations.* New York: St. Martin's, 1987.

Nordlinger, Eric A. *Conflict Regulation in Divided Societies.* Cambridge: Center for International Affairs, Harvard University, 1972.

Nuñéz Astrain, L. *The Basques: Their Struggle for Independence.* Wales: Welsh Academic Press, 1997.

Obradovic, Daniela. "Policy Legitimacy and the European Union." *Journal of Common Market Studies* 34 (1996): 191–221.

O'Brien, Conor Cruise. *Ancestral Voices: Religion and Nationalism in Ireland.* Dublin: Poolbeg, 1994.

O'Leary, Brendan. "Public Opinion and Northern Irish Futures." *Political Quarterly* 63 (1992): 143–170.

———. "The 1998 British-Irish Agreement: Power-Sharing Plus." *Scottish Affairs* 26 (1999): 14–35.

———, and John McGarry. *The Politics of Antagonism: Understanding Northern Ireland.* London: Athlone, 1993.

———. "Regulating Nations and Ethnic Communities." In *Nationalism and Rationality*, edited by Albert Breton, Gianluigi Galeotti, Pierre Salmon, and Ronald Wintrobe, 245–289. Cambridge: Cambridge University Press, 1995.

O'Neill, Michael. "Belgium: Language, Ethnicity and Nationality." *Parliamentary Affairs* 53 (2000): 114–134.

Osgood, Charles E. "Suggestions for Winning the Real War with Communism." *Journal of Conflict Resolution* 3 (1959): 295–325.

Patterson, Henry. *Class Conflict and Sectarianism: The Protestant Working Class and the Belfast Labour Movement 1868–1920.* Belfast: Blackstaff, 1980.

Payne, Stanley. *Basque Nationalism.* Reno, Nevada: University of Nevada, 1975.

———. *Spanish Catholicism: An Historical Overview*. Madison: University of Wisconsin Press, 1984.

———. *The Franco Regime: 1936–1975*. Madison: University of Wisconsin Press, 1987.

———. *Spain's First Democracy: The Second Republic, 1931–1936*. London: University of Wisconsin Press, 1993.

———. *Fascism in Spain, 1923–1977*. Madison: University of Wisconsin Press, 1999.

———. "Catalan and Basque Nationalism: Contrasting Patterns." In *Ethnic Challenges to the Modern Nation State*, edited by S. Ben-Ami and Y. Peled, 95–107. London: MacMillan, 2000.

Pérez-Díaz, Victor M. *The Return of Civil Society: The Emergence of Democratic Spain*. Cambridge: Harvard University Press, 1993.

PES Group. "Policy Papers: Political Priorities for the Second Term of Office (1998–2002)." *Committee of the Regions*. http://www.cor. eu.int/presentation/down/Pes/PolicyPapers.html.

Posen, Barry R. "The Security Dilemma and Ethnic Conflict." *Survival* 35 (1993): 27–47.

Preston, Paul, ed. *España en crisis: La evolución y decadencia del régimen de Franco*. Madrid: Fondo de cultura económica, 1977.

———. *The Coming of the Spanish Civil War: Reform, Reaction and Revolution in the Second Republic, 1931–1936*. London: Macmillan, 1978.

———. *The Triumph of Democracy in Spain*. London: Methuen, 1986.

———. *Franco: A Biography*. London: HarperCollins, 1993.

———. *The Coming of the Spanish Civil War: Reform, Reaction and Revolution in the Second Republic*. London: Routledge, 1994.

———. *A Concise History of the Spanish Civil War*. London: HarperCollins, 1996.

Preuss, Ulrich K. "Citizenship in the European Union: A Paradigm for Transnational Democracy?" In *Re-imagining Political Community: Studies in Cosmopolitan Democracy*, edited by Daniele Archibugi, David Held, and Martin Kohler, 138–51. Stanford: Stanford University Press, 1998.

Pruitt, Dean G. "Definition of the Situation as a Determinant of International Action." In *International Behavior: A Social-Psychological Analysis*, edited by Herbert C. Kelman, 393–432. New York: Holt, Rinehart and Winston, 1965.

Raento, Paulina. "The Geography of Spanish Basque Nationalism." In *Nested Identities: Nationalism, Territory and State*, edited by Guntram H. Herb and David H. Kaplan, 219–235. Lanham, MD: Rowman and Littlefield, 1999.

Rath, Sharda. *Federalism Today: Approaches, Issue and Trends*. New Delhi: Sterling Publishers Private, 1984.

Rees, Merlyn. *Northern Ireland: A Personal Perspective*. London: Methuen, 1985.

Requejo, Ferran. "Cultural Pluralism, Nationalism and Federalism: A Revision of Democratic Citizenship in Plurinational States." *European Journal of Political Research* 35 (1999): 255–286.

Reynolds, Andrew. "A Constitutional Pied Piper: The Northern Irish Good Friday Agreement." *Political Science Quarterly* 114 (1999–2000): 613–367.

Rhodes, Carolyn. *Pivotal Decisions: Selected Cases in Twentieth-Century International Politics*. Fort Worth: Harcourt College Publishers, 2000.

Richards, Michael. "Constructing the Nationalist State: Self-Sufficiency and Regeneration in the Early Franco Years." In *Nationalism and the Nation in the Iberian Peninsula: Competing and Conflicting Identities*, edited by Clare Mar-Molinero and Angel Smith, 149–167. Oxford: Berg, 1996.

———. "Collective Memory, the Nation-State and Post-Franco Society." In *Contemporary Spanish Cultural Studies*, edited by B. Jordan and R. Morgen-Tamosunas, 38–47. New York: Oxford University Press, 2000.

Romero Salvadó, Francisco. "The Failure of the Liberal Project of the Spanish Nation-State, 1909–1938." In *Nationalism and the Nation in the Iberian Peninsula: Competing and Conflicting Identities*, edited by Clare Mar-Molinero and Angel Smith, 119–132. Oxford: Berg, 1996.

———. *Twentieth-Century Spain: Politics and Society in Spain, 1898–1998*. New York: St. Martin's Press, 1999.

Ros, Maria, Carmen Huic, and Angel Gomez. "Comparative Identity, Category Salience and Intergroup Relations." In *Social Identity Processes: Trends in Theory and Research*, edited by D. Capozza and R. Brown, 89–95. London: Sage, 2000.

Ross, Cameron. "Federalism and Democratization in Russia." *Communist and Post-Communist Studies* 33 (2000): 403–420.

Rothbart, Myron. "Intergroup Perception and Social Conflict." In *Conflict Between People and Groups: Causes, Processes, and Resolutions*, edited by Stephen Worchel and Jeffrey A. Simpson, 93–109. Chicago: Nelson-Hall, 1993.

Ruane, Joseph, and Jennifer Todd. *The Dynamics of Conflict in Northern Ireland: Power, Conflict and Emancipation*. Cambridge: Cambridge University Press, 1996.

Sánchez-Albornoz, Nicolas, ed. *The economic modernization of Spain, 1830–1930*. New York: New York University Press, 1987.

Sandholtz, Wayne. "Membership Matters: Limits of the Functional Approach to European Institutions." *Journal of Common Market Studies* 34 (September 1996): 403–429.

Schopflin, George. "The Rise and Fall of Yugoslavia." In *The Politics of Ethnic Conflict Regulation*, edited by John McGarry and Brendan O'Leary, 172–203. London: Routledge, 1993.

Senelle, Robert. "The Reform of the Belgian State." In *Federalizing Europe?* edited by J. Hesse and V. Wright, 266–324. Oxford: Oxford University Press, 1996.

Shabad, Goldie. "After Autonomy: The Dynamics of Regionalism in Spain." In *The Politics of Democratic Spain*, edited by S. G. Payne, 111–180. Chicago: Chicago Council of Foreign Relations, 1986.

Shafer, Mark. "Images and Policy Preferences." *Political Psychology* 18, 4 (1997): 813–829.

Shafir, Gershon. *Immigrants and Nationalists: Ethnic Conflict and Accommodation in Catalonia, the Basque Country, Latvia, and Estonia*. Albany: State University of New York Press, 1995.

Shore, Chris. "Inventing the 'People's Europe': Critical Approaches to European Community 'Cultural Policy.'" *Manchester Journal of the Royal Anthopological Institute* 28 (1993): 779–800.

———. "Transcending the Nation-State?: The European Commission and the (Re)-Discovery of Europe." *Journal of Historical Sociology* 9 (1996): 473–496.

Shubert, Adrian. *A Social History of Modern Spain*. London: Unwin Hyman, 1990.

Siguan, Miquel. *Multilingual Spain*. Amsterdam: Swets and Zeitlinger, 1993.

Smith, Anthony D. "National Identity and the idea of European Unity." *International Affairs* 68 (1992): 55–76.

Smith, Graham. "Mapping the Federal Condition: Ideology, Political Practice and Social Justice." In *Federalism: The Multiethnic Challenge*, edited by Graham Smith, 1–28. London: Longman, 1995.

Smith, Joseph. *The Spanish-American War: Conflict in the Caribbean and the Pacific, 1895–1902*. London: Longman, 1994.

Solé-Tura, Jordi. *Nacionalidades y Nacionalismos en España: Autonomias Federalismo Autodeterminacion*. Madrid: Alianza Editorial, 1985.

Solé-Vilanova, J. "Spain: Developments in Regional and Local Government." In *Territory and Administration in Europe*, edited by R. Bennett, 205–229. London: Pinter, 1989.

Stern, Paul C. "Why Do People Sacrifice for Their Nations?" *Political Psychology* 16 (1995): 217–235.

Suberu, Rotimi T. *Federalism and Ethnic Conflict in Nigeria*. Washington, DC: United States Institute of Peace, 2001.

Sullivan, John. *ETA and Basque Nationalism: The Fight for Euskadi*. London: Routledge, 1988.

Sutton, Malcolm. *Bear in Mind These Dead . . . : An Index of Deaths from the Conflict in Ireland, 1969–1993*. Belfast: Beyond the Pale Publications, 1994.

Tajfel, Henri. *Human Groups and Social Categories: Studies in Social Psychology*. Cambridge: Cambridge University Press, 1981.

Tannam, Etian. *Cross-Border Cooperation in the Republic of Ireland and Northern Ireland*. New York: St. Martin's, 1999.

Taylor, Rupert. "Northern Ireland: Consociation or Social Transformation?" In *Northern Ireland and the Divided World: The Northern Ireland Conflict and the Good Friday Agreement in Comparative Perspective*, edited by John McGarry, 36–52. Oxford: Oxford University Press, 2001.

Tejerina Montaña, Benjamin. "Language and Basque Nationalism: Collective Identity, Social Conflict and Institutionalisation." In *Nationalism and the Nation in the Iberian Peninsula: Competing and Conflicting Identities*, edited by Clare Mar-Molinero and Angel Smith, 221–236. Oxford: Berg, 1996.

Tetlock, Philip E. "Policy-Makers' Images of International Conflict." *Journal of Social Issues* 39, 1 (1983): 67–86.

Thomas, Hugh. *The Spanish Civil War*, 3rd ed. Harmondsworth: Penguin, 1986.

Torres Boursault, L. "La División de Poderes en la España de Hoy." *Sistema* 117 (1993): 19–34.

Townshend, Charles. *Political Violence in Ireland: Government and Resistance since 1848*. Oxford: Clarendon Press, 1983.

Trew, Karen. "The Northern Irish Identity." In *A Question of Identity*, edited by Anne J. Kershen, 60–76. Aldershot, England: Ashgate, 1998.

————, and Denny E. Benson. "Dimensions of Social Identity in Northern Ireland." In *Changing European Identities: Social Psychological Analyses of Social Change*, edited by Glynis M. Breakwell and Evanthia Lyons Speri, 123–143. Oxford: Butterworth-Heinemann, 1996.

Trumbore, Peter F. "Public Opinion as a Domestic Constraint in International Negotiations: Two-Level Games in the Anglo-Irish Peace Process." *International Studies Quarterly* 42 (1998): 545–565.

Tsebelis, George. *Nested Games: Rational Choice in Comparative Politics*. Berkeley and Los Angeles: University of California Press, 1990.

————. "The Power of the European Parliament as a Conditional Agenda Setter." *American Political Science Review* 88 (1994): 128–142.

Tuñón de Lara, Manuel. *La II República*. Madrid: Siglo XXI, 1976.

————. *Poder y sociedad en España, 1900–1931*. Madrid: Colección Austral, 1992.

Urban, Lynn M., and Norman Miller. "A Theoretical Analysis of Crossed Categorization Effects: A Meta-Analysis." *Journal of Personality and Social Psychology* 74 (1998): 894–908.

Urwin, Derek W. *A Dictionary of European History and Politics 1945–1995*. London: Longman, 1996.

Van Schendenlen, M. P. C. M. "The Views of Arend Lijphart and Collected Criticisms." *Acta Politica* 19 (1984): 19–55.

Varela-Ortega, Jose. *Los amigos políticos: Partidos, elecciones y caciquismo en la Restauración, 1875–1900*. Madrid: Alianza Editorial, 1977.

————. "Aftermath of Splendid Disaster: Spanish Politics before and after the Spanish-American War of 1898." *Journal of Contemporary History* 15 (1980): 317–344.

Vincent, J. "Ethnicity and the State in Northern Ireland." In *Ethnicity and the State*, edited by J. D. Toland, 123–146. New Brunswick: Transaction Publishers, 1993.

Waever, Ole. "Identity, Integration and Security: Solving the Sovereignty Puzzle in E.U. Studies." *Journal of International Affairs* 48 (Winter 1995): 389–431.

Walt, Stephen M. *Revolution and War*. Ithaca: Cornell University Press, 1996.

Walter, Barbara F., and Jack Snyder, eds. *Civil Wars, Insecurity, and Intervention*. New York: Columbia University Press, 1999.

Watts, Ronald L. *Comparing Federal Systems*. 2d ed. Kingston, Ontario: McGill-Queen's University Press, 1999.

Weitzer, Ronald. "Policing and Security." In *Politics in Northern Ireland*, edited by Paul Mitchell and Rick Wilford, 170–194. Boulder, CO: Westview, 1999.

Wendt, Alexander. "Anarchy Is what States Make of It: The Social Construction of Power Politics." *International Organization* 46, 2 (Spring 1992): 391–425.

———. "Collective Identity Formation and the International State." *American Political Science Review* 88, 2 (June 1994): 384–396.

Wheare, K. C. *Federal Government*. 4th ed. London: Oxford University Press, 1963.

Whyte, John H. *Interpreting Northern Ireland*. Oxford: Clarendon, 1991.

Wiener, Antje. "Promises and Resources-the Developing Practice of 'European' Citizenship." In *European Citizenship: An Institutional Challenge*, edited by Massimo La Torre, 387–414. The Hague: Kluwer Law, 1998.

———, and Vincent Della Salla. "Constitution-making and Citizenship Practice-Bridging the Democracy Gap in the EU?" *Journal of Common Market Studies* 35 (1997): 595–614.

Wilford, Rick. "Regional Assemblies and Parliament." In *Politics in Northern Ireland*, edited by Paul Mitchell and Rick Wilford, 117–141. Boulder, CO: Westview, 1999.

———. "Epilogue." In *Politics in Northern Ireland*, edited by Paul Mitchell and Rick Wilford, 285–303. Boulder, CO: Westview, 1999.

Williams, Kristen P., and Neal G. Jesse. "Resolving Nationalist Conflicts: Promoting Overlapping Identities and Pooling Sovereignty-the 1998 Northern Irish Peace Agreement." *Political Psychology* 22 (2001): 571–599.

Woolard, Kathryn A. *Double Talk: Bilingualism and the Politics of Ethnicity in Catalonia*. Stanford: Stanford University Press, 1989.

Young, Michael D., and Mark Schafer. "Is There Method in Our Madness? Ways of Assessing Cognition in International Relations." *Mershon International Studies Review* 42 (1998): 63–96.

Zartman, I. William. "Putting Humpty-Dumpty Together Again." In *The International Spread of Ethnic Conflict: Fear,Diffusion, and Escalation* edited by David. A. Lake and Donald Rothchild, 317–336. Princeton: Princeton University Press, 1998.

Zulaika, Joseba. *Basque Violence: Metaphor and Sacrament*. Reno: University of Nevada, 1988.

Index

Index

SUNY series in Global Politics
James N. Rosenau, Editor

List of Titles

American Patriotism in a Global Society – Betty Jean Craige

The Political Discourse of Anarchy: A Disciplinary History of International Relations – Brian C. Schmidt

Power and Ideas: North-South Politics of Intellectual Property and Antitrust – Susan K. Sell

From Pirates to Drug Lords: The Post – Cold War Caribbean Security Environment – Michael C. Desch, Jorge I. Dominguez, and Andres Serbin (eds.)

Collective Conflict Management and Changing World Politics – Joseph Lepgold and Thomas G. Weiss (eds.)

Zones of Peace in the Third World: South America and West Africa in Comparative Perspective – Arie M. Kacowicz

Private Authority and International Affairs – A. Claire Cutler, Virginia Haufler, and Tony Porter (eds.)

Harmonizing Europe: Nation-States within the Common Market – Francesco G. Duina

Economic Interdependence in Ukrainian-Russian Relations – Paul J. D'Anieri

Leapfrogging Development? The Political Economy of Telecommunications Restructuring – J. P. Singh

States, Firms, and Power: Successful Sanctions in United States Foreign Policy – George E. Shambaugh

Approaches to Global Governance Theory – Martin Hewson and Timothy J. Sinclair (eds.)

After Authority: War, Peace, and Global Politics in the Twenty-First Century – Ronnie D. Lipschutz

Pondering Postinternationalism: A Paradigm for the Twenty-First Century? – Heidi H. Hobbs (ed.)

Beyond Boundaries? Disciplines, Paradigms, and Theoretical Integration in International Studies – Rudra Sil and Eileen M. Doherty (eds.)

International Relations – Still an American Social Science? Toward Diversity in International Thought – Robert M. A. Crawford and Darryl S. L. Jarvis (eds.)

Which Lessons Matter? American Foreign Policy Decision Making in the Middle East, 1979 – 1987 – Christopher Hemmer (ed.)

Hierarchy Amidst Anarchy: Transaction Costs and Institutional Choice – Katja Weber

Counter-Hegemony and Foreign Policy: The Dialectics of Marginalized and Global Forces in Jamaica – Randolph B. Persaud

Global Limits: Immanuel Kant, International Relations, and Critique of World Politics – Mark F. N. Franke

Money and Power in Europe: The Political Economy of European Monetary Cooperation – Matthias Kaelberer

Why Movements Matter: The West German Peace Movement and U. S. Arms Control Policy – Steve Breyman

Agency and Ethics: The Politics of Military Intervention – Anthony F. Lang, Jr.

Life After the Soviet Union: The Newly Independent Republics of the Transcaucasus and Central Asia – Nozar Alaolmolki

Information Technologies and Global Politics: The Changing Scope of Power and Governance – James N. Rosenau and J. P. Singh (eds.)

Theories of International Cooperation and the Primacy of Anarchy: Explaining U. S. International Monetary Policy-Making After Bretton Woods – Jennifer Sterling-Folker

Technology, Democracy, and Development: International Conflict and Cooperation in the Information Age – Juliann Emmons Allison (ed.)

Systems of Violence: The Political Economy of War and Peace in Colombia – Nazih Richani

The Arab-Israeli Conflict Transformed: Fifty Years of Interstate and Ethnic Crises — Hemda Ben-Yehuda and Shmuel Sandler

Debating the Global Financial Architecture – Leslie Elliot Armijo

Political Space: Frontiers of Change and Governance in a Globalizing World – Yale Ferguson and R. J. Barry Jones (eds.)

Crisis Theory and World Order: Heideggerian Reflections – Norman K. Swazo

Political Identity and Social Change: The Remaking of the South African Social Order – Jamie Frueh

Social Construction and the Logic of Money: Financial Predominance and International Economic Leadership – J. Samuel Barkin

What Moves Man: The Realist Theory of International Relations and Its Judgment of Human Nature – Annette Freyberg-Inan

Democratizing Global Politics: Discourse Norms, International Regimes, and Political Community – Rodger A. Payne and Nayef H. Samhat

Landmines and Human Security: International Politics and War's Hidden Legacy – Richard A. Matthew, Bryan McDonald, and Kenneth R. Rutherford (eds.)

Collective Preventative Diplomacy: A Study of International Management – Barry H. Steiner

International Relations Under Risk: Framing State Choice – Jeffrey D. Berejikian

Globalization and the Environment: Greening Global Political Economy – Gabriela Kütting

Sovereignty, Democracy, and Global Civil Society – Elisabeth Jay Friedman, Kathryn Hochstetler, and Ann Marie Clark

Imperialism and Nationalism in the Discipline of International Relations – David Long and Brian C. Schmidt (eds.)

United We Stand? Divide and Conquer Politics and the Logic of International Hostility – Aaron Belkin

Globalization, Security, and the Nation State: Paradigms in Transition – Ersel Aydinli and James N. Rosenau (eds.)

Mediating Globalization: Domestic Institutions and Industrial Policies in the United States and Britain – Andrew P. Cortell

Globalizing Interests: Pressure Groups and Denationalization – Michael Zürn (ed., with assistance from Gregor Walter)